THOMAS JEFFERSON
GENIUS OF LIBERTY

THE PROVIDENTIAL DETECTION

THOMAS JEFFERSON
GENIUS OF LIBERTY

Introduction by Garry Wills

With Essays by
Joseph J. Ellis
Annette Gordon-Reed
Pauline Maier
Charles A. Miller
Peter S. Onuf

Viking Studio, New York
in association with the
Library of Congress, Washington, D.C.

Narrative by Amy Pastan, with historical assistance from Gerard W. Gawalt, curator of the exhibition *Thomas Jefferson: Genius of Liberty*.

Library of Congress Editorial Team:
W. Ralph Eubanks, Director of Publishing
Sara Day, Managing Editor
Linda Barrett Osborne, Research Editor and Scholars' Liaison
Heather Burke, Picture Editor

Design: Garruba | Dennis | Konetzka, Washington, D.C.

Frontispiece: *The Providential Detection*. Etching, ca. 1800. Courtesy, American Antiquarian Society.

Opposite: William Hamilton after George Noble. "The Manner in which the American Colonies Declared themselves Independant of the King of England, throughout the different Provinces, on July 4, 1776." Etching from Edward Barnard, *History of England* (London, 1783). Prints and Photographs Division, Library of Congress.

VIKING STUDIO
Published by the Penguin Group
Penguin Putnam Inc., 375 Hudson Street,
New York, New York 10014, U.S.A.
Penguin Books Ltd, 27 Wrights Lane,
London w8 5TZ, England
Penguin Books Australia Ltd, Ringwood,
Victoria, Australia
Penguin Books Canada Ltd, 10 Alcorn Avenue,
Toronto, Ontario, Canada M4V 3B2
Penguin Books (N.Z.) Ltd, 182-190 Wairau Road,
Auckland 10, New Zealand
Penguin Books Ltd, Registered Offices:
Harmondsworth, Middlesex, England

First published in 2000 by Viking Studio,
a member of Penguin Putnam Inc.

10 9 8 7 6 5 4 3 2 1

Library of Congress Cataloging-in-Publication Data

Thomas Jefferson, genius of liberty / introduction by Garry Wills ; with essays
by Joseph J. Ellis . . .[et al.].
p. cm.

ISBN 0-670-88933-4
1. Jefferson, Thomas, 1743–1826—Political and social views. 2. United States—Politics
and government—1775–1783. 3. United States—Politics and government—1783–1865.
I. Ellis, Joseph J. II. Library of Congress.
E332.2 .T47 2000
973.4 '6' 092—DC21   99-039115

Printed in the United States of America

The Manner *in which the* American Colonies *Declared themselves*
INDEPENDANT *of the* King *of* ENGLAND,
throughout the different Provinces, on July 4, 1776.

Contents

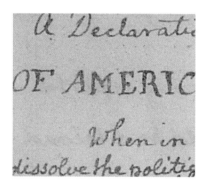

Chapter One 1
Self-Evident Truths
"Rebellion to Tyrants is
Obedience to God."

Chapter Two 31
The Passionate Idealist
"The first object of my heart
is my own country. In that is
embarked my family, my
fortune, & my own existence."

Chapter Three 63
The Power of Opinion
"The spirit of 1776 is not dead.
It has only been slumbering."

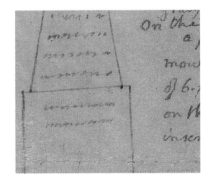

Chapter Four 89
A Second Revolution

"We are all republicans:
we are all federalists."

Chapter Five 115
Empire for Liberty

"I considered as a great public
acquisition the commencement
of a settlement on that point of
the Western coast of America,
& looked forward with
gratification to the time when its
descendants should have spread
themselves thro' the whole length
of that coast, covering it with free
and independant Americans."

Chapter Six 145
The Race of Life

"Here was buried
Thomas Jefferson
Author of the Declaration
of American Independance
of the Statute of Virginia
for religious Freedom
& Father of the University
of Virginia."

Preface

In 1776 Thomas Jefferson sounded the call for freedom in the Declaration of Independence with words that have come to symbolize liberty and equality to millions of people around the world. Jefferson's and America's ringing declaration, "We hold these Truths to be self-evident, that all Men are created equal, that they are endowed by their Creator with certain unalienable Rights, that among these are Life, Liberty, and the Pursuit of Happiness," has inspired the spirit of liberty around the world. From the French Declaration of the Rights of Man, to Thomas G. Masaryk's Czechoslovak Declaration of Independence, to freedom's cries from Tiananmen Square, Jefferson's words are still a "signal for arousing men . . . to assume the blessings and security of self-government."

This illustrated biography, *Thomas Jefferson: Genius of Liberty*, with essays by leading scholars, is the companion volume to the Library's major exhibition on Thomas Jefferson. This exhibition is also part of the celebration of the two hundredth anniversary of the founding of the Library of Congress. Testimonies to the enduring fascination with Thomas Jefferson and the founders and freedoms of the United States, both the book and the exhibition draw on the Library's unparalleled collection of Jefferson manuscripts and from his personal library acquired by the United States in 1815 as the core of the Library of Congress.

Indeed, the Library of Congress is one of Thomas Jefferson's principal legacies. The wide range of his interests determined the universal and diverse nature of the Library's collections and services. Founded in 1800 as the national government prepared to move from Philadelphia to the new capital city, the Library of Congress owned 740 books and 3 maps a year later. While he was president of the United States from 1801 to 1809, Jefferson took a keen interest in the Library of Congress and its collections, including approving the first law defining the role and functions of the new institution. He personally recommended books for the Library and appointed the first two librarians of Congress, John J. Beckley (1802-1807) and Patrick Magruder (1807-1815).

After the British army invaded Washington in 1814 and burned the Capitol, including the by now 3,000-volume Library of Congress, Jefferson offered to sell his personal library at Monticello to Congress to "re-commence" its collection. Anticipating the argument that his library might be too comprehensive, he emphasized that there was "no subject to which a member of Congress might not have occasion to refer." The purchase of Jefferson's 6,487 volumes for $23,940 was approved in 1815. Jefferson oversaw the packing of the books, leaving them in their pine bookshelves. Books and shelves were transported to Washington in ten horse-drawn wagons and were received and organized by new Librarian of Congress George Waterston in the temporary Capitol, Blodget's Hotel. The Library adopted Jefferson's personal classification system of forty-four categories of knowledge and used it for the remainder of the century.

Not only did the library that Jefferson sold to Congress include more than twice the number of volumes that had been destroyed, it further expanded the commitment of the fledgling Library of Congress to a broadly based collection, far beyond the usual scope of a legislative library. Jefferson was a man of encyclopedic interests; his library included works on architecture, the arts, science, literature, and geography. It contained books in French, Spanish, German, Latin, Greek, and one three-volume statistical work in Russian. Recognizing that the Jefferson collection was a national treasure, the committee on the Library acquired new materials across the subject range to maintain its comprehensiveness. Today's Library of Congress epitomizes Jefferson's belief in the power of knowledge to inform citizens and shape democracy. Its collections and programs reflect Jefferson's deep appreciation for the arts and his passionate devotion to music. At the dawn of the twenty-first century, as the Library celebrates its bicentennial, it houses more than 115 million items in nearly every known language and format.

What is less well known to the general public is that almost two-thirds of Jefferson's original collection of books was destroyed in a disastrous fire on Christmas Eve of 1851. While many of those volumes have subsequently been replaced, there are still hundreds of titles missing. Another Library bicentennial project is under way to raise the necessary funds and rebuild Jefferson's library. Through a world-wide search, the Library is making every effort to replace the missing volumes in the same editions as those owned by Jefferson. All the replaced books will be featured in the Jefferson exhibition.

At the same time, a monumental effort is under way to digitize the voluminous Jefferson Papers and put them online via the Library's American Memory website. Jefferson's words, the evidence that leads each new generation of historians to a different interpretation of this most complex of men, and also the animating impulse of the exhibition and this book, will then be available to all people.

James H. Billington
Librarian of Congress

Acknowledgments

This book is a companion volume to the major exhibition *Thomas Jefferson: Genius of Liberty*, curated by Gerard W. Gawalt, manuscript historian in the Manuscript Division of the Library of Congress. The book is based on the object list and themes of the exhibition. Dr. Gawalt helped the editorial team and writer-editor Amy Pastan to develop the framework of the narrative and select the featured documents and letters, based on his knowledge of the Jefferson Papers. He also assisted the editorial team in identifying scholars to write on themes suggested by the exhibition. He would like to thank F. Lee Shepard of the Virginia Historical Society, Jim McClure at the Thomas Jefferson Papers, and William Fowler at the Massachusetts Historical Society for their assistance.

Director of Publishing W. Ralph Eubanks thanks Martha Kaplan, who served as the Library's agent on this project. He also wishes to express his gratitude to the scholars—Joseph J. Ellis, Annette Gordon-Reed, Pauline Maier, Charles A. Miller, Peter S. Onuf, and Garry Wills—for agreeing to write essays when their schedules were already very busy. It was also a pleasure to work with our editor at Viking Studio, Christopher Sweet, who gave his whole-hearted support to this project from the start. Viking's production manager, Roni Axelrod, worked closely with the book's designer, Mike Konetzka of Garruba|Dennis|Konetzka, to ensure the highest quality.

Sara Day served as managing editor for the book, leading an excellent team of text and picture editors; arbitrating on questions of content, fact, and style; and liaising with the publisher, designer, and historian. Amy Pastan produced a readable, lively, and yet authoritative story from the immensely complicated facts of Jefferson's long life. Linda Barrett Osborne ensured the high integrity of the book by checking all these facts against some of the bibles of Jeffersonian scholarship, including the six volumes of Dumas Malone's landmark *Jefferson and His Time*. She also spent many hours discussing essay themes and acting as liaison with the scholars. Heather Burke achieved the monumental task of researching and gathering in from the Library's divisions and from other institutions more than 150 illustrations

The "PERFEC" STEREOGRAPH.
(Trade Mark)

H. C. WHITE CO., Publishers,
North Bennington, Vt., U.S.A.

114 Library of Congress, Washington, D. C.
COPYRIGHT 1902 BY H. C. WHITE CO.

H. C. White Co., *Library of Congress,*
Washington, D.C. **Stereograph, 1902.**
Prints and Photographs Division,
Library of Congress.

for the book against very tight deadlines and also pursued or checked innumerable facts and details for the captions.

Many individuals within the Library deserve individual thanks for their help. In the Rare Book and Special Collections Division: Cynthia Earman and Clark Evans. In the Geography and Map Division: Ron Grim, Jim Flatness, Edward Redmond, and Kathryn Engstrom. The reference staffs of the Serials and Government Publications Division, Prints and Photographs Division, Rare Book and Special Collections Division, and Manuscript Division provided consistent support over many weeks. Jim Higgins and Yusef El Amin of the Photoduplication Service photographed the Library materials and Cheryl Regan of the Interpretive Programs Office allowed key documents to be removed from exhibit cases for photography. In the Publishing Office, Nawal Kawar and Gloria Baskerville-Holmes also assisted in obtaining illustrations from outside institutions.

Many institutions gave permission for the reproduction of Jefferson materials. Among the staff members who gave more than regular assistance were John B. Rudder, Assistant Curator, and Carolyn Book and Whitney Espich, of the Office of Public Affairs and Development, at the Thomas Jefferson Memorial Foundation/Monticello; Nicole Wells at the New-York Historical Society; Erika Piola at the Library Company of Philadelphia; Joseph Benford, Head of the Print and Picture Collection at the Free Library of Philadelphia; Georgia Barnhill, Curator of Graphic Arts, and Jenna Loosemore, Curatorial Assistant of Graphic Arts, at the American Antiquarian Society; Rob Cox, Curator of Manuscripts at the American Philosophical Society; Tom Ford at the Houghton Library, Harvard University; Claudia Jew at the Mariners' Museum; Regina Rush and Margaret Rhabe at the Alderman Library, University of Virginia. William K. Geiger photographed two key images for the book, including the image of the Houdon bust on the cover.

The Goddess of Liberty with a portrait of Thomas Jefferson. Salem, Massachusetts, January 15, 1807.
Mabel Brady Garvan Collection, Yale University Art Gallery.

Jefferson is shown in this allegorical print, made late in his second administration, as "the Favorite of the People." While Liberty points to his portrait on her shield and crushes the symbols of monarchy with her foot, she gazes at a commemorative portrait of George Washington, remembering his services to the country. As a symbol of the fight for independence, Liberty/America began to be portrayed as a goddess from the Revolutionary War period on, following the classical tradition of Minerva, goddess of war. Since symbolic Geniuses (for example, the cupids here are the Genius of Peace and the Genius of Gratitude) were often portrayed dancing attendance on Liberty, then perhaps we can call Jefferson in this context "Liberty's Genius." "Genius" to Jefferson meant natural talent or "lively imagination," as in: "Those persons, whom nature hath endowed with genius and virtue, should be rendered by liberal education . . . able to guard the sacred deposit of the rights and liberties of their fellow citizens." (TJ, A Bill for the More General Diffusion of Knowledge, 1778)

Jefferson's Genius

Those of us who grew up in the middle of this century thought that Jefferson's star could never be dimmed, much less flicker or go out. In fact, we were surprised to learn that in the early decades of the century the star had disappeared behind clouds of hostility. Theodore Roosevelt described our saint as a "scholarly, timid and shifting doctrinaire" and described any cult of him as "a discredit to my country." (Merrill Peterson, *The Jefferson Image in the American Mind*, 1960) Roosevelt reflected the imperial mood in which America ended the nineteenth century, with naval adventurism into Cuba, the Philippines, and the Far East. The prophet of naval power at that time, Alfred Thayer Mahan (surely the only Admiral who was ever the president of the American Historical Association), joined others in seeing the active government envisaged by Alexander Hamilton as the vehicle for America's rise to the status of a world power. Henry Adams, though he did not share his fellow imperialists' admiration for Hamilton, made endless fun of Jefferson for his belief that America could sustain a realistic foreign policy with the help of a few shore-hugging gun boats. (*History of the United States of America during the Administrations of Thomas Jefferson*, 1889-91)

As the country moved from turn-of-the-century imperialism into the Progressive Era, reformers found that they, too, needed Hamilton's strong government for the remaking of society. The leading voice here was that of Herbert Crowley, who found in Jefferson's libertarian ideals only "individual aggrandizement and collective irresponsibility." (*Jefferson Image*) Well into the twenties, Americans were assured that ordinary people were incapable of conducting their own affairs in a time of rapid and necessary technological innovation. Robert and Helen Lynd, famed for *Middletown* (their sociological study of Muncie, Indiana), concluded that the bewildered modern housewife could not keep up with the new tools and markets she must use, and turned her over to the advice of experts to be specially created for her guidance. Walter Lippmann, in *The Phantom Public* (1927), claimed that the average voter could not judge complex issues involved in modern public policy, and wanted boards of experts to make the real decisions, which voters would simply ratify.

It was only with the crash of the high hopes for governmental omnicompetence—it was only with the Great Depression—that a new emphasis on the plight and dignity of common people led to a resurgence of the great celebrator of the American yeoman, the plowman, the common man, the citizen. By the 1940s both political parties were invoking Jefferson—even Republicans now remembered that their own greatest president, Abraham Lincoln, called Jefferson, in his 1854 speech on the Kansas-Nebraska Act, the man "who was, is, and perhaps will continue to be the most distinguished politician of our history." They had discovered the whole founding dream of America in Jefferson's words. The dedication of the Jefferson Memorial on April 13, 1943—the two hundredth anniversary of his birth—lodged him in that high stellar place where my contemporaries first encountered him. It seemed there would be no further wavering on the place of Jefferson at the center of America's historical commitments.

Yet Jefferson's formerly unquestioned greatness is now very thoroughly questioned. There are several confluent reasons for this, but the greatest is no doubt a deeper awareness of our national sin of slavery. When I first went to Monticello in the late 1950s, the role of slaves at that plantation complex was muted and made barely visible. The civil rights movement made such historical evasiveness impossible. The presence of slaves, their crucial labors (in a double sense), began to be marked, not only at Monticello, but at Mount Vernon, Williamsburg, and other sacred places in our history. In itself, this new clarity about our racial history should have told no more against Jefferson than against other presidents who ever owned slaves—Washington, Madison, Monroe, Jackson, Harrison, Tyler, Taylor, Andrew Johnson. But there are three things that add a special note of hypocrisy to Jefferson's purchasing and sale of human beings:

1. He was more passionate and effective in his calls for human freedom than was any other Founder.

2. He maintained an extravagant lifestyle that kept him heavily indebted (to the very banks he called sources of corruption), and this made it impossible for him to free any but a few slaves (unlike Washington, who stayed solvent and could support the slaves he freed at his wife's death). Debt forced Jefferson to sell slaves in ways that disrupted family life, a step some other slave owners deplored and Washington was able to avoid.

3. The charge that Jefferson had a secret affair with his own slave, Sally Hemings, and lied about it, gained new plausibility as a result of DNA testing.

A shift in the climate of any reputation leads to sharper looks at other aspects of the person's life than the one that caused that shift in the first place. So, even on issues not directly related to slavery, Jefferson's credentials have come under increasing challenge. Contradictions in his policies toward Native Americans have received harsh new scrutiny, notably by Anthony Wallace in his *Jefferson and the Indians: The Tragic Fate of the First Americans* (1999). James Morton Smith's running commentary on the Jefferson-Madison correspondence suggests that Madison was not only the deeper thinker but that he may have been a more consistent defender of liberty. (Smith, *The Republic of Letters: The Correspondence between Thomas Jefferson and James*

Madison, 1995) A romantic picture of Jefferson the democrat who received diplomats in his slippers was dealt a blow by the great Monticello exhibit and catalogue of 1993, which revealed how elite was the life he led, abroad and at home, in Virginia and in Washington. (Susan R. Stein, *The Worlds of Thomas Jefferson at Monticello*) A guest at one of his famous White House dinners wrote:

His maitre-d'hotel had served in some of the finest families abroad, and understood his business to perfection. The excellence and the superior skill of his French cook was acknowledged by all who frequented his table, for never before had such dinners been given in the President's House, nor such a variety of the finest and most costly wines. (Margaret Bayard Smith, The First Forty Years of Washington Society, *1906)*

We can no longer forget that the fine wines, like the almost frantic collecting of art works, books, and furniture, were paid for with money wrung from the bodies of Jefferson's human property. This can only make us shake our heads when Jefferson professes a creed of thrift: "would a missionary appear who would make frugality

the basis of his religious system, and go thro the land preaching it up as the only road to salvation, I would join his school . . . ." (TJ to John Page, May 4, 1786)

Pauline Maier's recent reappraisal of Jefferson's claim to authorship of the Declaration of Independence is evidence that Jefferson's image is under assault. She even once nominated him as "the most overrated person in American history . . . but only because of the extraordinary adulation (and sometimes execration) he has received and continues to receive." (Maier, *American Scripture: Making the Declaration of Independence*, 1997) Conor Cruise O'Brien, in his book on Jefferson and the French Revolution, adds the final insult when he calls Jefferson the son of the Parisian Terror and the father of the Oklahoma City terror bombing. And, as has happened in the past, a sinking of Jefferson's claims has been paired with a concomitant lifting of Hamilton's. Though Hamilton's biographer, Henry Cabot Lodge, was not entirely justified in claiming that all Americans are either Jeffersonians or Hamiltonians, the two men's reputations do tend to move in contrary directions, if not quite on an historical seesaw, then as part of a sensitively poised Calder mobile.

Can we, in this climate, continue to hold that Jefferson is our "genius of liberty"? Certainly not, if that means denying some of the critical insights gained in recent years. But a reconsideration of the man may indicate that we misconceived his greatness rather than that he lacked greatness. Many people in the past thought of

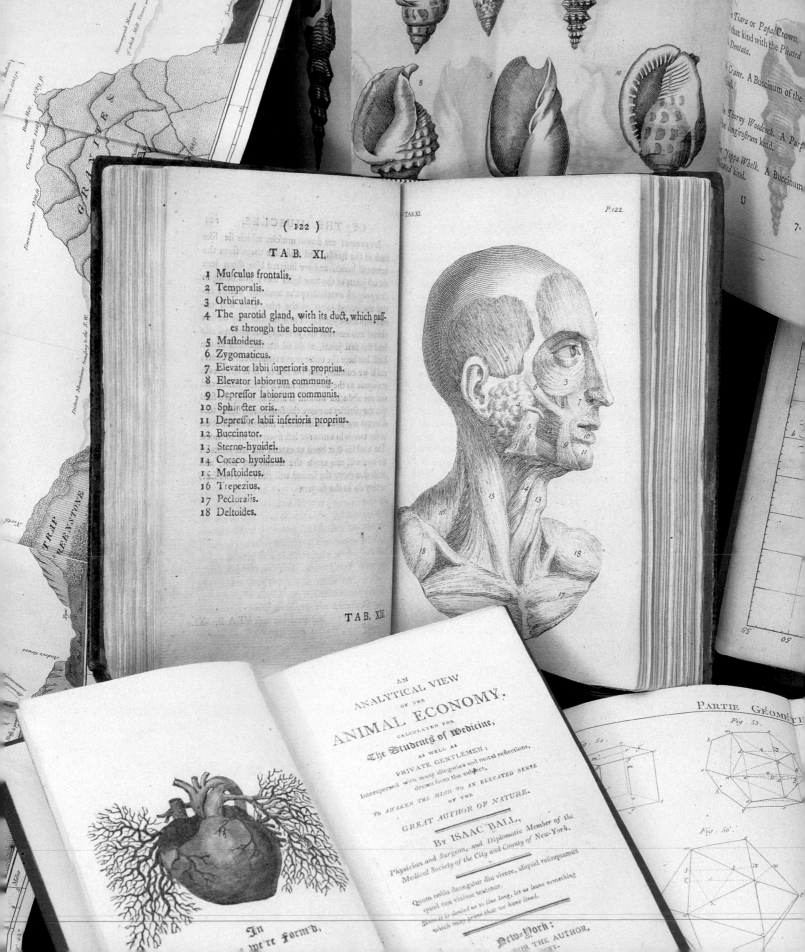

TAB. XI.

1 Musculus frontalis.
2 Temporalis.
3 Orbicularis.
4 The parotid gland, with its duct, which passes through the buccinator.
5 Mastoideus.
6 Zygomaticus.
7 Elevator labii superioris proprius.
8 Elevator labiorum communis.
9 Depressor labiorum communis.
10 Sphincter oris.
11 Depressor labii inferioris proprius.
12 Buccinator.
13 Sterno-hyoidei.
14 Coraco hyoideus.
15 Mastoideus.
16 Trepezius.
17 Pectoralis.
18 Deltoides.

TAB. XII.

TAB. XI.   P. 122.

AN
ANALYTICAL VIEW
OF THE
ANIMAL ECONOMY;
CALCULATED FOR
The Students of Medicine,
AS WELL AS
PRIVATE GENTLEMEN;
Interspersed with many allegories and moral reflections,
drawn from the subject,
TO AWAKEN THE MIND TO AN ELEVATED SENSE
OF THE
GREAT AUTHOR OF NATURE.

By ISAAC BALL,
Physician and Surgeon, and Diplomatic Member of the
Medical Society of the City and County of New-York.

Quam nobis denegatur diu vivere, aliquid relinquamus
quod nos vixisse testatur.
Since it is denied us to live long, let us leave something
which may prove that we have lived.

New-York:
FOR THE AUTHOR,

PARTIE GÉOMÉTRIE
Fig. 53.

Jefferson as a theoretician, a French rationalist, even a metaphysician—timid, as Theodore Roosevelt thought, because so airily abstract and scholarly. Actually, of course, Jefferson despised metaphysicians. He lumped them together with the Platonists who had corrupted with their abstractions the plain moral instincts of Jesus. (TJ to John Adams, July 5, 1814) Jefferson was not a rigorous thinker. He was a rhetorician, an artist, an aesthete bordering on the dilettante. Henry Adams went right to the heart of this paradox when he spoke of Jefferson's "intellectual sensuousness." In discussing hypotheses, Jefferson would not sacrifice to scientific accuracy their symmetry and elegance. Even his handwriting—amply illustrated throughout this book—showed his compulsion to the chaste ordering of shapes (uppercase letters were not allowed to violate the letters' formal ranks). He evened off his letters as he evened off the generations of men at a tidy nineteen years. He wanted "natural" measures of American weights and moneys, disregarding irregular intrusions of friction in his means of arriving at these all-too-neat numbers. (TJ to James Madison, September 9, 1798)

Not only was he an architect of talent, he was a *romantic* architect. His plantation was highly impractical because he placed it high above sublime views, where he could "ride above the storms!" (and above mundane tasks), "to look down into the workhouse of nature, to see her clouds, hail, snow, rain, thunder, all fabricated at our feet!" (TJ to Maria Cosway, October 12, 1786) Despite his years of obsessively collecting meteorological data, he never formulated a theory from them, as Franklin did from the experience of one storm at sea. (I. Bernard Cohen, *Science and the Founding Fathers*, 1995) Jefferson was the observer, who wanted to be awed by nature in its purity. When he compares his view from Monticello with other sights, they are all of untouched nature—"the Falling spring, the Cascade of Niagara, the Passage of the Potowmac thro the Blue mountains, the Natural bridge." (Cosway)

In his aesthetic primitivism, Jefferson wanted to get back to a pure state of nature—pre-feudal, pre-urban, pre-monetary. The religion of Jesus was sound because non-institutional, non-theological, non-professional. It had no priests or ceremonies. Debts must be abolished periodically, to start over, to have a clean slate. America was superior to Europe, in Jefferson's eyes, because closer to nature. Europeans must be admitted into this paradise only slowly and grudgingly, if at all, lest they bring the evil fruit of their training, foreign to the ethos of our law, to "warp and bias its direction, and render it a heterogeneous, incoherent, distracted mass." (TJ, "Query VIII," *Notes on the State of Virginia*, 1781-82) For the same reason, wrote Jefferson from France, young Americans should not be allowed to study in Europe, where, in an atmosphere of monarchs and priests, they may come to feel "the hollow, unmeaning manners of Europe to be preferable to the simplicity and sincerity of our own country." (TJ to Thomas Walker Maury, August 19, 1785) The encroachments of "civilization" must be fought off as long as possible, since "when they [Americans] get piled upon one another in large cities, as in Europe, they will become corrupt as is Europe." (TJ to James Madison, December 29, 1797) Since even the Bible has been corrupted by the priests, children should not be allowed to read it before they have been taught the self-evident maxims of honesty. (*Notes on the State of Virginia*) Then they will accept from it only "the facts [that] are within the ordinary course of nature." (TJ to Peter Carr, August 10, 1787)

A selection of scientific books from Jefferson's library. Rare Book and Special Collections Division, Library of Congress.

Jefferson's choice of scientific treatises reflects the wide-ranging interests of this son of the Enlightenment over his lifetime. He continued to collect books for "amusement" after Congress purchased his nearly 6,500 volumes in 1815 and, while he willed the majority of this third collection to the library at the University of Virginia, many of those left to private individuals have continued to supplement his library at the Library of Congress. Shown here are **(center)** *William Cheselden's* The Anatomy of the Human Body *(London, 1763), and* **(clockwise, from top left)** *Samuel Akerly's* An Essay on the Geology of the Hudson River, and the Adjacent Regions *(New York, 1820); Emanuel Mendes da Costa's* Elements of Conchology: or an Introduction to the Knowledge of Shells *(London, 1776); James Benignus Winslow's* An Anatomical Exposition of the Structures of the Human Body *(London, 1756); Le Cen. Haüy's* Traité de Minéralogie *(Paris, 1801); and Isaac Ball's* An Analytical View of the Animal Economy *(New-York, 1808).*

Thomas Jefferson. Elevation of the first Monticello. Drawing, pen and ink, 1769-70. Monticello/Thomas Jefferson Memorial Foundation, Inc.

Architecture was one of Jefferson's greatest passions and talents. A romantic before the Age of Romanticism, he built his neoclassical villa on top of a mountain, in the style of the Greeks, with sublime views in every direction. Even before his stay in Europe, he was heavily influenced by the drawings of Andrea Palladio—a principal catalyst of the Italian renaissance of classical form—which he found in the many books on architecture that he began acquiring as a student. Monticello became a laboratory for his experiments in architecture and design, an innovative blend of form and function.

In Jefferson's primitivism we can discover the moral aspect of his aesthetics. For the encyclopedists in France, for Shaftesbury in England, for Hume and Hutcheson in Scotland, the perception of moral beauty was closely allied with the aesthetic sense. That is why Jefferson thought that the sublime vistas of nature not only uplift but educate. Though he upheld harsh removal measures for the Native American, he thought that "his sensibility is keen" because he lives close to nature, while his natural self-control makes him "endeavour to appear superior to human events." The Indians' aesthetic sense led to "the most sublime oratory" in leaders like the Mingo chief, Logan. The link between this aesthetic sensibility and moral probity was seen in the fact that "crimes are very rare among them." ("Queries VI, XIV, and XI," *Notes on the State of Virginia*)

Here we have to ask how Jefferson could at times be so appreciative of Native American dignity under conquest yet so blind to human worth in the oppressed African Americans. People have thrashed about looking for a basis in intellect for this distinction, but have neglected the regnant principle with Jefferson, his sense of beauty. He found that blacks lack "the circumstance of superior beauty" that is taken into account even in animal husbandry:

Is it [skin color] not the foundation of a greater or less share of beauty in the two races? Are not the fine mixtures of red and white, the expressions of every passion by greater or less suffusions of colour in the one, preferable to that eternal monotony, which reigns in the countenances, that immoveable veil of black which covers all the emotions of the other race? ("Query XIV," Notes on the State of Virginia)

This is Jefferson's aestheticism at its worst. But he had the strengths of his weaknesses. He thought that his "beautiful people," the ordinary white yeomen, had a sense of order that was at once artistic and moral. His treatise of prosody says that all people are able to sense the order of accents that is most pleasing because of "the construction of the human ear." Why do rules jump out at us from the very nature of the English language? "The reason is that it has pleased God to make us so." Even the whole complex of grammatical constructions was grasped without rules by those who spoke Anglo-Saxon, that pre-learned language of nature that he recommended to students at his university. (TJ to J. Evelyn Denison, November 9, 1815) It was such natural beauty, existing before theories, that he thought he discerned in the poems of the Scottish bard Ossian. (TJ to Charles McPherson, February 25, 1773)

This complex of aesthetic notions about natural perception gave Jefferson the assurance for one of his most famous democratic statements: "state a moral case to a ploughman & a professor. the former will decide it as well, & often better than the latter, because he has not been led astray by artificial rules." (TJ to Peter Carr, August 10, 1787) It was in the context of his letter on the sublimities of nature that Jefferson told Maria Cosway: "morals were too essential to the happiness of man to be risked on the incertain combinations of the head. she [nature] laid their foundation therefore in sentiment, not in science." The head must make "combinations," create a chain of linked arguments, in order to reach a point that the heart leaps to directly. Jefferson even attributes the American Revolution to the direct perception of right that bypassed the head's more timid reflections:

you [the head] began to calculate & to compare wealth and numbers: we threw up a few pulsations of our warmest blood; we supplied enthusiasm against wealth and numbers; we put our existence to the hazard when the hazard seemed against us, and we saved our country: justifying at the same time the ways of Providence, whose precept is to do always what is right, and leave the issue to him.

His estimate of the heart's moral certitudes also made Jefferson prefer the emotional yeoman of the South to the scheming banker of the North. When he listed the attributes of the two regions, he said that southerners were "generous," "candid," and "without attachment or pretensions to any religion but that of the heart," while the "chicaning" northerners were "superstitious and hypocritical in their religion." (TJ to marquis de Chastellux, September 2, 1785)

For Jefferson, then, the preservation of the heart's moral instinct is the true aim of education. That is why aesthetic response to a novel is a mode of moral formation:

we are therefore wisely framed to be as warmly interested for a fictitious as for a real personage. the field of imagination is thus laid open to our use and lessons may be formed to illustrate and carry home to the heart every moral rule of life. (TJ to Robert Skipwith, August 3, 1771)

Tears for another's plight, even for an imaginary character in a sentimental novel, show how the moral sense turns pain into the pleasures of benevolence: "And what more sublime delight than to mingle tears with one whom the hand of heaven hath smitten ! . . ." (TJ to Cosway)

Jefferson the aesthete, then, is not really Jefferson the dilettante but Jefferson the moralist. *And* the democrat. He felt that human beings respond nobly to nature if their contact with it is not broken by adventitious accretions to it—by institutional religion, by systems of financial credit and debit, by cities, by theories, by governments. The defense of freedom, for him, meant not obtruding on natural man an artificial compulsion. As he wrote to Abigail Adams (February 22, 1787):

the spirit of resistance to government is so valuable on certain occasions, that I wish it to be always kept alive. it will often be exercised when wrong, but better so than not to be exercised at all. I like a little rebellion now and then. it is like a storm in the Atmosphere.

That last sentence returns us to the storms brewing in the "laboratory" below Monticello's height, and to the basically artistic sense Jefferson had of politics. In his oddly mandarin way he had arrived at the basic democratic insight—that every human being is Humanity itself. It is an insight that G. K. Chesterton put in many earthy ways—that we do not shout that "a Nobel Prize winner is drowning," but that "a man is drowning"; that the jury system expresses the truth that ordinary

Thomas Jefferson. "A Map of the country between Albemarle Sound and Lake Erie, comprehending the whole of Virginia, Maryland, Delaware and Pensylvania, ..." Colored engraving from his *Notes on the State of Virginia* (London, 1787). Rare Book and Special Collections Division, Library of Congress.

Jefferson's map of Virginia and environs, based on his father's earlier map, was the sole illustration to his only book, Notes on the State of Virginia. *In their attempts to reach an understanding of his principles and attitudes and the influences upon him, historians have drawn heavily on this compendium of Jefferson's responses to questions from François de Marbois, secretary to the French legation, on a broad range of issues.*

Gilbert Stuart. Thomas Jefferson. Oil on wood. Washington, D.C., 1805. National Portrait Gallery, Smithsonian Institution; Gift of the Regents of the Smithsonian Institution, the Thomas Jefferson Memorial Foundation, and the Enid and Crosby Kemper Foundation. Owned jointly with Monticello.

Jefferson was well served by the quality of the portraits made of him during his lifetime, ensuring that his image is one of the best known among the pantheon of American leaders. Prints of Stuart's portrait were widely dispersed and, by late in Jefferson's second term, had displaced Rembrandt Peale's earlier image of the president in popularity. When the Stuart likeness, in the form of the replica painted by John Doggett, was adopted as the official Jeffersonian image for stamps, currency, and certificates in 1867, it became his preeminent icon.

persons should be the judges of moral truth; that "democracy is like blowing your nose, you may not do it well but you ought to do it yourself." The contradictions of Jefferson had their dark side, but they also had this one dramatically benign side as well: he was the most uncommon of men, but he had a deep faith in the common man. For all his own elite lifestyle, he was anti-elitist in principle—anti-priest, anti-banker, anti-theoretician, anti-politician. No other Founder had his deep reverence for the dignity and freedom of the individual.

Naturally, the nation has expanded on his insights—but it is to those insights it recurred when the work of expansion was to be done. The rights he found in his idealized yeoman are the model for those we try to uphold for every person in America. He voiced his faith in a rhetoric that has resonated far beyond any results he could have expected himself. The statement that "all men are created equal" is one of those formulations that ends up meaning more than it meant to mean. It became the lodestar to Lincoln, who taught us to read the Constitution itself in the light of the Declaration of Independence. It was appealed to by Martin Luther

King, Jr. The legacy of Jefferson, as passed on by Lincoln, is at the very heart of the American love of freedom. Here is the way Lincoln phrased the matter:

The principles of Jefferson are the definitions and axioms of free society . . . All honor to Jefferson—to the man who, in the concrete pressure of a struggle for national independence by a single people, had the coolness, forecast, and capacity to introduce into a merely revolutionary document, an abstract truth, applicable to all men and all times, and so to embalm it there, that to-day, and in all coming days, it shall be a rebuke and stumbling-block to the very harbingers of re-appearing tyranny and oppression. (Lincoln to Henry L. Pierce, April 6, 1859)

In Lincoln's own version of the American melting-pot concept, expressed in a July 10, 1859 speech in Chicago, he says that people who come from different countries, cultures, and status will be made equal in their American liberties by the Declaration. The statement that all men are equal "is the electric cord in that Declaration that links the hearts of patriotic and liberty-loving men together, that will link those patriotic hearts as long as the love of freedom exists in the minds of men throughout the world."

Drawing on the new generation of Jeffersonian scholarship, with its debunking of mythology and its attempt to determine his true legacy, *Thomas Jefferson: Genius of Liberty* takes a fresh look at Jefferson's ideas and principles, and the words he used to express them, in the context of the public and private realities he faced and the choices he made. Reflecting the wide range of opinion on Jefferson, both during his lifetime and in subsequent scholarship, it leaves an image of a complex and contradictory man of enduring fascination, whose most transcendent gift may have been the gift of expression.

Jefferson's words continue to express what is deepest and best in America's struggle toward equality for all. They are applied to blacks in ways that Jefferson did not intend, and have reached others going beyond his own anticipation—women, gays, the disabled, minorities of all kinds. He intuited, with his fine sensibility, an ethos he could not always act on himself, but he conjured it up with undispellable words. That ethos was liberty, and he remains its genius. Even Henry Adams, often Jefferson's critic, had to admit that the privately visionary words of Jefferson embodied, in time, the shared public vision of the American citizenry.

(opposite) Thomas Jefferson. Codicil to will, March 17, 1826. Special Collections Department, University of Virginia Library, on deposit from the Albemarle County Circuit Court.
Jefferson freed just five slaves in this codicil to his will made less than four months before his death; of these, three were Hemingses, and two, Madison and Eston, were allegedly his sons with Sally Hemings. Their other two children, Beverly (another son) and Harriet, had been allowed to go free four years earlier.
The timing of the departure of the two older children and the freeing of the younger two seems to corroborate allegations that Jefferson had made a promise that Sally Hemings's children would be freed when they reached the age of twenty-one.

I give a gold watch to each of my grand children who shall not have already received one from me, to be purchased and delivered by my executor, to my grandsons at the age of 21. and grand-daughters at that of sixteen.

I give to my good, affectionate and faithful servant Burwell his freedom, and the sum of three hundred Dollars to buy necessaries to commence his trade of painter and glazier, or to use otherwise as he pleases. I give also to my good servants John Hemings and Joe Fosset their freedom at the end of one year after my death: and to each of them respectively all the tools of their respective shops or callings: and it is my will that a comfortable log house be built for each of the three servants so emancipated on some part of my lands convenient to them with respect to the residence of their wives, and to Charlottesville and the University; where they will be mostly employed, and reasonably convenient also to the interests of the proprietor of the lands; of which houses I give the use of one, with a curtilage of an acre to each, during his life or personal occupation thereof.

I give also to John Hemings the service of his two apprentices, Madison and Eston Hemings, until their respective ages of twenty one years, at which period respectively, I give them their freedom. and I humbly and earnestly request of the legislature of Virginia a confirmation of the bequest of freedom to these servants, with permission to remain in this state where their families and connections are, as an additional instance of the favor, of which I have received so many other manifestations, in the course of my life, and for which I now give them my last, solemn, and dutiful thanks.

In testimony that this is a Codicil to my will of yesterday's date, and that it is to modify so far the provisions of that will, I have written it all with my own hand, on two pages, to each of which I subscribe my name this 17th day of March one thousand eight hundred and twenty six.

Th Jefferson

Attributed to André Basset l'aîné. *La Destruction de la Statue Royale a Nouvelle Yorck.*
Die Zerstorung der Koniglichen Bild Saule zu Neu Yorck. **Hand-colored etching. Paris, [177?].**
Prints and Photographs Division, Library of Congress.

An imaginary scene created in Paris after accounts reached Europe and widely reprinted there shows a crowd of soldiers
and civilians pulling down this statue of George III on Bowling Green. The statue was later melted down to provide lead for badly
needed bullets for the Continental Army.

"Rebellion to tyrants is obedience to God."

FROM DESIGN FOR U.S. SEAL

A Declaration by the Representatives of the UNITED STATES OF AMERICA, in General Congress assembled.

When in the course of human events it becomes necessary for one people to dissolve the political bands which have connected them with another, and to assume among the powers of the earth the separate and equal station to which the laws of nature & of nature's god entitle them, a decent respect to the opinions of mankind requires that they should declare the causes which impel them to the separation.

We hold these truths to be self-evident; that all men are created equal, that they are endowed by their creator with equal rights, some of which are inherent & inalienable, among these are the life, & liberty, & the pursuit of happiness; that to secure these rights, governments are instituted among men, deriving their just powers from the consent of the governed; that whenever any form of government becomes destructive of these ends, it is the right of the people to alter or to abolish it, & to institute new government, laying it's foundation on such principles & organising it's powers in such form, as to them shall seem most likely to effect their safety & happiness. prudence indeed will dictate that governments long established should not be changed for light & transient causes: and accordingly all experience hath shewn that mankind are more disposed to suffer while evils are sufferable, than to right themselves by abolishing the forms to which they are accustomed. but when a long train of abuses & usurpations [begun at a distinguished period &] pursuing invariably the same object, evinces a design to reduce them under absolute Despotism, it is their right, it is their duty, to throw off such + & to provide new guards for their future security. such has been the patient sufferance of these colonies; & such is now the necessity which constrains them to expunge their former systems of government. the history of the present king of Great Britain is a history of unremitting injuries and usurpations, [among which appears no solitary fact to contradict the uniform tenor of the rest, but all have] in direct object the establishment of an absolute tyranny over these states. to prove this, let facts be submitted to a candid world, for the truth of which we pledge a faith yet unsullied by falsehood.

Self-Evident Truths

THE VISION THAT AMERICANS have of their country is largely derived from a single document—the Declaration of Independence. Brown parchment replicas of this revolutionary statement are sold at museums and gift shops throughout the country. Children who can barely read are taught that the words on the fragile scroll are by Thomas Jefferson. Although many now believe that Jefferson drew on other sources to create his ringing denunciation of the British King George III, his extraordinary eloquence has gone undisputed for generations. His ability to articulate and assert the revolutionary ideals of his time won him a place not only at the Second Continental Congress of the United States in 1776 but also in the pantheon of American history. His unflinching vision of the American republic, however flawed or unrealistic, is our American dream. The fact that his ideals were coupled with brilliance in many fields, from philosophy and science to literature and architecture, only contributes to his lofty status.

Thomas Jefferson. "Original Rough draught" of the Declaration of Independence. Philadelphia, June 1776. Manuscript Division, Library of Congress.

Photographed from the original in the Jefferson Papers at the Library of Congress, this is the document submitted by Jefferson to Congress after corrections and additions were made by Adams, Franklin, and others on the Committee of Five. Brackets indicate the parts stricken out by Congress. Long after, perhaps in the nineteenth century, Jefferson went back to the document and annotated in the margins some of the changes made by Adams and Franklin. From the "original Rough draught" a "fair," or clean, copy was made.

It is difficult, therefore, to realize that Jefferson's first public appearances were so low key. At only thirty-three years of age, Jefferson was one of the junior members of the Virginia delegation to the Continental Congress. Tall for his time—about six feet, two inches—he was impressive in stature but shy in demeanor. In fact, there is no record of Jefferson ever delivering a single speech at the Continental Congress, and John Adams recalled, "during the whole Time I sat with him in Congress, I never heard him utter three sentences together." If he was overshadowed by the oratorical brilliance of fellow Virginians Patrick Henry, Edmund Pendleton, and Richard Henry Lee, Jefferson was not forgotten. For although the red-haired Virginian sat silently in the Pennsylvania State House that July in 1776, it is his contribution to the assembly that is most remembered.

As the debate over Jefferson's rough draft of the Declaration of Independence took center stage on July 2, 1776, he may have reflected on the path that led him, a

John Trumbull. *Declaration of Independence, 4 July 1776*. Oil on canvas. Begun Paris, 1787. Yale University Art Gallery, Trumbull Collection.

Jefferson's likeness was painted by Trumbull from life during the winter of 1787-1788 at Jefferson's home, the Hôtel de Langeac in Paris. It is said that Jefferson proposed the subject of the work to Trumbull and greatly aided the rising artist by helpfully recounting details of the event at the State House (later Independence Hall). Considered the most clear and faithful depiction of the presentation of the Declaration to Congress, it shows Jefferson as he was in 1776, with unpowdered hair and in the costume of the time. Trumbull later made several miniature copies of this portrait of Jefferson, one of which was sent to the statesman's intimate friend Maria Cosway.

> "the debates having taken up the greater parts of the 2ᵈ. 3ᵈ. & 4ᵗʰ. days of July, were, in the evening of the last, closed; the declaration was reported by the commee; agreed to by the house; & signed by every member except mr Dickinson."
>
> *TJ to James Madison, Notes on Congress drafting the Declaration, June 1, 1783*

Edward Savage and/or Robert Edge Pine. *Congress voting its Independence*. Oil on canvas. Philadelphia, ca. 1788. The Historical Society of Pennsylvania (HSP).

Pine's and/or Savage's depiction of the scene of independence is perhaps not as famous but certainly is as valuable as the Trumbull image. It presents a different, and some say more accurate, view of the actual Assembly Room in which the Declaration was approved. Jefferson, flanked by committee members Adams, Sherman, and Livingston, presents the document to John Hancock, while Benjamin Franklin is seated to their right.

member of the British colonial establishment, to the verge of a radical republican rebellion. The eldest son of Peter Jefferson and Jane Randolph, Jefferson was born April 13, 1743 at Shadwell plantation in Goochland, later Albemarle County, Virginia. Peter Jefferson was a prominent planter and surveyor. He taught his son about nature and imbued him with a sense of wonder about the Indian cultures and unexplored lands that lay to the west. Jane Randolph belonged to a prominent and influential family of the Virginia aristocracy, which proved helpful to her son early in his career. Jefferson's father died in 1757, when he was just fourteen. He was sent to boarding school to learn Latin and Greek. In 1760, he entered the College of William and Mary in Williamsburg. There, William Small became his most valued teacher and mentor. Through Small, he was first exposed to science and mathematics and to a world order described by philosophers of the Enlightenment:

it was my great good fortune, and what probably fixed the destinies of my life that Dr Wm. Small of Scotland was then professor of Mathematics, a man profound in most of the useful branches of science, with a happy talent of communicn, correct & gentlemanly manners, & an enlarged & liberal mind. he, most happily for me, became soon attached to me & made me his daily companion when not engaged in the school; and from his conversation I got my first views of the expansion of science & of the system of things in which we are placed. (TJ, "Autobiography," 1821)

J. Trenchard after Charles Willson Peale. "A N.W. View of the State House in Philadelphia taken 1778." Etching from *The Columbian Magazine*, July 1787. Rare Book and Special Collections Division, Library of Congress.

When this image, after Peale's drawing, appeared in The Columbian Magazine *just two years after the signing of the Declaration, it was accompanied by a description that referred to the State House as "a building which will, perhaps become more interesting in the history of the world than any of the celebrated fabrics of Greece or Rome." Aside from being the site of American independence, the upstairs was used during the Revolutionary War as a hospital for the wounded. During the occupation of British troops in Philadelphia, the soldiers quartered at the State House showed their disdain for their enemy by ransacking and vandalizing the premises.*

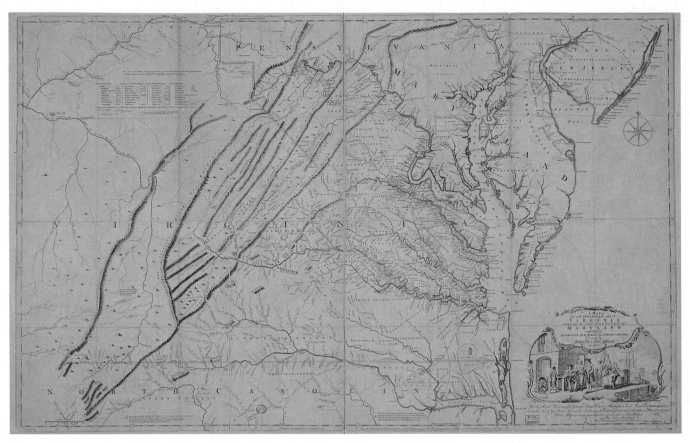

Thomas Jefferys after Joshua Fry and Peter Jefferson. *A Map of the most Inhabited part of Virginia containing the whole Province of Maryland with Part of Pensilvania, New Jersey and North Carolina.* **Engraving. London, 1755. Geography and Map Division, Library of Congress.**

Thomas Jefferson was eight years old when his father and surveyor Joshua Fry drew the original of this map of Virginia. It shows Albemarle County much the way it was in Jefferson's youth. Shadwell, the Jefferson family farm, is indicated at upper right of the county. The Jefferson estate known as Poplar Forest (not shown) was located between Peaks of Otters and Blackwater Creek (middle left). Jefferson used this map as a source for his own in Notes on the State of Virginia. *He called it, "the 1st accurate map of Virginia which had ever been made."*

John Trumbull. *Geo Wythe Esq.* **Drawing, pen and ink. Williamsburg, April 25, [17]91. Print and Picture Collection, The Free Library of Philadelphia.**

George Wythe, the man and mentor to whom Jefferson was forever indebted, is shown here as an older man. In his day he was considered one of the most learned lawyers in Virginia, and like his young protégé, was a lover of the classics. Even when others doubted Jefferson, Wythe remained his ardent supporter, which may have been why Jefferson called him "my second father."

The "Bodleian plate" of Williamsburg, Virginia. Modern print from the Bodleian copperplate owned by Colonial Williamsburg Foundation. Between 1723 and 1747. Prints and Photographs Division, Library of Congress.

The original copperplate from which this print was made was bequeathed to the Bodleian Library at Oxford University in 1755. Known as the "Bodleian Plate," it has become of primary importance to students and researchers because it is the only contemporary image we have of colonial Williamsburg. Recognizing its importance to the modern restoration led by John D. Rockefeller, Jr., the Bodleian Library presented the plate to him. In the top panel are the Wren building and formal topiary garden at the College of William and Mary, appearing as they would have when Jefferson attended classes there. The middle panel shows the colonial capitol, the Wren building, and the governor's palace.

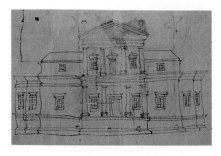

Thomas Jefferson. Elevation of the first Monticello. Drawing, pen and ink, 1769-70. Monticello/Thomas Jefferson Memorial Foundation, Inc.

Jefferson once admitted, "Architecture is my delight, and putting up and pulling down, one of my favorite amusements." This design for the first of Monticello's many incarnations reveals Jefferson's indebtedness to Andrea Palladio, the sixteenth-century Italian whose manifesto of classical architecture, Quattro Libri, *was reportedly referred to by Jefferson as "the Bible." Jefferson proved to be innovative in his design, combining Palladio's theories of symmetry and proportion with his own thoughts on aesthetics and function.*

Thomas Jefferson. "On the instructions given to the 1st delegation of Virginia to Congress in August 1774." Manuscript, ca. 1809. Manuscript Division, Library of Congress.

The eloquent language and radical ideas in Jefferson's draft instructions to the Virginia delegates to the Continental Congress in August 1774, later published as A Summary View of the Rights of British America, *helped win Jefferson the job of drafting the Declaration of Independence. When John Marshall, in his biography of George Washington, challenged the right of Virginia and Jefferson to claim preeminence in the early revolutionary movement, Jefferson wrote this explanation of his and Virginia's calls for national action in 1774 and attached it to a copy of his original draft, which had been lost.*

A serious and compulsive student, Jefferson sometimes studied fifteen hours a day and spent the few hours away from his books practicing the violin. After graduation, he became a law apprentice to George Wythe and then a local attorney representing landholders, primarily in cases including land-claims, debts, wills, and deeds. Edmund Randolph, a fellow attorney, wrote this recollection:

Until about the age of twenty-five years he had pursued general science, with which he mingled the law, as a profession, with an eager industry and unabated thirst. His manners could never be harsh, but they were reserved toward the world at large. To his intimate friends he shewed a peculiar sweetness of temper and by them was admired and beloved . . . He panted after the fine arts and discovered a taste in them not easily satisfied with such scanty means as existed in a colony . . . But it constituted a part of Mr. Jefferson's pride to run before the times in which he lived. (Edmund Randolph, History of Virginia, *Arthur H. Shaffer, ed., 1970)*

Jefferson's decision to run for political office in 1768 was a fateful one. Had he not been elected in 1769 to the House of Burgesses, he might have become Virginia's most well-read and cultured planter. But opposition to the British parliament had been brewing ever since the Stamp Act of 1765, and like other founders of the new American nation, Jefferson was presented with certain opportunities made possible by a spirit of rebellion that was spreading throughout the colonies.

The act that launched Jefferson onto the public stage was executed with his strongest and most incisive instrument—the pen. The reticent lawyer volunteered to draft instructions for the first Virginia delegation to the Continental Congress. Illness prevented Jefferson from attending the Virginia Convention, but his pamphlet *A Summary View of the Rights of British America* was published later in 1774 by the convention leaders in Williamsburg. This elegantly written—some said intemperate—condemnation of British treatment of the colonists, as well as staunch defense of American freedom and self-government, not only furthered the revolutionary cause, but secured Jefferson's reputation as a fine writer. His dramatic style conjured a convincing black-and-white picture, in which the king and his parliament were villains and the colonists their slaves.

> **"And this his majesty will think we have reason to expect when he reflects that he is no more than the chief officer of the people, appointed by the laws, and circumscribed with definite powers, ..."**
>
> *TJ,* A Summary View of the Rights of British America, *1774*

Single acts of tyranny may be ascribed to the accidental opinion of a day; but a series of oppressions, begun at a distinguished period, and pursued unalterably through every change of ministers, too plainly prove a deliberate and systematical plan of reducing us to slavery.

Jefferson's *Summary* was indeed a radical view. It asserted that the colonies were subject only to the laws adopted by their own legislatures and that their natural rights had been violated by Great Britain. The document called for a repeal of taxes and a lifting of the ban on American trade and manufacturing. Many of the charges

Mulberry Row, site of slave quarters at Monticello. Photograph by James T. Tkatch. Monticello/Thomas Jefferson Memorial Foundation, Inc.

This chimney is all that remains of the original slave quarters at Monticello, located on what was known as Mulberry Row. Most of Jefferson's slaves lived in log cabins with earthen floors and fireplaces for heating and cooking. They were provided with cooking utensils, bedding, clothing, and a weekly food ration, which they could supplement with crops from their own gardens.

(above right) *Run away from the subscriber* . . . . Advertisement placed by Thomas Jefferson. From *The Virginia Gazette*. Williamsburg, September 14, 1769. Virginia Historical Society, Richmond, Virginia.

The author of the Declaration of Independence was a slave owner, and as this ad would prove, regarded his African servants as valuable property. His livelihood very much depended on their labors. Still, Jefferson wrestled with the injustice of slavery. In interviews conducted years after Jefferson's death, some of his former slaves remembered him as a benevolent master.

leveled at Great Britain in *A Summary View* were strong, and one in particular—at least for a planter of the southern aristocracy—was quite unanticipated and bold:

The abolition of domestic slavery is the great object of desire in those colonies, where it was unhappily introduced in their infant state. But previous to the enfranchisement of the slaves we have, it is necessary to exclude all further importations from Africa; yet our repeated attempts to effect this by prohibitions, and by imposing duties which might amount to a prohibition, have been hitherto defeated by his majesty's negative: Thus preferring the immediate advantages of a few African [changed to "British" by Jefferson on his copy] *corsairs to the lasting interest of the American states, and to the rights of human nature, deeply wounded by this infamous practice . . . this is so shameful an abuse of a power trusted with his majesty for other purposes, ...*

Even Jefferson, a slaveowner himself, later came to realize that "tamer sentiments were preferred." Nevertheless, several of the other grievances set forth in that pamphlet were later incorporated into the Declaration of Independence.

The foundation of Jefferson's assertion in *A Summary View* that "the British parliament has no right to exercise authority over us" was not accepted by all. Most colonists agreed that Parliament had the right to regulate trade, but not impose taxes for the purposes of earning revenue. Jefferson went so far as to draw a parallel between the experiences of the British emigrants to America and the emigrations of the Saxons and Danes to England centuries before:

. . . our ancestors, before their emigration to America, were the free inhabitants of the British dominions in Europe, and possessed a right which nature has given to all men, of departing from the country in which chance, not choice, has placed them, of going in quest of new habitations, and of there establishing new societies, under such laws and regulations as to them shall seem most likely to promote public happiness.

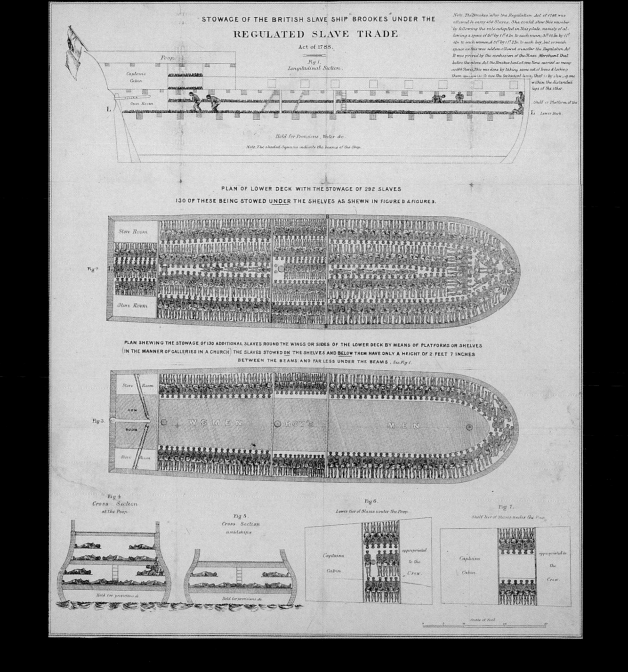

***Stowage of the British Slave Ship "Brookes" Under the Regulated Slave Trade Act of 1788.* Broadside. London, ca. 1790.**
Rare Book and Special Collections Division, Library of Congress.

The fate of African slaves—seen here as human cargo in a coffin-like ship—is the subject of this broadside issued by British abolitionist Thomas Clarkson in protest of the Regulated Slave Trade Act passed in 1788. The Act allowed British ships, like the Brookes, *to densely pack adult males into 6' x 14" of space, adult females into 5' 10" x 11" of space, and boys into compartments of 5' x 12". Such horrifying conditions produced an outcry from antislavery groups. The Declaration of Independence ignored the problem of slavery and Jefferson found it impossible to resolve this divisive issue in his*

Jefferson's views on government and the natural rights of man were not wholly original but took shape from his studies of the leaders of the Enlightenment, particularly John Locke. Jefferson proclaimed Locke, along with Isaac Newton and Francis Bacon, to be "the greatest men that have ever lived without exception." (TJ to John Trumbull, February 15, 1789) Jefferson regarded Locke's *Two Treatises on Government* (1690) as a key work and referred to Algernon Sidney's *Discourses Concerning Government* (1763) as "a rich treasure of republican principles." But his claim that the original colonists in America came as expatriates, with no allegiance to or charter from the king, was totally of his own devising. In fact, none—with the exception of his law tutor George Wythe—agreed with his imaginative twist on history in his own time or thereafter.

Thomas Jefferson and John Dickinson. *A Declaration By the Representatives of the United Colonies of North-America, now met in General Congress At Philadelphia, Setting forth the Causes and Necessity of their taking up Arms*. Broadside. Portsmouth, New Hampshire [?] [1775]. The Historical Society of Pennsylvania (HSP).

Only days after arriving in Philadelphia to take Peyton Randolph's place in Congress, Jefferson drafted the original version of this printed broadside revised by the moderate John Dickinson, which rallied the colonists to take up arms against the king. Adopted on July 6, 1775, it was considered the most important document of the first session of the Second Continental Congress.

A
DECLARATION
By the Repreſentatives of the
United Colonies
Of NORTH-AMERICA, now met in
General Congreſs
AT PHILADELPHIA,
Setting forth the CAUSES and NECESSITY
OF THEIR TAKING UP
ARMS.

A View of that great and flouriſhing City of BOSTON, when in its purity, and out of the Hands of the Philiſtines.

IF it was poſſible for Men, who exerciſe their Reaſon, to believe, that the Divine Author of our Exiſtence intended a Part of the human Race to hold an abſolute Property in, and an unbounded Power over others, marked out by his infinite Goodneſs & Wiſdom, as the Objects of a legal Domination, never rightfully reſiſtible, however ſevere and oppreſſive, the Inhabitants of theſe Colonies might at leaſt require from the Parliament of Great Britain, ſome Evidence, that this dreadful Authority over them has been granted to that Body. But a Reverence for our Great CREATOR, Principles of Humanity, and the Dictates of common Senſe, muſt convince all thoſe who reflect upon the Subject, that Government was inſtituted to promote the Welfare of Mankind, and ought to be adminiſtered for the Attainment of that End. The Legiſlature of Great-Britain, however ſtimulated by an inordinate Paſſion for a Power not only unjuſtifiable, but which they know to be peculiarly reprobated by the very Conſtitution of that Kingdom, and deſperate of Succeſs in any Mode of Conteſt, where Regard ſhould be had to Truth, Law, or Right, have at length, deſerting thoſe, attempted to effect their cruel and impolitic Purpoſe of enſlaving theſe Colonies by Violence, and have thereby rendered it neceſſary for us to cloſe with their laſt Appeal from Reaſon to Arms.—Yet however blinded that Aſſembly may be, by their intemperate Rage for unlimited Domination ſo to ſlight Juſtice and the Opinion of Mankind, we eſteem ourſelves bound by Obligations of Reſpect to the reſt of the World, to make known the Juſtice of our Cauſe.

Our Foreſathers, Inhabitants of the Iſland of Great-Britain, left their native Land to ſeek on theſe Shores a Reſidence for civil and religious Freedom. At the Expence of their Blood, at the Hazard of their Fortunes, without the leaſt Charge to the Country from which they removed, by unceaſing Labor and an unconquerable Spirit, they effected Settlements in the diſtant & inhoſpitable Wilds of America, then filled with numerous and warlike Nations of Barbarians.—Societies or Governments, veſted with perfect Legiſlatures, were formed under Charters from the Crown, and an harmonious Intercourſe was eſtabliſhed between the Colonies and the Kingdom from which they derived their Origin.—The mutual Benefits of this Union became in a ſhort Time ſo extraordinary, as to excite Aſtoniſhment: It is univerſally confeſſed, that the amazing Increaſe of the Wealth, Strength and Navigation of the Realm, aroſe from this Source; and the Miniſter who ſo wiſely and ſucceſsfully directed the Meaſures of Great-Britain in the late War, publicly declared, that theſe Colonies enabled her to triumph over her Enemies.—Towards the Concluſion of that War, it pleaſed our Sovereign to make a Change in his Counſels.—From that fatal Moment, the Affairs of the Britiſh Empire began to fall into Confuſion, and gradually ſliding from the Summit of glorious Proſperity to which they had been advanced by the Virtues and Abilities of one Man, are at length diſtrated by the Convulſions that now ſhake it to its deepeſt Foundations.— The new Miniſtry finding the brave Foes of Britain, though frequently defeated, yet ſtill contending, took up the unfortunate Idea of granting them a haſty Peace, and of then ſubduing her faithful Friends.

Theſe devoted Colonies were judged to be in ſuch a State, as to preſent Victories without Bloodſhed, and all the eaſy Emoluments of ſtatuteable Plunder.— The uninterrupted Tenor of their peaceable and reſpectful Behaviour from the Beginning of Colonization, their dutiful, zealous and uſeful Services during the War, though ſo recently and amply acknowledged in the moſt honorable Manner by his Majeſty, by the late King, and by Parliament, could not ſave them from the meditated Innovations.— Parliament was influenced to adopt the pernicious Project, & aſſuming a new Power over them, have in the Courſe of eleven Years, given ſuch deciſive Specimens of the Spirit and Conſequences attending this Power, as to leave no Doubt concerning the Effects of Acquieſcence under it. They have undertaken to give and grant our Money without our Conſent, tho' we have ever exerciſed an excluſive Right to diſpoſe of our own Property; Statutes have been paſſed for extending the Juriſdiction of Courts of Admiralty and Vice Admiralty beyond their ancient Limits: For depriving us of the accuſtomed and ineſtimable Privilege of Trial by Jury in Caſes affecting both Life and Property; for ſuſpending the Legiſlature of one of the Colonies; for interdicting all Commerce of another; and for altering fundamentally the Form of Government eſtabliſhed by Charter, and ſecured by Acts of its own Legiſlature ſolemnly confirmed by the Crown; for exempting the "Murderers" of Coloniſts from legal Trial, and in Effect, from Puniſhment; for erecting in a neighbouring Province acquired by the joint Arms of Great Britain and America, a Deſpotiſm dangerous to our very Exiſtence; and for quartering Soldiers upon the Coloniſts in Time of profound Peace. It has alſo been reſolved in Parliament, that Coloniſts charged with committing certain Offences, ſhall be tranſported to England to be tried.

But why ſhould we enumerate our Injuries in Detail? By one Statute it is declared, that Parliament can "of Right make Laws to bind us IN ALL CASES WHATSOEVER." What is to defend us againſt ſo enormous, ſo unlimited a Power? Not a ſingle Man of thoſe who aſſume it, is choſen by us; or is ſubject to our Controul or Influence: but on the contrary, they are all of them exempt from

Operation of ſuch Laws, and an American Revenue, if not diverted from the oſtenſible Purpoſes for which it is raiſed, would actually lighten their own Burdens in Proportion, as they increaſe ours. We ſaw the Miſery to which ſuch Deſpotiſm would reduce us. We for ten Years inceſſantly and ineffectually beſieged the Throne as Supplicants; we reaſoned, we remonſtrated with Parliament in the moſt mild and decent Language. But Adminiſtration, ſenſible that we ſhould regard thoſe oppreſſive Meaſures as Freemen ought to do, ſent over Fleets and Armies to enforce them. The Indignation of the Americans was rouſed it is true; but it was the Indignation of a virtuous, loyal, and affectionate People. A Congreſs of Delegates from the united Colonies was aſſembled at Philadelphia, on the fifth Day of laſt September. We reſolved again to offer an humble and dutiful Petition to the King, and alſo addreſſed our Fellow Subjects of Great Britain. We have purſued every temperate, every reſpectful Meaſure, we have even proceeded to break off our commercial Intercourſe with our Fellow Subjects, as the laſt peaceable Admonition, that our Attachment to no Nation upon Earth ſhould ſupplant our Attachment to Liberty.— This, we flattered ourſelves, was the ultimate Step of the Controverſy: But ſubſequent Events have ſhewn, how vain was this Hope of finding Moderation in our Enemies.

Several threatening Expreſſions againſt the Colonies were inſerted in his Majeſty's Speech; our Petition, though we were told it was a decent one, that his Majeſty had been pleaſed to receive it graciouſly, and to promiſe laying it before his Parliament, was huddled into both Houſes amongſt a Bundle of American Papers, and there neglected. The Lords and Commons in their Addreſs, in the Month of February laſt, ſaid, "that a Rebellion at that Time actually exiſted within the Province of Maſſachuſetts Bay; and that thoſe concerned in it, had been countenanced and encouraged by unlawful Combinations and Engagements, entered into by his Majeſty's Subjects in ſeveral of the other Colonies; and therefore they beſought his Majeſty, "that he would take the moſt effectual Meaſures to inforce due Obedience to the Laws and Authority of the ſupreme Legiſlature."— Soon after the commercial Intercourſe of whole Colonies, with foreign Countries and with each other, was cut off by an Act of Parliament; by another, ſeveral of them were intirely prohibited from the Fiſheries in the Seas near their Coaſts, on which they always depended for their Suſtenance; and large Re-inforcements of Ships and Troops were immediately ſent over to General Gage.

Fruitleſs were all the Entreaties, Arguments and Eloquence of an

(overleaf) Thomas Jefferys after George Heap and Nicholas Scull. "An East Prospect of the City of Philadelphia." Engraving from Jefferys, *A general topography of North America and the West Indies* (London, 1768). Geography and Map Division, Library of Congress.

This view of Philadelphia, taken from the Jersey Shore of the Delaware River, does not differ significantly from the city Jefferson knew as a delegate to the Second Continental Congress twenty years later. The street plan shows the location of the State House on Chestnut Street, and the image in the lower right is a detailed view of the façade. The text reads like a chamber of commerce ad for the thriving and prosperous colonial capital, calling the harbor "one of the safest & most commodious that is known."

Still, Jefferson's fine and fiery repudiation of arbitrary royal and parliamentary powers earned him election to the Second Continental Congress when he was chosen as an alternate to Peyton Randolph, at the convention formulating state government in Richmond in 1775. While the colonies were still reeling from encounters with British troops at Lexington and Concord, the southern gentleman, who had expanded his land and slave holdings through marriage to Martha Wayles Skelton, arrived in Philadelphia accompanied by his personal servants. Jefferson took his seat at the Second Continental Congress on June 21. His first achievement there was drafting a critical document, "A Declaration . . . Setting forth the Causes and Necessity of their taking up Arms." Afterwards, Jefferson returned to his home at Monticello, a full-fledged revolutionary.

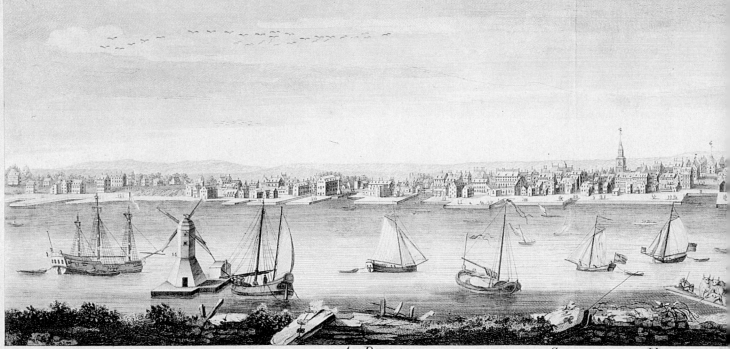

An EAST PROSPECT of the CITY of PHILADELPHIA; taken by GEORGE HEAP from the JERSEY Sh...

A DESCRIPTION OF THE SITUATION, HARBOUR

PHILADELPHIA, the Capital of Pennsylvania, is situate on the West side of the River Delaware, on a high and pleasant Plain; the City is laid out in form of an Oblong, two Miles in length, and one in breadth, bounded on the East by Delaware River, and on the West by the River Schuylkill, the Streets are all strait and parallel to the sides of the Plan, and consequently cut each other at right Angles, none of which are less than 50 and the widest 100 feet in breadth, the Houses are built with Brick, and are from two to three and four Stories high; the Buildings are extended on Delaware's Front a considerable distance North and South

beyond the Verge of the City the depth of several Streets to the Westward. The Harbour is one of the safest & most commodious that is known, where Ships of the greatest Burthen may safely Anchor in seven or eight Fathom at Low Water, & may unlade close to the Wharfs without the least Danger, & as this Harbour is at least thirty Miles above Salt Water, it must consequently be free from the Ship Worm; The Tides rise and fall here seven or eight feet, and flow up the River thirty Miles above the Town; the great distance of Philadelphia from the Sea adds much to its Security, as the Channel is intricate & long, and is a natural Fortification, which together

REFER...

1. Christ Church. 2. State House. 3. Academy. 4. Presbyterian Church. 5. Dutch Calvinist Church. 6. The Court House. 7. Quakers Meeting House. 8. High Street Wharf

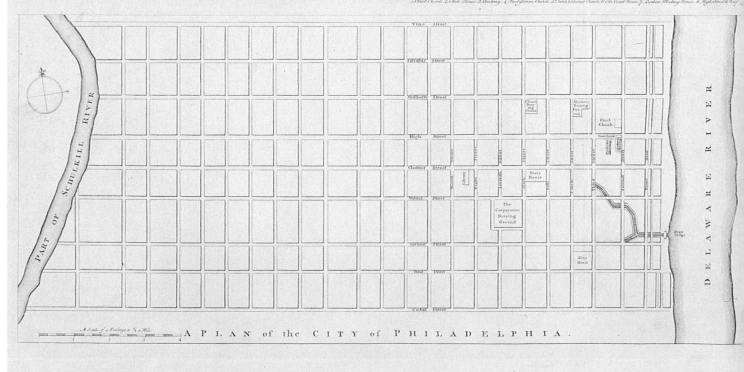

A PLAN of the CITY of PHILADELPHIA.

ORE, under the Direction of NICHOLAS SCULL Surveyor General of the PROVINCE of PENNSYLVANIA.

&c. OF THE CITY AND PORT OF PHILADELPHIA.

with a Battery a little below the Town, of twenty seven pieces of large Cannon, is thought a sufficient defence against an attack by Sea. This flourishing City was founded by the hon.ble William Penn first Proprietor of the Province of Pennsilvania & Counties of Newcastle, Kent & Sussex on Delaware, in the Year 1682, & has increased so fast, that in the Year 1753 the number of dwelling Houses were near two thousand two hundred & The City is govern'd by a Mayor, Recorder, Aldermen & Common Council, so very full of Inhabitants, & the trade so extensive that there was in the Month of October last one hundred & Seventen Sea Vessels in the harbour at one time, & the Export from December 25, 1751, to December

RENCES.

27, 1752, by the Naval Office appears to be as follows, Wheat 86,500 Bushels, 325,960 barrels of Flour 90,733 Bushels of Indian Corn, 589 Hogsheads, 80 Furos, 18,258 Barrels, 788 quarter Casks and 219 Tons of Bread, 925 Barrels of Beef, 3,130 Barrels of Pork, 1,802, 933 Staves, 1,491 Tons, 891 Tons of Bar and 203 Tons of Pig Iron, 505 Chests, 32 half Chests and 15 quarter Chests of Wine & Yarn, 57 Chests, 1121 Barrels & Boxes of Wax and 5 Hogsheads of Gins 19,985 Hogsheads 451 half Hogsheads, 591 Tierces and 221 Barrels of Flaxseed, & the Import from England to Philadelphia for 3 Years from Christmas 1748 to Christmas 1751 amounted to 617, 267, 8, 9, of which 178, 582, 5, 5, was the Product & Manufacture of G.t Britain.

9, Mulberry Street. 10, Safsafras Street. 11 Vine Street. 12, Chesnut Street. The other Streets are not to be seen from the point of Sight. 18, Front ridge. 14, Cornmill.

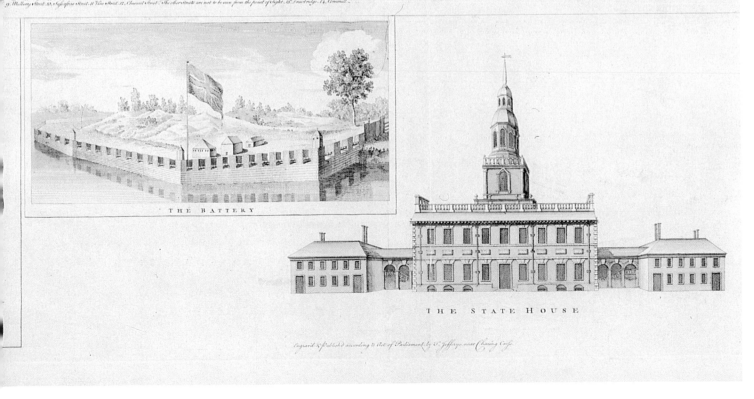

THE BATTERY

THE STATE HOUSE

Engrav'd & Publish'd according to Act of Parliament, by T. Jefferys near Charing Cross.

Thomas Paine. *Common Sense* **(Philadelphia, 1776). Rare Book and Special Collections Division, Library of Congress.**

Paine's rousing pamphlet, an instant best-seller in its time, had sold 129,000 copies only six months after its publication date in January 1776. Paine's argument that no reconciliation with Britain would resolve the colonists' grievances urged Americans toward revolution and ultimately aided the efforts of the Second Continental Congress to approve the Declaration of Independence. In Paine's lifetime the book sold half a million copies.

COMMON SENSE;

ADDRESSED TO THE

INHABITANTS

OF

AMERICA,

On the following interesting

SUBJECTS.

I. Of the Origin and Design of Government in general, with concise Remarks on the English Constitution.

II. Of Monarchy and Hereditary Succession.

III. Thoughts on the present State of American Affairs.

IV. Of the present Ability of America, with some miscellaneous Reflections.

Man knows no Master save creating HEAVEN,
Or those whom choice and common good ordain.
THOMSON.

PHILADELPHIA;

Printed, and Sold, by R. BELL, in Third-Street.

MDCCLXXVI.

G.W. *Fashion Before Ease;—or,—a good Constitution sacrificed, for a Fantastick Form.* **London, January 2, 1793. Prints and Photographs Division, Library of Congress.**

Even after the American Revolution, British and American hostilities continued to surface, as in this entertaining political cartoon, in which radical writer Thomas Paine is rudely bracing his foot against Britannia's posterior while tightening the laces of her corset. His face is red with exertion, and she clings desperately to a large tree so she will not fall. In his pocket Paine has a pair of scissors as well as a measuring tape labeled "Rights of Man." A sign on the cottage in the background reads "Thomas Pain, Stay Maker from Thetford, Paris Modes by Express." Without the final "e" in his surname, Paine is the perfect Anglo-American to exact justice for past injuries inflicted on the colonies by the British Empire. But the suggestion in this sketch is that Paine's were cosmetic efforts that only led his country to sacrifice "a good Constitution."

Although Monticello was Jefferson's haven from his public life, he could not ignore that war was enveloping Virginia. After the January 1776 publication of Thomas Paine's pamphlet *Common Sense* entreating colonists to proclaim their independence from the crown, the Virginia convention voted to form its own government and set about writing its own constitution. Jefferson, back in Philadelphia for the Congress to which he was reelected, longed to be back in Williamsburg. While George Mason crafted Virginia's Declaration of Rights, Jefferson labored at a distance. He wrote at least three drafts of a Virginia constitution, which he forwarded to friends in Williamsburg. Although Jefferson's version came too late to be adopted, the Virginia legislature did use his preamble.

One can look at *Summary View*, "Declaration of Necessity," and the Virginia Constitution as try-outs for Jefferson's stellar performance as author of the Declaration of Independence. On June 7, 1776, when Richard Henry Lee introduced the resolution calling on Congress "to declare that these United colonies are & of right ought to be free and independent states," Congress did not take an immediate vote, but appointed a five-man committee to draft a declaration of independence for its consideration. With Lee returning to Virginia to establish the new state government, his junior colleague was appointed, along with John Adams of Massachusetts, Roger Sherman of Connecticut, Benjamin Franklin of Pennsylvania, and Robert R. Livingston of New York, to serve on the committee. Fortunately, Jefferson brought along his notes, his now-famous portable desk, and his violin to his new quarters in Jacob Graff's house. Designated principal draftsman of the document, he was in for some long nights.

It seems odd to us now that the senior members of the Virginia government sent a junior member to Philadelphia at such a critical moment, but in 1776 the Virginia delegates felt that the key to independence was the establishment of a secure state government. Home was where the great debates were to be held and where history would be made. The task of writing the Declaration was not perceived as a great honor. In his autobiography, John Adams recalled that he passed the task of writing the Declaration on to Jefferson so that the draft would not suffer the criticism of Adams's political opponents. Jefferson had never led a debate on the floor, and he belonged to no faction. His words would be received purely for the principles they conveyed.

Holed up in his second-floor lodgings in the Graff house on Seventh and Market Streets, Jefferson set out to apply all his knowledge about individual freedom and

> "... that whenever any form of government becomes destructive of these ends, it is the right of the people to alter or to abolish it, & to institute new government."
>
> *"Original Rough draught," Declaration of Independence*

Graff House. So. West corner of Seventh and Market Sts., Philadelphia. Photograph by James E. McClees. Philadelphia, ca. 1880. The Library Company of Philadelphia.
We can imagine Jefferson spending long nights laboring over his rough draft in the second floor bedroom and parlor of this house, which he rented from bricklayer Jacob Graff. Located at Seventh and Market Streets, and generally known as the Graff House, the building was demolished in 1883, shortly after this photograph was taken. A reconstruction of the house was later built on the original site. It is now a museum and recreates the setting in which Jefferson composed the Declaration of Independence.

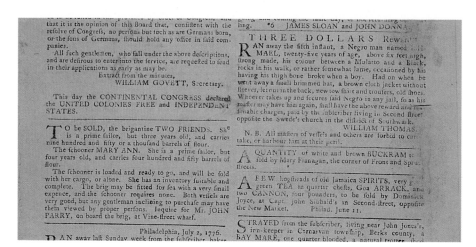

natural order to his vision of the new nation. Later in life, he recalled, somewhat defensively, that he endeavored:

not to find out new principles, or new arguments, never before thought of, not merely to say things which had never been said before; but to place before mankind the common sense of the subject; [in] terms so plain and firm as to command their assent, and to justify ourselves in the independant stand we [were] compelled to take. neither aiming at originality of principle or sentiment, nor yet copied from any particular and previous writing, it was intended to be an expression of the American mind, and to give to that expression the proper tone and spirit called for by the occasion. (TJ to Henry Lee, May 8, 1825)

Drawing on his earlier writings, he produced in just a few days the first draft of the masterful document. He then made a clean or "fair" copy of the composition document, which became the foundation of the document labeled by Jefferson as "the original Rough draught." Revised first by Franklin and Adams, and then by the full committee, a total of forty-seven alterations, including the insertion of three complete paragraphs, was made on the text before it was presented to Congress on June 28. After voting for independence on July 2, Congress continued to refine the document, making thirty-nine additional revisions to the committee draft before its final adoption on the morning of July 4.

Jefferson's "original Rough draught" embodies the multiplicity of corrections, additions, and deletions that were made at each step. Although most of the alterations are in Jefferson's handwriting (he later indicated which changes he believed were made by Adams and Franklin), he felt slighted by the way Congress "mangled" the manuscript. In fact, as Congress neared completion of the document, Jefferson could only write in the margin "a different phraseology inserted." To console his young colleague, Benjamin Franklin told him this now-famous account of the editorial process:

I have made it a rule, . . . whenever in my power, to avoid becoming the draftsman of papers to be reviewed by a public body. I took my lesson from an incident which I will relate to you. When I was a journeyman printer, one of my companions, an apprentice hatter, having served out his time was about to open shop for himself. His first concern was to have a handsome signboard with a proper inscription. He composed it in these words: "John Thompson, hatter, makes and sells hats for ready money," with a figure of a hat subjoined. But he thought he would submit it to his friends for their amendments. The first he showed it to thought the word "hatter" tautologous, because followed by the words, "makes hats" which show he was a hatter. It was struck out. The next observed that the word "makes" might as well be omitted, because the customers would not care who made the hats. If good and to their mind, they would buy, by whomever made. He struck it out. A third said he thought the words "for ready money" were useless, as it was not the custom of the place to sell on credit. Everyone who purchased expected to pay. They were parted with, and the inscription now stood: "John Thompson sells hats." "Sells hats?" says his next friend. "Why, nobody will expect you to give them away. What then is the use of that word?" It was stricken out; and "hats" followed it, the rather as there was one painted on the board. So his inscription was reduced ultimately to "John Thompson" with the figure of a hat subjoined. (Carl Van Doren, Benjamin Franklin, 1939)

Jefferson remained bitter about the changes made to the Declaration of Independence right up to his death. Again, he found opposition to his view on expatriation, as he had in *Summary View*, and he was disappointed that the Congress was unwilling to endorse his rousing farewell to his "British brethren":

we must endeavor to forget our former love for them, and to hold them as we hold the rest of mankind, enemies in war, in peace friends. we might have been a free & a great people together; but a communication of grandeur & of freedom it seems is below their dignity. be it so, since they will have it: the road to happiness & to glory is open to us too; we will tread it apart from them, ... (TJ, "Original Rough draught," Declaration)

Of course, the greatest words attributed to Jefferson—the words most school children can recite—are, "We hold these truths to be self-evident, that all men are created equal, that they are endowed by their Creator with certain unalienable Rights, that among these are Life, Liberty, and the pursuit of Happiness—." (engrossed copy, National Archives) Our national identity is expressed by this statement, and its author is our national icon. His vision, whether borrowed from the British philosophers or recycled from his previous writings, became the hope of a new republic and ultimately the dream of all Americans, those born here and those who left foreign oppression to make "the land of liberty" their home.

John Dunlap, a Philadelphia printer, produced the first typeset text of the Declaration of Independence, now called the "Dunlap Broadside," probably during the night of July 4–5. The next day John Hancock, president of the Continental Congress, began dispatching copies of the Declaration to America's political and military leaders. The *Pennsylvania Evening Post* published the first newspaper edition of the Declaration on July 6. On July 9, General George Washington ordered that his personal copy of "the Dunlap Broadside," of which only two-thirds now survives, be read to the assembled American army in New York. After many celebratory toasts, the raucous troops went to the foot of Broadway at the Bowling Green and pulled down the statue of George III. The lead figure was melted into bullets for the American army.

On July 19, after New York's assent, Congress added "Unanimous" to the title, "The unanimous Declaration of the thirteen united States of America," and ordered the production of an engrossed (officially inscribed) copy, which Jefferson and his colleagues, including some who had not voted for its adoption, began to sign on August 2, 1776.

Wounded to the core by the concessions he was forced to make to Congress in the final Declaration, and worried by news from Monticello of Martha's failing health (she was enduring her third difficult pregnancy), Jefferson had already asked to return to Virginia:

I am sorry the situation of my domestic affairs renders it indispensably necessary that I should sollicit the substitution of some other person here in my room. the delicacy of the house will not require me to enter minutely into the private causes which render this necessary. (TJ to Edmund Pendleton, ca. June 30, 1776)

By July 29, he was desperate. He wrote to Richard Henry Lee:

for god's sake, for your country's sake, & for my sake, come. I receive by every post such accounts of the state of mrs Jefferson's health, that it will be impossible for me to disappoint her expectation of seeing me at the time I have promised . . . I pray you to come. I am under a sacred obligation to go home. (TJ to Richard Henry Lee, July 29, 1776)

It wasn't until September 1776 that Richard Henry Lee came to replace him in Philadelphia. Stung by critics of the Declaration, he returned to his family, his farm, and his books. At Monticello, he took a much-needed sabbatical from public life.

William Hamilton after George Noble. "The Manner in which the American Colonies Declared themselves Independant of the King of England, throughout the different Provinces, on July 4, 1776." Etching from Edward Barnard, *History of England* (London, 1783). Prints and Photographs Division, Library of Congress.

In an imaginary scene made for a later history of England, a mounted officer reads the Declaration of Independence to an enthusiastic hat-waving crowd. On the wall at left there is a sign declaring "America Independant 1776."

IN CONGRESS, JULY 4, 1776.

A DECLARATION

BY THE REPRESENTATIVES OF THE

UNITED STATES OF AMERICA,

IN GENERAL CONGRESS ASSEMBLED.

WHEN in the Course of human Events, it becomes neceſſary for one People to diſſolve the Political Bands which have connected them with another, and to aſſume among the Powers of the Earth, the ſeparate and equal Station to which the Laws of Nature and of Nature's God entitle them, a decent Reſpect to the Opinions of Mankind requires that they ſhould declare the cauſes which impel them to the Separation.

We hold theſe Truths to be ſelf-evident, that all Men are created equal, that they are endowed by their Creator with certain unalienable Rights, that among theſe are Life, Liberty, and the Purſuit of Happineſs—That to ſecure theſe Rights, Governments are inſtituted among Men, deriving their juſt Powers from the Conſent of the Governed, that whenever any Form of Government becomes deſtructive of theſe Ends, it is the Right of the People to alter or to aboliſh it, and to inſtitute new Government, laying its Foundation on ſuch Principles, and organizing its Powers in ſuch Form, as to them ſhall ſeem moſt likely to effect their Safety and Happineſs. Prudence, indeed, will dictate that Governments long eſtabliſhed ſhould not be changed for light and tranſient Cauſes; and accordingly all Experience hath ſhewn, that Mankind are more diſpoſed to ſuffer, while Evils are ſufferable, than to right themſelves by aboliſhing the Forms to which they are accuſtomed. But when a long Train of Abuſes and Uſurpations, purſuing invariably the ſame Object, evinces a Deſign to reduce them under abſolute Deſpotiſm, it is their Right, it is their Duty, to throw off ſuch Government, and to provide new Guards for their future Security. Such has been the patient Sufferance of theſe Colonies; and ſuch is now the Neceſſity which conſtrains them to alter their former Syſtems of Government. The Hiſtory of the preſent King of Great-Britain is a Hiſtory of repeated Injuries and Uſurpations, all having in direct Object the Eſtabliſhment of an abſolute Tyranny over theſe States. To prove this, let Facts be ſubmitted to a candid World.

He has refuſed his Aſſent to Laws, the moſt wholeſome and neceſſary for the public Good.

He has forbidden his Governors to paſs Laws of immediate and preſſing Importance, unleſs ſuſpended in their Operation till his Aſſent ſhould be obtained; and when ſo ſuſpended, he has utterly neglected to attend to them.

He has refuſed to paſs other Laws for the Accommodation of large Diſtricts of People, unleſs thoſe People would relinquiſh the Right of Repreſentation in the Legiſlature, a Right ineſtimable to them, and formidable to Tyrants only.

He has called together Legiſlative Bodies at Places unuſual, uncomfortable, and diſtant from the Depoſitory of their public Records, for the ſole Purpoſe of fatiguing them into Compliance with his Meaſures.

He has diſſolved Repreſentative Houſes repeatedly, for oppoſing with manly Firmneſs his Invaſions on the Rights of the People.

He has refuſed for a long Time, after ſuch Diſſolutions, to cauſe others to be elected; whereby the Legiſlative Powers, incapable of Annihilation, have returned to the People at large for their exerciſe; the State remaining in the mean time expoſed to all the Dangers of Invaſion from without, and Convulſions within.

He has endeavoured to prevent the Population of theſe States; for that Purpoſe obſtructing the Laws for Naturalization of Foreigners; refuſing to paſs others to encourage their Migrations hither, and raiſing the Conditions of new Appropriations of Lands.

He has obſtructed the Adminiſtration of Juſtice, by refuſing his Aſſent to Laws for eſtabliſhing Judiciary Powers.

He has made Judges dependent on his Will alone, for the Tenure of their Offices, and the Amount and Payment of their Salaries.

He has erected a Multitude of new Offices, and ſent hither Swarms of Officers to harraſs our People, and eat out their Subſtance.

He has kept among us, in Times of Peace, Standing Armies, without the conſent of our Legiſlatures.

He has affected to render the Military independent of and ſuperior to the Civil Power.

He has combined with others to ſubject us to a Juriſdiction foreign to our Conſtitution, and unacknowledged by our Laws; giving his Aſſent to their Acts of pretended Legiſlation:

For quartering large Bodies of Armed Troops among us:

For protecting them, by a mock Trial, from Puniſhment for any Murders which they ſhould commit on the Inhabitants of theſe States:

For cutting off our Trade with all Parts of the World:

For impoſing Taxes on us without our Conſent:

For depriving us, in many Caſes, of the Benefits of Trial by Jury:

For tranſporting us beyond Seas to be tried for pretended Offences:

For aboliſhing the free Syſtem of Engliſh Laws in a neighbouring Province, eſtabliſhing therein an arbitrary Government, and enlarging its Boundaries, ſo as to render it at once an Example and fit Inſtrument for introducing the ſame abſolute Rule into theſe Colonies:

For taking away our Charters, aboliſhing our moſt valuable Laws, and altering fundamentally the Forms of our Governments:

For ſuſpending our own Legiſlatures, and declaring themſelves inveſted with Power to legiſlate for us in all Caſes whatſoever.

He has abdicated Government here, by declaring us out of his Protection and waging War againſt us.

He has plundered our Seas, ravaged our Coaſts, burnt our Towns, and deſtroyed the Lives of our People.

He is, at this Time, tranſporting large Armies of foreign Mercenaries to compleat the Works of Death, Deſolation, and Tyranny, already begun with circumſtances of Cruelty and Perfidy, ſcarcely paralleled in the moſt barbarous Ages, and totally unworthy the Head of a civilized Nation.

He has conſtrained our fellow Citizens taken Captive on the high Seas to bear Arms againſt their Country, to become the Executioners of their Friends and Brethren, or to fall themſelves by their Hands.

He has excited domeſtic Inſurrections amongſt us, and has endeavoured to bring on the Inhabitants of our Frontiers, the mercileſs Indian Savages, whoſe known Rule of Warfare, is an undiſtinguiſhed Deſtruction, of all Ages, Sexes and Conditions.

In every ſtage of theſe Oppreſſions we have Petitioned for Redreſs in the moſt humble Terms: Our repeated Petitions have been anſwered only by repeated Injury. A Prince, whoſe Character is thus marked by every act which may define a Tyrant, is unfit to be the Ruler of a free People.

Nor have we been wanting in Attentions to our Britiſh Brethren. We have warned them from Time to Time of Attempts by their Legiſlature to extend an unwarrantable Juriſdiction over us. We have reminded them of the Circumſtances of our Emigration and Settlement here. We have appealed to their native Juſtice and Magnanimity, and we have conjured them by the Ties of our common Kindred to diſavow theſe Uſurpations, which would inevitably interrupt our Connections and Correſpondence. They too have been deaf to the Voice of Juſtice and of Conſanguinity. We muſt, therefore, acquieſce in the Neceſſity, which denounces our Separation, and hold them, as we hold the reſt of Mankind, Enemies in War, in Peace, Friends.

We, therefore, the Repreſentatives of the UNITED STATES OF AMERICA, in GENERAL CONGRESS, Aſſembled, appealing to the Supreme Judge of the World for the Rectitude of our Intentions, do, in the Name, and by Authority of the good People of theſe Colonies, ſolemnly Publiſh and Declare, That theſe United Colonies are, and of Right ought to be, FREE AND INDEPENDENT STATES; that they are abſolved from all Allegiance to the Britiſh Crown, and that all political Connection between them and the State of Great-Britain, is and ought to be totally diſſolved; and that as FREE AND INDEPENDENT STATES, they have full Power to levy War, conclude Peace, contract Alliances, eſtabliſh Commerce, and to do all other Acts and Things which INDEPENDENT STATES may of right do. And for the ſupport of this Declaration, with a firm Reliance on the Protection of divine Providence, we mutually pledge to each other our Lives, our Fortunes, and our ſacred Honor.

Signed by ORDER and in BEHALF of the CONGRESS,

JOHN HANCOCK, PRESIDENT.

ATTEST.
CHARLES THOMSON, SECRETARY.

PHILADELPHIA: PRINTED BY JOHN DUNLAP.

In Congress, July 4, 1776. A Declaration By the Representatives of the United States of America, In General Congress Assembled. Broadside. Philadelphia, July 4–5, 1776. Rare Book and Special Collections Division, Library of Congress.

John Hancock sent a copy of the "Dunlap Broadside" to General George Washington on July 6, 1776. When Washington had the text read to his troops in New York on July 9, they celebrated by destroying a bronze and lead statue of King George III that stood at Broadway on the Bowling Green.

Benjamin Randolph after Thomas Jefferson. Portable writing desk. Philadelphia, 1776.
The National Museum of American History, Smithsonian Institution.

Even in his lifetime this mahogany lap desk, designed by Jefferson and made to his specifications by Philadelphia cabinetmaker Benjamin Randolph, held great significance. It is the desk on which Jefferson composed the Declaration of Independence and wrote a daunting number of letters. In giving this valuable possession to his granddaughter Ellen and grandson-in-law Joseph Coolidge, Jr. at their marriage, Jefferson wrote, "Politics as well as Religion has its superstitions. these, gaining strength with time, may, one day, give imaginary value to this relic, for its association with the birth of the Great Charter of our Independance." (TJ, affidavit, November 18, 1825) Coolidge was suitably grateful for the "faithful depository of your cherished thoughts" and said he would consider the desk "no longer inanimate, and mute, but as something to be interrogated and caressed." (Coolidge to TJ, February, 27, 1826)

Thomas Jefferson, 1776: Draftsman and Author

by Pauline Maier

"I HAVE SOMETIMES ASKED myself," Thomas Jefferson wrote in late 1800, "whether my country is the better for my having lived at all? I do not know that it is." During the previous fifty-seven years he had "been the instrument" of several notable deeds, but "they would have been done by others; some of them, perhaps, a little better." Among the accomplishments he mentioned were a series of legislative reforms he had proposed for Virginia, some of which were never passed, some of which were enacted only through the agency of others after he had left the legislature. Jefferson's list included the Declaration of Independence, but his emphasis lay elsewhere—on his efforts to make the Rivanna River navigable, his sending a number of fine olive trees from Marseilles to South Carolina and Georgia, his obtaining "a cask of heavy upland rice" from Africa in the hope that it might be planted and "supersede the culture of wet rice, which renders South Carolina and Georgia so pestilential in the summer." The greatest service anyone could render his country, Jefferson said, was to add a "useful plant to its culture," particularly a "bread grain" or, only slightly less useful, an oil, which the olive trees could provide. (TJ memorandum to himself on public services, ca. September 1800)

Obviously Jefferson had no idea that he would become the most admired American of his generation. Like modern historians who assume that eminence should turn on things done, on concrete accomplishments that left a mark on the world, Jefferson scoured his life for acts that might merit the gratitude of posterity—and found the results distressingly meager. Finally, in 1826, he reduced his nominations to a short list of three. The inscription he proposed for his tombstone read:

Here was buried
Thomas Jefferson
Author of the Declaration of American Independance
of the Statute of Virginia for religious freedom
& Father of the University of Virginia

It was a strange epitaph for a man who had been governor of Virginia, American minister to France, secretary of state, vice president, and president of the United States. By failing to mention those offices, Jefferson perhaps recognized that his administrative career was, in general, undistinguished. Even his splendid first term in the White House failed to produce the kind of achievements that Jefferson could comfortably have chiseled on his tombstone: the glory of the Lewis and Clark expedition went more to the explorers than to its sponsor, and the Louisiana Purchase, which doubled the size of the United States, required that Jefferson violate his own strict construction principles. Then, thanks to the Embargo, his second term ended disastrously. "never did prisoner, released from his chains, feel such relief," he wrote, "as I shall on shaking off the shackles of power." (TJ to Pierre du Pont de Nemours, March 2, 1809)

What Jefferson cited is almost as striking as what he excluded. Many distinguished American institutions of higher education predated the University of Virginia, and by 1826 student unrest had already undermined Jefferson's idealistic plans for a community of self-regulating, autonomous scholars, which might have distinguished Virginia from its predecessors. To be sure, Jefferson's Statute of Religious Freedom had significance far beyond Virginia: it began a dismantling of state religious establishments that spread, separating church and state, and so, despite the militant protestantism of eighteenth-century America, helped rescue the United States from divisions that would blight the history of Ireland. But by 1826 Jefferson's primary claim to fame was as "author of the Declaration of American Independence." And, for reasons that are in good part of his doing, it is that role for which he is primarily remembered.

Why did the Declaration seem so notable an achievement in 1826? A half century earlier, the Second Continental Congress considered other pressing tasks of greater importance—gathering votes for independence, holding out against a new British military offensive, and designing a possible treaty with France. After the Declaration carried news of independence to the far reaches of the United States, it was all but forgotten. Members of Jefferson's own Republican Party first rescued it from obscurity in the 1790s, and later, after the War of 1812, it became a national icon that Americans revered like a sacred object. That made it a text well worth claiming by a man worried about his historical legacy.

Jefferson probably emphasized his role as "author" of the Declaration—a claim missing in the 1800 list—because that role had been questioned. The publication in 1819 of the "Mecklenburg Declaration of Independence" inspired charges that Jefferson had copied much of his text from resolutions adopted over a year earlier by militiamen in Mecklenburg County, North Carolina. Jefferson dismissed the charge, as have most subsequent historians. But his claim of authorship remains open to question on different grounds. He overlooked contributions made by other members of the five-man drafting committee Congress appointed on June 11, 1776, by the Congress as a whole, by earlier writers whose words fed into the document, and by younger Americans who in 1826 had already begun reshaping the Declaration of Independence, giving it a function it was not originally meant to serve.

In the early nineteenth century, John Adams recalled that the committee held several meetings in which members discussed the document, divided it into sections or "articles," and committed their conclusions to paper as "minutes" or instructions for its draftsman. That makes sense: a committee appointed to draft a document would not meet and appoint a draftsman without first discussing what he should do. But from there on, Jefferson insisted in 1823, the text was almost entirely his. He prepared a draft, then showed it to John Adams and Benjamin Franklin, who made only a few verbal changes. After incorporating those suggestions into a "fair copy," he submitted it to the committee, which, he said, passed it on to Congress with no further changes.

Jefferson was confident of his account because it was based not on memory but evidence from the time still in his possession, including the "original Rough draught" of the Declaration, which is now in the collections of the Library of Congress. It shows the text as Jefferson first presented it to other committee members and all subsequent editorial changes, which, except for a few by Adams and Franklin, are in Jefferson's handwriting. He probably concluded that they were therefore entirely of his doing, forgetting that some of those changes were mandated by the committee (which also included Connecticut's Roger Sherman and R. R. Livingston of New York). On a "Friday morn" in June of 1776, Jefferson wrote Franklin that the committee had asked him to change "a particular sentiment or two," which he had done. He proposed to submit the revised draft to the committee the next morning with whatever additional alterations Franklin might propose. Clearly the committee played a far more active role than Jefferson recalled almost five decades later.

And Congress? After adopting resolutions endorsing independence on July 2, it spent the better part of two days editing the draft Declaration, moving words, changing phrases, chopping out large blocks of text, and rewriting much of the last paragraph. During that process Jefferson suffered so visibly that, he later recalled, Franklin tried to console him with a story about a hat-maker who solicited from friends comments on a sign he proposed to hang outside his shop. Gradually they struck out everything but the man's name and the image of a hat. The story, as Franklin put it, illustrated the peril of "becoming the draughtsman of papers to be reviewed by a public body." Later, Jefferson made at least six copies of the committee draft, to show correspondents the "mutilations" Congress had imposed on his work. He had no idea that the cause of so much pain and humiliation would someday be a source of pride.

Those who defend Jefferson's "authorship" of the Declaration point out that Congress's editorial pen fell hardest on the latter parts of the text, not the opening section that posterity most admires. The delegates left unchanged the Declaration's first paragraph, which began "When in the course of human events," a spectacular improvement over the "whereas" that opened similar documents. And Congress made only a handful of alterations in the second paragraph, whose long, powerful first sentence begins "We hold these truths to be self evident . . . ." In composing that famous line Jefferson probably used a draft Declaration of Rights for Virginia by George Mason, a fellow planter, that appeared in the *Pennsylvania Gazette* on June 12, 1776, about the time the committee first met. Step by step he compressed Mason's language so it fit a defined eighteenth-century rhetorical form by which one phrase was piled on another in a long sequence, the meaning of which became clear only at the end. Jefferson's sentence ended with an assertion of the people's right to "alter or abolish" a form of government that fails to secure their rights and to found another that they consider "most likely to effect their safety and happiness"—with an assertion of the right of revolution, which the Americans were exercising in 1776. For Jefferson, on into the final weeks of his life, the Declaration remained first and foremost a revolutionary manifesto, a "signal" that might arouse men everywhere to "burst the chains" that bound them and to "assume the blessings and security of self-government." (TJ to Roger Weightman, June 24, 1826)

The editing of the Declaration did not, however, end on July 4, 1776. Today Jefferson's assertion of the right of revolution has been all but excised from the document. What Americans remember is a shortened version of Jefferson's long rhetorical sentence—like the quotation on the Jefferson Memorial:

WE HOLD THESE TRUTHS TO BE SELF-EVIDENT: THAT ALL MEN ARE CREATED EQUAL, THAT THEY ARE ENDOWED BY THEIR CREATOR WITH CERTAIN INALIENABLE RIGHTS, AMONG THESE ARE LIFE, LIBERTY AND THE PURSUIT OF HAPPINESS, THAT TO SECURE THESE RIGHTS GOVERNMENTS ARE INSTITUTED AMONG MEN.

Cutting off Jefferson's sentence in the middle alters its meaning and that of the document. It ceases to be a revolutionary manifesto and becomes akin to a bill of rights, a statement of principles for an established state that affirms men's original equality and their rights to life, liberty, and the pursuit of happiness—which went unmentioned in the Constitution of 1787 and its first ten amendments—and the fundamental obligation of government to protect those rights.

Today Jefferson often receives credit not only for writing the Declaration but for the principles of equality and rights that it asserted, as if they were of his invention and so part of his personal legacy to the nation. He himself made no such claim. The Declaration of Independence, he said, was meant to be "an expression of the American mind." There is, however, strong evidence that the Declaration's assertion of equality and rights coincided with his own convictions. It lies in a draft constitution for Virginia that he composed in 1776 immediately before drafting the Declaration of Independence. Jefferson was author, not draftsman, of that draft constitution since he wrote it alone, with no committee or Congress to direct and edit his text and no mandate to express any convictions but his own. At the time, moreover, he considered the constitution a work of first importance. The establishment of a new form of government, he wrote Thomas Nelson, was "the whole object of the present controversy; for should a bad government be instituted for us . . . it had been as well to have accepted at first the bad one offered to us from beyond the water without the risk and expence of contest." (TJ to Nelson, May 16, 1776)

The story of Jefferson's draft constitution began the day after he arrived in Philadelphia after taking a five-month "break" from his congressional duties in Virginia. On May 15, 1776, Congress called on the states to suppress all authority under the Crown and establish new governments founded firmly on the authority of the people. That meant, Jefferson correctly concluded, that Virginia would write a new state constitution, and he wanted desperately to participate. Why, he wrote Nelson the very next day, didn't Virginia recall its congressional delegates for a short period, perhaps leaving one or two to speak for the state? He didn't get his way. Jefferson remained at Congress when, on June 13, two other delegates, Richard Henry Lee and George Wythe, left for the Virginia convention. Wythe, however, carried with him a "bill for new-modelling the form of Government" that Jefferson had written on his own initiative in late May and early June.

It was a remarkable document that contained prototypes of all three American "fundamental documents": its preamble declared Virginia's independence from Britain, the body of the text provided a plan of government or constitution proper, and its final section, which Jefferson labeled "Rights Private and Public," constituted, in effect, a bill of rights. Jefferson's preamble—most of which the Virginia convention tacked onto the constitution it had already agreed upon when Jefferson's draft arrived—condemned George III with words inspired by the English Declaration of Rights (1688/89), but had an ideological explicitness that the earlier document lacked. By his "several acts of misrule," it said, the king had "forfeited the kingly office." Moreover, since "all experience" had shown that monarchy was "inveterately inimical" to "public liberty," Jefferson would have explicitly abolished it in Virginia "forever."

The government Jefferson proposed formally separated the legislative, executive, and judiciary, but centered power in the lower house of the legislature, whose members chose the senate, the "administrator" (or governor), and a privy coun-cil as well as the state's treasurer and attorney general. Later, in his *Notes on the State of Virginia*, Jefferson complained that the constitution Virginia adopted in 1776 placed too much power in the legislature and so created an "elective despotism." His plan of government was not much better, but both designs were produced at a time, as he later put it, when Americans were "new and unexperienced in the science of government." In the context of 1776, however, his scheme was at once distinctly "democratical" and radically egalitarian. It rested power not on both houses of the legislature, as did the constitution Virginia adopted, but on the state's house of representatives, which would be annually elected by an electorate that included more small property-holders than qualified under Virginia's established rules. Jefferson also would have made county representation in the legislature proportional to population, and so ended a system of unequal power that favored Virginia's eastern, Tidewater counties, despite westerners' ardent complaints, on into the nineteenth century. And he insisted that the people should ratify the constitution directly, making it an act of the sovereign people, not of the legislature, which anticipated what would soon become standard American practice.

The greatest distinction of Jefferson's "new modelling" of Virginia's government lay, however, in its proposed egalitarian social reforms and specification of rights. The document lacked the powerful assertion that "all men are born equally free and independent" and had "certain inherent natural rights" that Mason included in his draft Virginia Declaration of Rights. But where Mason stated rights with a peculiarly tentative language taken straight from the English Declaration of Rights, Jefferson asserted them in a direct way appropriate to the Americans' understanding of their nature. Where Mason, for example, said "that standing armies, in time of peace, should be avoided, as dangerous to liberty," Jefferson wrote "there shall be no standing armies but in time of actual war." His draft constitution said "printing presses shall be free," except insofar as private injuries prompted private legal

(opposite) Thomas Jefferson. Notes on the Virginia Constitution. June 1776. Manuscript Division, Library of Congress.

Jefferson may have been busy in Philadelphia in June 1776, but he still had time to convey his thoughts on the Virginia Constitution to the delegates laboring back in Williamsburg. These notes were sent to George Wythe for delivery to the Virginia convention, but arrived too late to be incorporated into the final document. However, the delegates did draw on Jefferson's suggestions in these notes in writing amendments.

this conduct ... at this time ... permitting their ... chief magistrate ... send over ... soldiers of our own ... but foreign mercenaries ... this is too much ... we must endeavor to forget our former love for them and to hold them as the rest of mankind, enemies in war, in peace friends. we might have been a free & a great people together, but ... happiness ... apart be it so, since they will have it: the road to ... happiness is open to us too, we will climb it ... & acquiesce in the necessity which ... our ... eternal separation.

649

suits, that "all persons shall have full and free liberty of religious opinion" and could not be compelled to "frequent or maintain any religious institution," and that "no freeman shall be debarred the use of arms within his own lands or tenements." Carrying semi-automatic rifles in public places would not, it seems, come under his definition of the right to bear arms.

Jefferson also tried to enhance equality among Virginians in one way after another. His article on "Rights Private and Public" granted poor and propertyless persons fifty acres of land, which they would hold "in full and absolute dominion, of no superior whatsoever," and demanded the purchase of Indian lands "on behalf of the public"—not by private land speculators—before they were appropriated. He provided that women's inheritance rights would equal those of men, ended the importation of slaves, and eased naturalization procedures so immigrants who gave satisfactory proof of their intention to reside in the state and subscribed to its fundamental laws could become residents with "all the rights of persons natural born." Where a provision failed to make its way into the Virginia constitution, Jefferson often later tried to secure its implementation by acts of the legislature—with mixed results, as he acknowledged in the memorandum of 1800 on his public services.

Jefferson was, in retrospect, an appropriate if unconventional hero for a nation of doers—a man of restless energy who threw himself whole-heartedly into one project after another. Many of his proposals were—as Joseph Ellis said of Jefferson's plans for the University of Virginia—"magisterial in conception, admirable in intention, unworkable in practice." That only a handful went into effect without substantial revision has, however, detracted very little from his reputation. Americans admire the range of his interests, the strength of his dreams, the power with which he stated ideals that we share but, like Jefferson, often have difficulty realizing in practice. And the widespread association of Jefferson with the cause of equality and rights is well founded. The proof lies, however, less in the celebrated Declaration of Independence that he drafted for Congress than in the little-known constitution he proposed for the state of Virginia—only part of which was adopted.

(opposite) Thomas Jefferson. Fragment of earliest known draft of the Declaration of Independence (obverse and reverse). Philadelphia, June 1776. Manuscript Division, Library of Congress.

This original manuscript in Thomas Jefferson's hand is the only known surviving fragment of the earliest draft of the Declaration of Independence. Although only a small part of the text is represented, it gives a sense of the laborious editing process the document went through before Jefferson was able to prepare the "original Rough draught" for Adams's and Franklin's scrutiny. One can track the path of many changes, for instance, in the "original Rough draught," Franklin changed Jefferson's "deluge us in blood," shown in this fragment (obverse image, third line) to "destroy us." Oddly, those are the very words Jefferson had first put down and then crossed out.

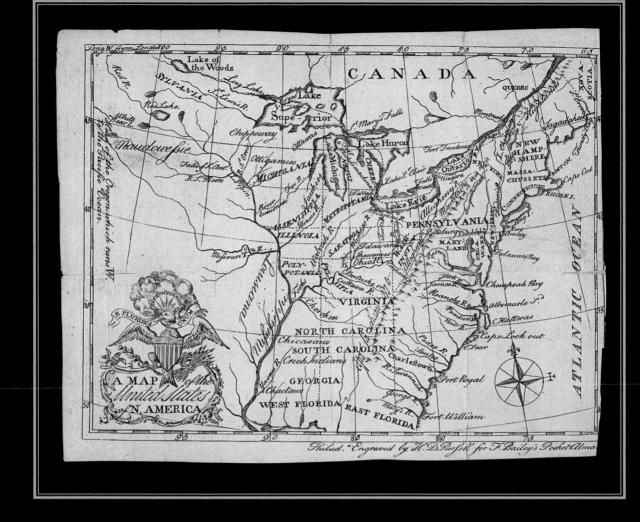

H. D. Pursell. "A Map of the United States of N. America." Engraving from *F. Bailey's Pocket Almanac* (Philadelphia, 1785).
Rare Book and Special Collections Division, Library of Congress.

When Jefferson became a member of Congress in 1783, he developed a plan for the creation of territories and new states which formed the basis of the Ordinance of 1784. His original plan envisioned fourteen states, to which he gave classicized names based on Native American words and geographical features, such as Cherronesus, Assenisippia, Pelisipia, Polypotamia, and Metropotamia, and historical names like Saratoga and Washington. Although most of his designations were not used, Michigania did evolve into Michigan and Illinoia became Illinois.
This map by H. D. Pursell was the first to show Jefferson's proposed names for the states (see page 41).

"the first object of my heart is my own country. in that is embarked my family, my fortune, & my own existence."

TJ TO ELBRIDGE GERRY, JANUARY 26, 1799

Chapter 2 | # The Passionate Idealist

THROUGHOUT HIS LIFE, Jefferson played tug-of-war with politics, and politics always won. His heart was in Monticello with his family, but his country needed him. He would pull away from the obligations of government, only to find himself unable to resist the opportunities to reassert the revolutionary principles that were so dear to him. In September 1776, Jefferson mistakenly believed that his national service was complete. He had not only drafted the Declaration of Independence and contributed to Virginia's state constitution, but had labored to prepare a great seal of the United States and articles of confederation before leaving Philadelphia. Soon after his return to Virginia, he was asked to serve with Benjamin Franklin and Silas Deane as one of the United States commissioners in Paris, an offer he refused. While Martha Jefferson's precarious health was certainly a factor in his decision, he realized that "the laboring oar was really at home." He wanted to have a personal hand in Virginia's transformation from colony to state.

Jefferson took his seat in the Virginia House of Delegates in October 1776 with the intention of establishing new individual freedoms. Consistent with his world view, he set about dismantling the framework of aristocratic society—class, religion, civil and criminal law, and slavery. Many of his proposals were defeated, but his successes meant a great deal to him. The abolition of primogeniture and entails—a system of inheritance that created a ruling class of wealthy landowners—was among his greatest contributions:

to annul this privilege, and instead of an Aristocracy of wealth, of more harm and danger, than benefit, to society, to make an opening for the aristocrasy of virtue and talent, which nature has wisely provided for the direction of the interests of society, & scattered with equal hand thro' all it's conditions, was deemed essential to a well ordered republic. (TJ, "Autobiography," 1821)

Mather Brown. Thomas Jefferson. Oil on canvas. London, 1786. National Portrait Gallery, Smithsonian Institution; Bequest of Charles Francis Adams.

Those who knew Jefferson did not think this portrait a good likeness of the sitter. His secretary and friend William Short said of the piece, "[the portrait] of Mr. Jefferson is supposed by every body here to be an étude. It has no feature like him." Considered one of Brown's finest compositions, it shows the American diplomat looking more like a European aristocrat. The iconography of the piece, showing the figure of Liberty with the familiar pole and Liberty cap, is indicative of Jefferson's growing reputation as the author of the Declaration of Independence and as a key player in America's battle for liberty. John Adams commissioned this copy from the artist before the original, which has been lost, was sent to Jefferson in Paris.

Benjamin Franklin. *Articles of Confederation and Perpetual Union, Between the Colonies of . . . . .* **Letterpress with pen and ink annotations by Thomas Jefferson. Philadelphia, [June–July 1775]. Manuscript Division, Library of Congress.**

Although Jefferson was silent throughout the debates on the articles of confederation, he took good notes, with a particular focus on the contentious issues of how much each state should contribute to support of the union and how large and small states should be fairly represented in Congress. Jefferson also annotated this copy of Benjamin Franklin's proposed articles of confederation. Of the final thirteen articles adopted by Congress on November 15, 1777—of which article 9 drastically limited the authority of the central government—Jefferson wrote, "but with all the imperfections of our present government, it is without comparison the best existing or that ever did exist."

"Seal of the United States of America MDCCLXXVI" (obverse) and "Rebellion to Tyrants is Obedience to God" (reverse). Wood engraving after drawings by Benson J. Lossing from *Harper's New Monthly Magazine*, July, 1856. General Collections, Library of Congress.

On July 4, 1776, in addition to approving the Declaration of Independence, Congress chose Jefferson, John Adams, and Benjamin Franklin to design a great seal for the new United States. Franklin proposed the phrase "Rebellion to tyrants is obedience to God," a sentiment Jefferson heartily embraced. He included it in the design for the Virginia seal and sometimes stamped it on the wax sealing his own letters. Although Congress rejected the elaborate seal endorsed by the trio, it retained the legend "E Pluribus Unum" beneath the shield and this, rather than "Rebellion to tyrants," became the country's motto.

ARTICLES

OF

CONFEDERATION AND PERPETUAL UNION,

BETWEEN THE COLONIES OF

NEW-HAMPSHIRE,
MASSACHUSETTS-BAY,
RHODE-ISLAND,
CONNECTICUT,
NEW-YORK,
NEW-JERSEY,
PENNSYLVANIA,

THE COUNTIES OF NEW-CASTLE,
KENT AND SUSSEX ON DELAWARE,
MARYLAND,
VIRGINIA,
NORTH-CAROLINA,
SOUTH-CAROLINA, AND
GEORGIA.

ART. I. THE Name of this Confederacy shall be "THE UNITED STATES OF AMERICA."

ART. II. The said Colonies unite themselves so as never to be divided by any Act whatever, and hereby severally enter into a firm League of Friendship with each other, for their common Defence, the Security of their Liberties, and their mutual and general Welfare, binding the said Colonies to assist one another against all Force offered to or attacks made upon them or any of them, on Account of Religion, Sovereignty, Trade, or any other Pretence whatever.

ART. III. Each Colony shall retain and enjoy as much of its present Laws, Rights and Customs, as it may think fit, and reserves to itself the sole and exclusive Regulation and Government of its internal police, in all matters that shall not interfere with the Articles of this Confederation.

ART. IV. No Colony or Colonies, without the Consent of the United States assembled, shall send any Embassy to or receive any Embassy from, or enter into any Treaty, Convention or Conference with the King or Kingdom of Great-Britain, or any foreign Prince or State; nor shall any Colony or Colonies, nor any Servant or Servants of the United States, or of any Colony or Colonies, accept of any Present, Emolument, Office, or Title of any Kind whatever, from the King or Kingdom of Great-Britain, or any foreign Prince or State; nor shall the United States assembled, or any Colony grant any Title of Nobility.

ART. V. No two or more Colonies shall enter into any Treaty, Confederation or Alliance whatever between them, without the previous and free Consent and Allowance

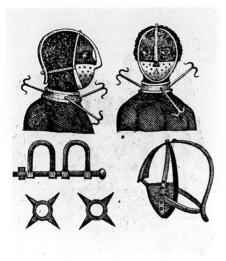

Virginia lawmakers may not have been prepared for all the changes proposed by their industrious colleague, but they must have been impressed by his untiring resolve to revamp Virginia's legal code. Working with a committee that included Edmund Pendleton and George Wythe, Jefferson submitted 126 bills for approval in under three years. Aside from updating archaic language and deleting all references to British rule, he took it upon himself to present several major reforms, the stickiest of which was the gradual abolition of slavery. Clearly an idea whose time had not come—particularly to Virginia's Tidewater planters—slavery remained a daunting and impenetrable hurdle throughout Jefferson's lifetime. A few years later, when asked to explain his position on slavery, Jefferson wrote this eloquent and insightful passage:

There must doubtless be an unhappy influence on the manners of our people produced by the existence of slavery among us. The whole commerce between master and slave is a perpetual exercise of the most boisterous passions, the most unremitting despotism on the one part, and degrading submissions on the other. Our children see this, and learn to imitate it; for man is an imitative animal . . . If a parent could find no motive either in his philanthropy or his self-love, for restraining the intemperance of passion towards his slave, it should always be a sufficient one that his child is present. But generally it is not sufficient. The parent storms, the child looks on, catches the lineaments of wrath, puts on the same airs in the circle of smaller slaves, gives a loose to his worst of passions, and thus nursed, educated, and daily exercised in tyranny, cannot but be stamped by it with odious peculiarities. The man must be a prodigy who can retain his manners and morals undepraved by such circumstances. And with what execration should the statesman be loaded, who permitting one half the citizens thus to trample on the rights of the other, transforms those into despots, and these into enemies, destroys the morals of the one part, and the amor patriae of the other . . . With the morals of the people, their industry also is destroyed. For in a warm climate, no man will labour for himself who can make another labour for him. This is so true, that of the proprietors of slaves a very small proportion indeed are ever seen to labour. And can the liberties of a nation be thought secure when we have removed their only firm basis, a conviction in the minds of the people that these liberties are of the gift of God? That they are not to be violated but with his wrath? Indeed I tremble for my country when I reflect that God is just: that his justice cannot sleep for ever: that considering numbers, nature and natural means only, a revolution of the wheel of fortune, an exchange of situation, is among possible events: that it may become probable by supernatural interference! The Almighty has no attribute which can take side with us in such a contest. (TJ, "Query XVIII," Notes on the State of Virginia, 1787 edition, written in 1781 and 1782)

The young statesman had greater success with the issue of religious freedom and considered passage of the Virginia statute for religious freedom among his greatest accomplishments. In Jefferson's Virginia, there was a long history of state support for the Church of England, which the first Anglican colonists had transported from the homeland, along with all its special privileges and legal advantages. However, as more immigrants of other faiths—Baptists, Lutherans, Methodists, and Presbyterians—multiplied in the colony, they resented having to contribute taxes to support a faith to which they did not subscribe. Jefferson felt that these dissenters were being tyrannized by the state. Still a student of the Enlightenment, he hoped to create a barrier between church and state, allowing individuals to pursue their own philosophical freedoms. Although he did not attend church regularly, he believed in a Supreme Being and respected the moral beliefs of others, which he

Thomas Jefferson. *An Act for establishing Religious Freedom; passed in the assembly of Virginia in the beginning of the year 1786* **[Paris, 1786]. Rare Book and Special Collections Division, Library of Congress.**

Jefferson was so proud of his efforts to secure religious freedom in his state that he chose the Virginia statute for religious freedom as one of the three achievements memorialized on his tombstone. The Virginia legislature altered Jefferson's preamble to tone down his enthusiastic praise of the supremacy of reason. Nevertheless, he was pleased enough with the final text of the act that he had it printed in Paris, where he was serving as minister. This copy is bound with a copy of his Notes on the State of Virginia *(Paris, 1785).*

Jefferson, Thomas.

An ACT for *establishing* RELIGIOUS FREEDOM; *passed in the assembly of Virginia in the beginning of the year* 1786.

WELL aware that Almighty God hath created the mind free; that all attempts to influence it by temporal punishments or burthens, or by civil incapacitations, tend only to beget habits of hypocrisy and meanness, and are a departure from the plan of the Holy Author of our religion, who, being Lord both of body and mind, yet chose not to propagate it by coercions on either, as was in his Almighty power to do; that the impious presumption of legislators and rulers civil, as well as ecclesiastical who, being themselves but fallible and uninspired men, have assumed dominion over the faith of others, setting up their own opinions and modes of thinking as the only true and infallible, and as such endeavouring to impose them on others, hath established and maintained false religions over the greatest part of the world, and through all time: That to compel a man to furnish contributions of money for the propagation of opinions which he disbelieves, is sinful and tyrannical; that even the forcing him to support this or that teacher of his own religious persuasion, is depriving him of the comfortable liberty of giving his contributions to the particular pastor whose thought were a private matter: ". . . it does me no injury for my neighbour to say there are twenty gods, or no god. It neither picks my pocket nor breaks my leg." (TJ, "Query XVII," *Notes on the State of Virginia*) In 1777, he drafted the Bill for establishing Religious Freedom, which sought to open the mind and free men's opinions from the controls of the state:

We the General Assembly of Virginia do enact, that no man shall be compelled to frequent or support any religious Worship place or Ministry whatsoever, nor shall be enforced, restrained, molested, or burthened in his body or goods, nor shall otherwise suffer on account of his religious opinions or belief, but that all men shall be free to profess, and by argument to maintain their opinions in matters of religion, and that the same shall in no wise diminish, enlarge, or affect their civil capacities. (Bill for establishing Religious Freedom, broadside, 1779, earliest printed text)

Initial efforts to pass the measure failed. The issue surfaced again in 1784-1786, while Jefferson was minister to France. His protégé James Madison was left in the Virginia Assembly to rally forces against the state coalition, which supported the established clergy. Led by Patrick Henry, with the support of George Washington and John Marshall, the opposition was daunting. But the Madison-led coalition—both tax opponents and religious reformers—successfully passed Jefferson's bill. In one of the many ironic twists in his life, staunch advocates of religion had passed Jefferson's plan to open people's minds to deism and secularism, in addition to traditional Christianity, while freeing them from the involuntary civil financial support of religious establishments.

Jefferson was more comfortable fighting a battle of ideas than waging a war with weapons. The three years he spent crafting laws for Virginia allowed him the time and luxury to apply his republican principles to the new nation, while never far from the sanctuary of Monticello. But the war's focus was shifting southward, and Jefferson had the misfortune of serving as governor of his state when the British landed four-square in Virginia. Management of troops, money, and supplies defied his concept of natural order, and his efforts to curtail the chaos of armed conflict failed.

Jefferson's term as governor (1779-1781) is considered to be a low point in his career. The ever-reluctant politician was a fiscally conservative and cautious executive, who was seen as a weak administrator and—even worse—a coward. But there is evidence that Jefferson was between a rock and a hard place when it came to defending Virginia—and particularly its new capital in Richmond—from invading British forces. When the South was in need, Jefferson had dutifully sent Virginia troops to reinforce state troops already sent by Washington to Charleston and

Charles Willson Peale. James Madison. Miniature, watercolor on ivory, with gold frame. Philadelphia, 1783. Rare Book and Special Collections Division, Library of Congress.

Fellow Virginian James Madison, known today as the "Father of the Constitution," was not only Jefferson's protégé, but his loyal ally in promoting republican principles. It was Madison who pushed Jefferson's statute for religious freedom through the Virginia legislature, kept Jefferson informed of the development of the Constitution while he was in Paris, and led the battle in Congress against the Federalists—those, like John Adams and Alexander Hamilton, who supported a centralized, powerful federal government.

Carte de La Partie de La Virginie . . . le 19 Octobre 1781. Hand-colored map. Paris, 1781. Geography and Map Division, Library of Congress.

The first major battles of the American Revolution were fought in the northern colonies, but by the time Jefferson assumed the governorship of Virginia in 1779, the war had moved south. Jefferson saw Virginia's role as supplier of troops and ammunition to the embattled Carolinas, rather than as a battle-ground itself. But the British thought otherwise, making several forays into the state when it was insufficiently defended by a small number of militia. This map, based on drawings made on site, records positions of strategic forts and the attacks of combined American and French army forces against Lord Cornwallis at Yorktown and of the French fleet under Admiral de Grasse against the British fleet on the Chesapeake Bay in October 1781.

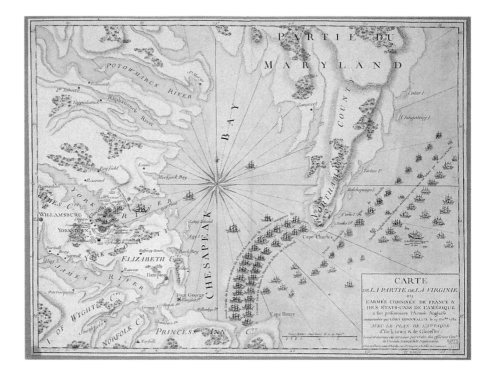

Reddition de l'Armée Angloises Commandée par Mylord Comte de Cornwallis . . . . Hand-colored etching. Paris, 1781. Geography and Map Division, Library of Congress.

With the help of the French navy, the Americans defeated the British under General Charles Cornwallis at Yorktown, Virginia, on October 19, 1781. This battle ended the Revolutionary War. However, the victory came too late to restore Jefferson's reputation as a war governor. He had ceased to serve in this post when his term expired in June, although the beleaguered House of Delegates was not able to elect Thomas Nelson, Jr. as his replacement until nearly a week later.

Camden, South Carolina, where together they sustained heavy losses. With British troops suddenly landing on the shores of the James River in October 1780, Jefferson faced a severe shortage of men to defend his state. The British, however, did little but settle in at Portsmouth.

With Cornwallis's troops to the south, the British fleet to the east, and the western frontier exposed to possible attack, the governor was again caught unprepared on the last day of 1780, when American turncoat Benedict Arnold began his advance up the James River to Richmond. Jefferson futilely called for enough militia to reinforce the small Continental force commanded by General Frederick von Steuben. He apparently rode in circles around Richmond trying to find his absent general while the British sacked the capital and destroyed public stores, state records, and the nearby foundry.

And his shame did not stop there. In the spring of 1781, British forces under Arnold and William Phillips, who had brought reinforcements, again sailed toward Richmond. They were contained by Virginia militia under von Steuben at Petersburg, where they burned some warehouses. At Manchester they were surprised by the daring and capable Lafayette, who marched his men from Baltimore in just ten days when he learned of the enemy's advance. The British were forced to retreat. Only a month later, however, Cornwallis sent elite troops under Colonel Banastre Tarleton to capture Jefferson and the retreating Virginia government. Jefferson was at Monticello when he was warned barely in time to elude capture; he literally escaped down the mountain as the British were riding up. Jefferson's critics fastened onto this as a sign of his inability to stand up to the British. He chose to end his term of office when it expired in June, before Cornwallis's surrender at Yorktown in October 1781 might have redeemed his damaged reputation.

On a motion put forward by George Nicholas of the Virginia Assembly, the House of Delegates voted to investigate Jefferson's conduct as governor during his last year in office. A weary Jefferson wrote a bitter letter to Nicholas on July 28, 1781:

> **"I hope you will not think me improper in asking the favor of you to specify to me the unfortunate passages in my conduct which you mean to adduce against me, ... "**
>
> *TJ to George Nicholas, July 28, 1781*

I am informed that a resolve on your motion passed the H. of D. requiring me to render account of some part of my administration without specifying the act to be accounted for. as I suppose that this was done under the impression of some particular instance or instances of ill conduct, and that it could not be intended just to stab a reputation by a general suggestion under a base expectation that facts might be afterwards hunted up to boulster it. I hope you will not think me improper in asking the favor of you to specify to me the unfortunate passages in my conduct which you mean to adduce against me, that I may be enabled to prepare to yield obedience to the house while facts are fresh in my memory and witnesses & documents are in existence.

He further expressed his distress in a letter to Edmund Randolph:

*were it possible for me to determine again to enter into public business there is no appointment what-
ever which would have been so agreeable to me. but I have taken my final leave of every thing of
that nature, have retired to my farm, my family & books from which I think nothing will ever more
separate me. a desire to leave public office with a reputation not more blotted than it has deserved
will oblige me to emerge at the next session of our assembly & perhaps to accept of a seat in it,
but as I go with a single object, I shall withdraw when that shall be accomplished. (TJ to Edmund
Randolph, September 16, 1781)*

Jefferson had to settle for a lukewarm note of thanks from the Virginia Assembly
for his vindication, modified during its composition as follows:

*RESOLVED, that the sincere Thanks of the General Assembly be given to our former Governor
Thomas Jefferson Esquire for his impartial, upright, and attentive administration ~~of the powers of
the Executive~~, whilst in office. ~~; popular rumours, gaining some degree of credence, by more pointed Accusations, rendered it necessary to make an enquirey into his conduct, and delayed that retri-
bution of public gratitude, so eminently merited; but that conduct having become the object of open
scrutiny, tenfold value is added to an approbation founded on a cool and deliberate discussion~~. The
Assembly wish ~~therefore~~ in the strongest manner to declare the high opinion which they entertain of
Mr. Jefferson's Ability, Rectitude and Integrity, as cheif Magistrate of this Commonwealth, and
mean by thus publicly avowing their Opinion, to obviate ~~all future~~, and to remove all ~~former~~ unmer-
ited Censure. (Draft resolution of thanks to TJ by the Virginia General Assembly, December 12, 1781)*

It was a sad irony that catapulted Jefferson back into public life after the debacle
of his governorship. On September 6, 1782, Martha Jefferson died. She had never
fully recovered from the difficult birth of their sixth child, Lucy Elizabeth, in May
1782. In the months she lay dying, Jefferson devoted himself to her care. In one of
history's more poignant scenes, husband and wife copied out the following lines
from *Tristram Shandy* in anticipation of their separation:

*Time wastes too fast: every letter I trace tells me with what rapidity life follows my pen. The days
and hours of it are flying over our heads like clouds of windy day never to return—more every thing
presses on—and every time I kiss thy hand to bid adieu, every absence which follows it, are prel-
udes to that eternal separation which we are shortly to make!" (Laurence Sterne,* The Life and
Opinions of Tristram Shandy, Gentleman, *Oxford, 1926, edition)*

Jefferson was inconsolable. Although he recorded in his account book merely
that "My dear wife died this day at 11 h-45' A.M.," he wrote a wrenching note to
the marquis de Chastellux on November 26 that reveals his true state of mind:
". . . your friendly letters . . . found me a little emerging from that stupor of mind
which had rendered me as dead to the world as she was whose loss occasioned it . . .
before that event my scheme of life had been determined. I had folded myself in
the arms of retirement and rested all prospects of future happiness on domestic &
literary objects. a single event wiped away all my plans and left me a blank which I
had not the spirits to fill up."

**Martha Jefferson's thread case.
Manuscript Division, Library of
Congress.**

*Just a few items remain to document the life
of Martha Wayles Jefferson, among them some
silver spoons, a layette pincushion, and this
thread case, essential to a colonial farmer's wife,
who was expected to have knowledge of a
variety of domestic arts. Martha was an able
partner in managing Monticello and kept a
meticulous account of plantation activities
until her final illness, despite poor health and
several pregnancies.*

**(opposite) Bell used by Martha
Wayles Jefferson. Monticello/Thomas
Jefferson Memorial Foundation, Inc.,
courtesy of Moorland-Spingarn
Research Center, Howard University.**

*The slave Sally Hemings was given this bell
after Martha Jefferson's death, according to the
oral history of the Hemings family. Martha
used to ring the bell when she needed one
of her servants. Hemings, then nine, helped her
mother Betty to care for Mrs. Jefferson before
she died. Sally and Martha were thought
to be half-sisters, both daughters of the planter
John Wayles.*

This British cartoon was published soon after the signing of the preliminary peace treaty ending the American Revolution, an event which delayed Jefferson's assignment in Paris. Although the figure of America, depicted here wearing an Indian headdress and carrying a flagpole with a liberty cap, triumphantly exclaims, "I have got all I wanted Empire!," her allies France, Holland, Spain, and Ireland cry over their unrequited demands for more territory after the war.

Jefferson's friends came to his aid. Led by James Madison, they sought to alleviate his grief by urging him back to public life. Their timing was fortuitous. Jefferson had declined an offer from Congress in 1781 to serve as peace commissioner. When Congress voted to reappoint him in November 1782, he accepted the post. Madison made a note of Jefferson's appointment:

The reappointment of Mr. Jefferson as Minister Plenipo. for negociating peace was agreed to unanimously and without a single adverse remark. The act took place in consequence of its being suggested that the death of Mrs. J. had probably changed the sentiments of Mr. J. with regard to public life, & that all the reasons which led to his original appointment still existed and indeed had acquired additional force from the improbablility that Mr. Laurens would actually assist in the negociation. (James Madison's notes of debates in Congress, November 12, 1782)

When the preliminary articles of peace were signed in Paris, Jefferson's departure was delayed indefinitely. Instead, Virginia elected him to the Confederation Congress where he joined in the work of outlining his country's future. One of Jefferson's contributions to the task was a report that became the basis for the Ordinance of 1784, which provided a legal structure by which the western lands could become territories and ultimately states. Congress did not accept Jefferson's recommendation that "after the year 1800 of the Christian æra, there shall be neither slavery nor involuntary servitude in any of the said states, otherwise than in punishment of crimes, whereof the party shall have been duly convicted to have been personally guilty" (Report of Committee of Congress, March 1, 1784), but they did approve the principle of creation and admission of new states, "That whensoever any of the said states shall have, of free inhabitants, as many as shall then be in any one of the least numerous of the thirteen original states, such state shall be admitted by it's delegates into the Congress of the United states, on an equal footing with the said original states: . . . ." (see page 30)

> "yet the American revolution seems first to have awakened the thinking part of the French nation in general from the sleep of despotism in which they were sunk."
>
> *TJ, "Autobiography," 1821*

Jefferson arrived in Paris at last in the late summer of 1784 as a minister plenipotentiary charged with negotiating treaties of friendship and commerce with European countries. One can only imagine how such a cultured and sensitive soul took to Parisian society. The grand art and architecture, plus rich food and wine, seemed to infuse him with new life. Undaunted by his poor French—which he read fluently but spoke poorly—he began to make Paris his home by plunging into the social and intellectual life of the city. In typical fashion, he spent some time getting settled, first renting and remodeling a house on cul-de-sac Taitbout, then spending more than his salary on lavish quarters at Hôtel de Langeac, near what is now the Arc de Triomphe. His daughter Martha, called Patsy, was the only one of his children to travel with him. She was enrolled in a convent school, the Abbaye Royale de Panthémont, while a complete staff of servants and advisers managed Jefferson's daily affairs. Later, after young Lucy Elizabeth died, Jefferson sent for his other surviving daughter, eight-year-old Mary (Maria or Polly), to join him and Patsy in Paris. She arrived in 1787, accompanied by her personal servant, fourteen-year-old Sally Hemings.

A new circle of relationships became important to Jefferson at this point in his

(above) Joseph Boze. Martha Jefferson. Miniature, oil on ivory. Paris, 1789. Diplomatic Reception Rooms, United States Department of State.

Martha was nearly twelve when she arrived in Paris with her father. His decision to enroll her in the convent school Abbaye Royale de Panthémont drew criticism from some, such as Abigail Adams. Yet Jefferson repeatedly insisted on the school's liberal attitude toward non-Catholic students. He had also chosen the school in the attempt to shelter his daughter from what he saw as the improprieties of Parisian society. Martha found herself quickly adjusting to her new environment and wrote to a friend in 1785, "At present I am charmed with my situation."

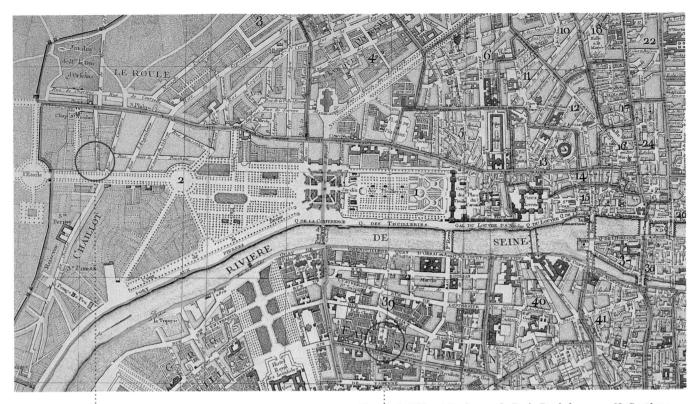

Plan de la Ville et Faubourg de Paris Devisé en ses. 48. Sections. Decreté par l'Assemblée Nationale le 22 Juin 1790 Et Sanctionné par le Roi (detail). **Hand-colored map. Paris, 1790. Geography and Map Division, Library of Congress.**

Though the building program carried out by Baron Georges Haussmann in the mid-nineteenth century would transform Paris into its present-day shape, the Paris Jefferson encountered still resembled a medieval city. He finally settled in the western outskirts of the city: his residence at the Hôtel de Langeac was located near the intersection of the Rue neuve de Berri and the Champs-Elysées, within view of the ancient Grille de Chaillot. His daughter Patsy attended school at the Abbaye Royale de Panthémont, located in the Faubourg Saint-Germain just across the Seine. Both are shown on this detail from a plan of Paris made in the period.

François Nicolas Martinet. "La Grille de Chaillot." Engraving from *Description Historique de Paris* (Paris, 1779). Bibliothèque Nationale, Paris.

This view of the Grille de Chaillot looks toward Paris down the Champs-Elysées. Jefferson took up residence at the Hôtel de Langeac, located on the left at the corner. He rented the entire building, lavishly accommodating himself and his entourage of servants and advisors at a cost far in excess of his 9,000 dollar annual salary.

Rembrandt Peale. William Short. Oil on canvas, 1806. Muscarelle Museum of Art, The College of William and Mary in Virginia, Gift of Mary Churchill Short, Fanny Short Butler, and William Short, 1938.004.

Short, whom Jefferson called his "adoptive son," was one of Jefferson's many younger protégés. Jefferson advised Short throughout his education and early career as a lawyer and took him to Paris as his personal secretary. Short remained there after Jefferson's return to America and reported to him on the political scene in Paris as the revolution unfolded. Despite his mentor's urging that he return to America, Short continued his diplomatic work abroad, only returning to settle in Philadelphia in 1810. The two maintained a close friendship until Jefferson's death.

Mather Brown. John Adams. Oil on canvas. London, 1788. Boston Athenæum.

Jefferson commissioned this portrait for his collection of "principal American characters." Adams is shown with "Jeffersons Hist. Of Virginia," first published as Notes on the State of Virginia *in 1785 while Jefferson was in Paris. Adams wrote to Jefferson about this book, ". . . I think it will do its Author and his Country great Honour. The passages upon slavery are worth Diamonds. They will have more effect than Volumes written by mere Philosophers." Upon its completion, the portrait, considered by the Adams family to be an excellent likeness, was sent from the artist's London studio to Jefferson in Paris.*

career. The homefront was manned by James Hemings, Sally's older brother and Jefferson's personal servant, who attended cooking classes to learn the art of French cuisine. Diplomatic and political issues were handled by David Humphreys, who had served on Washington's staff during the war, and William Short, a relative and protégé of Jefferson, who became his private secretary and, ultimately, financial adviser and life-long friend. In Paris, he was also reunited with two of his distinguished colleagues from 1776—John Adams and Benjamin Franklin. Together, the three statesmen offered French society the best America had to offer in terms of eloquence, intelligence, and wit. Adams was later dispatched to Great Britain, where he became America's first minister, but not before forming a deep personal relationship with Jefferson, which was to weather numerous political storms. When Franklin, who was nearly eighty, left Paris for America on July 12, 1785, Jefferson succeeded him as minister to France.

William Birch after William Hodges and Richard Cosway. *A View from Mr. Cosway's Breakfast-Room Pall Mall, with the Portrait of Mrs. Cosway.* **Stipple engraving. London, February 1, 1789. Print Collection, Miriam and Ira D. Wallach Division of Art, Prints and Photographs, The New York Public Library, Astor, Lenox and Tilden Foundations.**

Jefferson was enamored of French cuisine, architecture, and culture at large, but perhaps nothing so captivated him during his time in Paris as the young and beautiful Maria Cosway. Married to Richard Cosway, a noted miniature painter, Maria was also a painter of some reputation. Following their introduction by artist John Trumbull, Jefferson and Cosway were inseparable over the majority of the next few weeks, touring Paris and the surrounding areas together.

(right) Thomas Jefferson to Maria Cosway, Paris, October 12, 1786. Manuscript Division, Library of Congress.

Those heady weeks which Jefferson and Cosway spent together were effectively brought to an end by an accident in which Jefferson injured his right wrist, thereby forcing him, as he wrote to her, to "relinquish your charming company for that of the surgeon." News of the Cosways' impending return to London reached Jefferson during his convalescence. After their departure, he penned this now famous missive—with his left hand, of course—to his absent muse.

The conflicting elements of Jefferson's character created interesting—yet not insurmountable—problems for him throughout his life. His idealism often obscured reality, his tastes and obsessions led him to the brink of financial ruin, and, in Paris in 1786, his heart caused him to lose his head. The object of such abandon was Maria Cosway, wife of British painter Richard Cosway. Beautiful and intelligent, she captured Jefferson's passion. Jefferson, who had promised his dying wife that he would never remarry, was totally smitten. Heartbroken by Cosway's eventual return with her husband to London, Jefferson composed an emotional letter to her, including a now-famous imaginary dialogue between the head and the heart—reason and emotion:

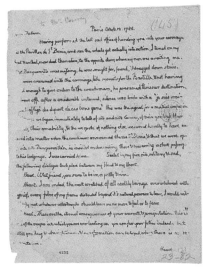

Head. Well, friend, you seem to be in a pretty trim.

Heart. I am indeed the most wretched of all earthly beings. overwhelmed with grief, every fibre of my frame distended beyond it's natural powers to bear, I would willingly meet whatever catastrophe should leave me no more to feel or to fear.

Head. These are the eternal consequences of your warmth & precipitation. this is one of the scrapes into which you are ever leading us. you confess your follies indeed: but still you hug & cherish them, & no reformation can be hoped, where there is no repentance.

Heart. Oh, my friend! this is no moment to upbraid my foibles. I am rent into fragments by the force of my grief! if you have any balm, pour it into my wounds if none, do not harrow them by new torments. spare me in this awful moment! at any other I will attend with patience to your admonitions. (TJ to Maria Cosway, October 12, 1786)

Although Jefferson and Maria Cosway corresponded throughout their lives, they never rekindled the intense relationship of 1786. In the wake of their affair, it is

1. L'Élan—2. Le Renne. Colored engraving from Georges Louis Leclerc, comte de Buffon, *Oeuvres complètes de Buffon.* Vol. 17 (Paris, 1830). Rare Book and Special Collections Division, Library of Congress.

Buffon's inquiries spanned the range of the natural sciences. Among the variety of animals documented in his work is the élan, or elk, seen here, the largest of the European deer. His observations on plant and animal life, interspersed with his theories on the order and workings of the natural world, established him as the leading naturalist of his day. Perhaps his most notable methodological shortcoming was his tendency to generalize, one example being his assertion of the overall degeneracy of species in America. These were precisely the grounds upon which Jefferson challenged him.

P. Mazell. *Elk, or Moose Deer.* Engraving from Thomas Pennant, *History of Quadrupeds.* Vol. 1 (London, 1793). Rare Book and Special Collections Division, Library of Congress.

In Notes on the State of Virginia, Jefferson challenged Buffon by citing examples of large American specimens documented by naturalists such as Pennant (he had a copy of this edition of Pennant's work in his library and was probably also familiar with the 1771 edition). Among these was the "Elk, or Moose Deer." Although Pennant's findings refuted Jefferson's supposition that the moose was unique to America, finding instead that the European elk and the American moose were virtually the same animal, he did support Jefferson in the matter of their comparative size. Pennant explained that, although some accounts of the animal's prodigious size in America may have been exaggerated, "the only thing certain is, that the Elk is common to both continents; and that the American, having larger forests to range in, and more luxuriant food, grows to a larger size than the European."

believed—though the evidence is not conclusive—that Jefferson began a long-term relationship with Sally Hemings, his slave, his daughter's personal servant, and his deceased wife's half-sister.

Despite the heady cultural and intellectual life of Paris, Jefferson's official duties proved frustrating. He and Adams tried unsuccessfully to arrange free passage for American ships and sailors with North African states in the Mediterranean. He also tried—again, unsuccessfully—to end the French tobacco monopolies. And a trip to London—where Adams presented him to King George III, who snubbed the author of the Declaration of Independence—made little headway in securing a commercial treaty with the former enemy.

If European governments did not yield to Jefferson's diplomacy, the European fruits of philosophy, architecture, and science were his for the taking. Jefferson was quick to counter assertions made by French naturalist Georges Louis Leclerc, comte

de Buffon, in his monumental *Histoire naturelle* that the natural species in America were inferior. In a classic case of "mine are bigger than yours," Jefferson arranged to have animal carcasses sent from the United States to prove his point. He wrote Buffon on October 1, 1787:

I really suspect you will find that the Moose, the Round horned elk, & the American deer are species not existing in Europe. the Moose is perhaps of a new class. I wish these spoils, Sir, may have the merit of adding any thing new to the treasures of nature which have so fortunately come under your observation, & of which she seems to have given you the key: they will in that case be some gratification to you.

In his zeal to exhibit the strength and diversity of American culture and natural bounty to the French, Jefferson maintained a demonstration garden of American vegetables at his house and arranged for the distribution of American seeds. He also allowed his *Notes on the State of Virginia*, which he had written at Monticello in 1781-82, to be released in a French translation. It was Jefferson's only published book, and reflected on all aspects of culture, nature, and the status of man.

(above) Thomas Jefferson. "A Map of the country between Albemarle Sound and Lake Erie, comprehending the whole of Virginia, Maryland, Delaware and Pensylvania, ..." Colored engraving from his *Notes on the State of Virginia* (London, 1787). Rare Book and Special Collections Division, Library of Congress.
Jefferson originally prepared this map for publication in the French edition of his Notes *in 1785. One of the cartographic sources upon which he drew heavily was the map of Virginia done in 1751 by his father Peter Jefferson and by Joshua Fry. In addition, Jefferson drew upon the mapmaker Nicholas Scull's map of Pennsylvania and upon Thomas Hutchins's work charting the watercourses west of the Allegheny.*

"Vue de l'extérieur de la maison quarrée." Engraving from Charles-Louis Clérisseau, *Monuments de Nismes*, Vol. 1, pt. 2 of his *Antiquités de la France* (Paris, 1804). Rare Book and Special Collections Division, Library of Congress.

While journeying through southern France in 1787, one of Jefferson's stops was at the first-century-A.D. Roman temple, the Maison Carrée, at Nîmes. Awed by this imposing classical structure, he recalled "gazing whole hours . . . like a lover at his mistress." (TJ to comtesse de Tessé, March 20, 1787) The year before his visit to the temple, Jefferson employed Charles-Louis Clérisseau, who had already published drawings of the antiquities of Nîmes, to make measured drawings of the building. Jefferson based his design for the state capitol at Richmond on this model, although the extent of Clérisseau's contribution to the final design is unclear.

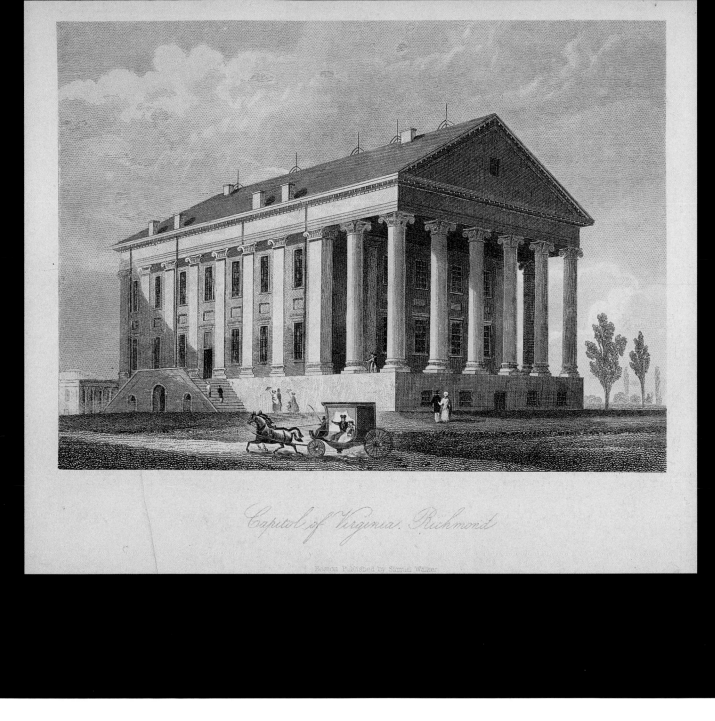

Capitol of Virginia. Richmond

Boston. Published by Samuel Walker

Capitol of Virginia. Richmond. Engraving. Boston, undated. Prints and Photographs Division, Library of Congress.

The Virginia Capitol was the first public building in the United States constructed in the neoclassical style, which subsequently took a strong hold in American architecture. Not only does the finished edifice demonstrate the elegance of the classical style which so impressed Jefferson, but it also evokes the cultural authority of the ancients, appropriating it for the state's new seat of power in Richmond and for the United States. He described the design as "a morsel of taste in our infancy promising much for our maturer age."

Jefferson's contradictory and complex nature again is evident in his reaction to Europe. The man who detested the aristocracy and opposed public obedience to an unchecked monarch plunged delightedly into a culture guilty of those very sins. He was enthralled by the Enlightenment movement in France and sought to capture its ideals in concrete forms and bring them home to America. He acquired thousands of books for his own library and for his friends, never minding the expense, which, of course, he couldn't afford. Paintings, statues, clocks, and furnishings were purchased, all of which had to be shipped back to Monticello, which ultimately became a center of European culture in the Virginia Piedmont.

Architecture was another love of Jefferson's, and he is often credited with the revival of classical architecture in the United States. While in Paris, he sent home plans for a new Virginia capitol, to be based on the Maison Carrée in Nîmes, France, "the most beautiful and precious morsel of architecture left us by antiquity." (TJ to Madison, September 20, 1785) Jefferson's design introduced several innovations, substituting Ionic for the traditional Corinthian columns and adding a simple, unadorned frieze. Jefferson's journals of his travels throughout Europe reveal his appreciation of even the most minute details, from antiquity to agriculture, including the various colors of European cows.

But immersion in European life did not shield Jefferson from the concerns of government back in America. Madison kept him well informed of the progress of the Federal Constitutional Convention, and Jefferson responded with his concern about one serious omission, "A bill of rights of what the people are entitled to against every government on earth."(TJ to Madison, December 20, 1787) He later recalled:

This Convention met at Philadelphia on the 25th of May '87. it sate with closed doors, and kept all it's proceedings secret, until it's dissolution on the 17th of September, when the results of their labors were published all together. I recieved a copy in early November, and read and contemplated it's provisions with great satisfaction. as not a member of the Convention however, nor probably a single citizen of the Union, had approved it in all it's parts, so I too found articles which I thought objectionable. the absence of express declarations ensuring freedom of religion, freedom of the press, freedom of the person under the uninterrupted protection of the Habeas corpus, & trial by jury in civil, as well as in criminal cases excited my jealousy; and the re-eligibility of the President for life, I quite disapproved. (TJ, "Autobiography," 1821)

Other news from home provoked quintessentially Jeffersonian comments from the French minister. On hearing of Shays's Rebellion, in which Revolutionary War

**Elkanah Tisdale. "Convention at Philadelphia. 1787."
Engraving from Rev. Charles A. Goodrich, *A History of
the United States* (Hartford, 1823). Rare Book and Special
Collections Division, Library of Congress.**

*In May of 1787 delegates from the thirteen states convened in
Philadelphia to overhaul the Articles of Confederation adopted by the
Continental Congress in 1777 but not ratified by all the states until 1781.
Agitation for a stronger federal government had led to the Annapolis
Convention of 1786 and now the Federal Constitutional Convention.
The flawed Articles were quickly abandoned and replaced by the principles
of a newly strengthened central government articulated by James Madison
in a federal Constitution. After its adoption by the delegates on September
17, 1787, the Constitution was sent to the states for ratification.*

**Thomas Jefferson to William Smith, Paris, November
13, 1787. Manuscript Division, Library of Congress.**

*Jefferson's doubts about the soundness of the new Constitution were
expressed in this letter to John Adams's son-in-law. Fearing that
Americans had been influenced by tales of anarchy fanned by the
British after Shays's Rebellion, he countered with the now famous
words, "the tree of liberty must be refreshed from time to time with the
blood of patriots & tyrants." To Jefferson, the Constitution's attempt
to control anarchy by providing for a chief judge empowered
to serve for life was an unnecessary and even potentially dangerous
overreaction.*

**Thomas Jefferson to James Madison, Paris, December 20,
1787. Manuscript Division, Library of Congress.**

*The newly drafted federal Constitution would greatly augment the powers
of the central government. Jefferson, concerned by the danger posed to the
sovereignty of individuals, voiced his alarm to his colleague at the center
of the debate in Philadelphia, James Madison. Although Jefferson found
himself on the periphery of this fundamental reassessment of the principles
of government, he nonetheless succeeded in voicing his objections to the
newly drafted system, chief among them being the absence of a bill of
rights which could not be encroached upon by the central government.*

J. M. Moreau le Jeune. *Ouverture des États-Généraux a Versailles, le 5 Mai 1789.* **Etching. Paris, 1789. Print Collection, Miriam and Ira D. Wallach Division of Art, Prints and Photographs, The New York Public Library, Astor, Lenox and Tilden Foundations.**

When King Louis XVI called the États-Généraux or Estates General, composed of three estates—the clergy, the nobles, and the commons—to address the financial crises facing the country, many expected it to be a forum for dealing with the grievances of the people and for legislating constitutional reforms. Jefferson traveled from Paris to Versailles to observe the debates. The following month, when such reforms were not forthcoming, the third estate—whose deputies equaled those from the clergy and nobles combined—broke with the body and declared itself the National Assembly, an act of defiance which can be said to have launched the French Revolution.

Joseph Boze. **Marie Joseph Paul Yves Roch Gilbert de Motier, marquis de Lafayette. Oil on canvas. Paris, 1789. Massachusetts Historical Society.**

After serving with distinction on behalf of the American fight for independence, Lafayette returned to fight for liberty in his own country, where the call for a more representative form of government was gathering strength. In the face of rising tensions, Lafayette's popularity and his position as a moderate aristocrat enabled him to promote compromise between conflicting political factions. Jefferson greatly admired Lafayette and the two remained close friends throughout his time in Paris. It was Jefferson who commissioned this copy of Boze's portrait.

veteran Daniel Shays led an insurrection in Massachusetts to protest new taxes levied by Boston, Jefferson assured Abigail Adams, "the spirit of resistance to government is so valuable on certain occasions, that I wish it to be always kept alive. it will often be exercised when wrong, but better so than not to be exercised at all. I like a little rebellion now and then. it is like a storm in the Atmosphere." (TJ to Abigail Adams, February 22, 1787) And to Adams's future son-in-law, William S. Smith, he commented, "the tree of liberty must be refreshed from time to time with the blood of patriots & tyrants." (TJ to Smith, November 13, 1787)

Interestingly, Jefferson's idealism found a home in France, too. With revolution brewing, Jefferson, allied with the marquis de Lafayette, provided moral support for the Patriot party. In mid-summer, as the newly formed National Assembly debated a new constitution for France, Jefferson opened his home for a secret meeting where the Patriots planned their strategy. He apologised to the French foreign minister the next day for this diplomatic breach of neutrality, only to be assured that the minister, too, welcomed his participation. Seeing a parallel between the French cause and his own country's battle for individual freedom, Jefferson also helped Lafayette draft a declaration of the rights of man for submission to the French Assembly. The Bastille was stormed soon after, on July 14, 1789. In August, the Declaration of the Rights of Man and Citizen was adopted by the National Assembly. Jefferson, believing that a transfer of power would be achieved peacefully in his adopted country, requested permission to take a leave from his post in order to see to financial matters in Virginia. He missed the violent turmoil of the French Revolution and never returned to Paris. As it turned out, his government needed him more at home.

(left) Marie Joseph Paul Yves Roch Gilbert de Motier, marquis de Lafayette. Draft of a declaration of the rights of man, July 1789. Manuscript Division, Library of Congress.

When Lafayette came to compose the document which articulated the tenets of the revolutionary movement and the inalienable rights of French citizens, who better to help him than the author of America's declaration of independence? Jefferson was deeply involved in the drafting of Lafayette's declaration, and in his annotation on this copy—which is not in Lafayette's handwriting—he recommends instituting a division of power between legislative, judiciary, and executive branches of the government. Lafayette submitted another copy of the declaration to the National Assembly on July 11, 1789, and it was adopted by that body on August 26, 1789. The Declaration of the Rights of Man and Citizen would serve as the preamble to the French constitution of 1791.

(opposite) *De par Le Roy*. Thomas Jefferson's passport upon his return from France. Signed by King Louis XVI, Versailles, September 18, 1789. Manuscript Division, Library of Congress.

In his autobiography, Jefferson recalled his departure from France, saying, "I cannot leave this great and good country without expressing my sense of it's preeminence of character among the nations of the earth. a more benevolent people I have never known, nor greater warmth & devotedness in their select friendships . . . so ask the traveled inhabitant of any nation, In what country on earth would you rather live?—Certainly in my own, where are all my friends, my relations, and the earliest & sweetest affections and recollections of my life. Which would be your second choice? France."

E 1789 Sept 18

De par le Roy

A tous Gouverneurs et nos Lieutenans Généraux en nos Provinces et Armées, Gouverneurs particuliers et Commandans de nos Villes, Places et Troupes, et à tous autres nos Officiers, Justiciers et Sujets qu'il appartiendra, Salut. Nous voulons et vous mandons très expressément que vous ayez à laisser librement passer le Sieur Jefferson, Ministre plénipotentiaire des Etats-unis de l'Amérique septentrionale près notre Personne, retournant par congé en Amérique avec sa famille, ses Domestiques bagages et Equipages sans lui donner ni souffrir qu'il lui soit donné aucun empêchement; le présent passeport valable pour deux mois seulement. Car tel est notre plaisir.

Donné à Versailles le 18 7bre 1789.

Louis

Par le Roy

[de Montmorin]

Vû au Comité de Police de l'hôtel de Ville de Paris le 19. 7bre 1789.

Gratis Dufresne Desjardins

Jeffersonia diphylla, The Twinleaf. Hand-colored version of the engraving in Benjamin Smith Barton, "A Botanical Description of the Podophyllum diphyllus of Linnaeus," *Transactions of the American Philosophical Society*, **1793. Dellafield Collection, American Philosophical Society.**

In 1792, Jefferson's friend, botanist Benjamin Smith Barton, challenged the Linnean classification of a plant indigenous to the southern Appalachians. He asserted that it belonged to a distinct genus, which he named Jeffersonia. Through his involvement with the American Philosophical Society, Jefferson was in contact with many of the American thinkers of his day, from botanists to philosophers. He became president of the Society in 1797, an office he held for almost twenty years.

The Rich Fields of Nature

by Charles A. Miller

JEFFERSON'S LONGEST LASTING love affair was with Nature, in all her tempting guises. From his student commonplace book, filled with extracts from authors he was reading, through his single book, *Notes on the State of Virginia*, and his mature political writings, to the letters of his old age, Jefferson's infatuation with Nature is spread across the record of his life. Perhaps no American political figure before or since has gone to nature as much as he did in order to explain his intellectual universe.

Like most Americans, I grew up on Jefferson and Liberty. It was not until I was thirty that I discovered Jefferson and Nature in *Notes on Virginia*, bought to celebrate the purchase of property in Virginia's Shenandoah Valley. I read chapters on rivers and mountains, examined a table of rainfall, temperature, and winds, and studied in awe a list of 130 vegetables categorized as medicinal, esculent, ornamental, or useful for fabrication. I was swept up by Jefferson's scientific refutation of the claim of the French naturalist Buffon that animals in Europe were larger than those in America.

Reading *Notes on Virginia* soon led to the discovery that nature meant more to Jefferson than plants and animals. Nature, the word and the many ideas associated with it, became the key to his intellectual mansion. In *Jefferson and Nature: An Interpretation* I organized his uses of "nature" under Being (physical nature and human nature), Value (the natural basis of the good and the beautiful, as well as its uses in politics and economics), and Action. The essay here samples, and in several instances revises, the arguments made there. As to the word "nature," it is capitalized or not according to context. In Jefferson's time, when English orthography was not standardized, nouns such as "Nature" were often capitalized. But Jefferson was of the opposite habit, normally lower-casing even though he knew that, as with "nature and nature's god," printers might ignore his preference.

When Jefferson is quoted in this essay, the word appears as he wrote it.

How did Jefferson's devotion to nature come about and what were the consequences on his life and thought? The world into which he was born teemed with nature—as American environmental fact and as European cultural idea. Raised in sight of the Blue Ridge Mountains, the son of a surveyor and mapmaker who had his eyes on the West, Jefferson could hardly have avoided wide interests out of doors. How different this was from his northern urban contemporaries, Franklin, Adams, and Hamilton. His best known Virginia compatriots certainly did know the out-of-doors, but Washington was not a natural historian nor a philosopher of nature; and Madison was both less of a farmer than Jefferson (albeit a more successful one) and too sophisticated a political thinker to find nature the touchstone for social analysis.

The Europeans whom Jefferson drew on for his ideas extended back to ancient Rome and Lucretius's *De rerum natura*. He was deeply influenced by several strains of the Enlightenment. He embraced the British empiricists (his heroes were Bacon, Newton, and Locke), the Scottish moral sense school, and the continental jurists who founded international law in the law of nature. His ideas were fortified by French thinkers of his own day, some of whom he knew personally. Devoted to natural science, Jefferson also believed in a natural religion, a natural morality, a natural aesthetics, and a natural basis of politics and economics.

From this mix of environmental and intellectual sources Jefferson became the most prominent exponent of the United States as a nation founded on nature. He justified American independence under "the laws of nature and nature's god." National defense was assured by our being "kindly separated by nature . . . from the exterminating havoc of one quarter of the globe." (First Inaugural Address, March 4, 1801) Nature stimulated exploration and science in the Lewis and Clark expedition. It encouraged immigration and western expansion in a "chosen country, with room enough for our descendants to the thousandth and thousandth generation." (First Inaugural) It championed farmers as "the chosen people of God." (*Notes on the State of Virginia*)

Above all, American nature served Jefferson as a cultural response to European history and society. In place of social classes fixed by convention, America boasted independent citizens who were republican by nature. From them, a "natural aristocracy" would emerge, superior to the artificial aristocracy of Europe. Indians were expressions of American nature in human form. In place of European monuments and architecture, America—that is, Virginia—countered with the Natural Bridge and the confluence of the Potomac and Shenandoah Rivers, which were sublime products of Nature, and the Ohio River, which Jefferson called without ever having seen it, "the most beautiful river on earth." (*Notes on Virginia*) In fact, the whole of *Notes on Virginia*—what one correspondent suggested might more aptly be titled, "A Natural History of North America"—successfully celebrates American nature. Nature may be found in nearly every one of the book's twenty-two chapters, whether about science or society, natural history or natural law.

Perhaps the greatest of Jefferson's successes with the use of nature was the grounding of the Declaration of Independence in "the laws of nature and of nature's god." Jefferson may not have been a genius of liberty, but with the aid of Nature he was certainly a genius of the rhetoric of liberty. Another undoubted written success was the application of nature in his "Dialogue Between My Head & My Heart." This was composed for Maria Cosway, the woman he fell in love with in Paris in 1786. In the "Dialogue," one side of Jefferson, the Stoical Head, contemplates in solitude what may reasonably be condensed to nature and nature's god: "truth & nature, matter & motion, the laws which bind up their existence, & that eternal being who made & bound them up by those laws." (TJ to Cosway, October 12, 1786) Jefferson's other side, the Epicurean Heart, enjoys the scenes of nature in the company of a friend. The "Dialogue," especially the Heart, presents its author as much in love with nature as with Mrs. Cosway.

As Jefferson's Heart acknowledged to Mrs. Cosway, however, there is "no rose without it's thorn," and, as we examine three further uses of nature by Jefferson, the thorns become increasingly prevalent. We are no longer in the world of a public appeal to sacred universals, a love letter as philosophic discourse, or a book of scholarship and speculation. Instead, we find nature as the basis for admirable but futile public policy (on weights and measures), dubious political theory (on the rights of the "living generation"), and moral turmoil (on slavery and race).

Notes on Virginia contains only a single sentence on weights and measures in the state: they are the same as those in England. But in a memorandum prepared for his personal copy of the book Jefferson recorded his speculative pursuit of weights and measures through European history. He claimed to have discovered an invariable ratio between the basic components of the modern avoirdupois and troy systems, the ratio "which Nature has established between the weights of water and wheat." In awe of what History had accomplished with the aid of Nature, his conclusion was that "a more natural, accurate, and curious reconciliation of the two systems . . . could not have been imagined."

As secretary of state a few years later, Jefferson continued the search for a natural system of measurement when he prepared for Congress a "Plan for Establishing Uniformity in the Coinage, Weights, and Measures of the United States." (July 4, 1790) Introducing the plan, he leaped beyond current practices because, although derivable from nature long ago, they did not meet criteria that modern society should demand and modern science could put into practice. He therefore shifted from natural history, the "particular nature" of water and wheat, to natural philosophy, and the universal nature of the solar day. He hoped to find a standard for length "fixed by nature, invariable, and accessible to all nations." (TJ to Dr. Robert Patterson, November 10, 1811)

Confident that a rod-shaped pendulum, of such length that it oscillated in one second, would establish the best standard from universal nature, Jefferson offered Congress two options for dividing this length into units. One, a decimal ratio, would continue his universalist creed by bringing "the calculation of the principal affairs of life within the arithmetic of every man." The other option, which he reluctantly recognized as more realistic, was based not on the universal nature that he thought a decimalized system reflected, but on the particular nature of the United States, "the established habits of a whole nation." The results were what he feared, a congressional decision—or indecision—which is still with us, imperfect nature and no metric system.

As an exponent of a natural basis for weights and measures Jefferson is at his most persuasive. His historical speculation is plausible. His policy proposals are either obviously sound (the standard for length) or meritorious, if debatable (the decimalized system). However, when he turned to nature, as natural right, in his political theory that "the earth belongs to the living," only he seemed to smell the rose; others found mainly thorns.

While in France in the late 1780s, Jefferson had become convinced, correctly, that the tax burdens sapping the regime of Louis XVI originated in the debts incurred for wars of an earlier generation. Proposing his theory to James Madison several weeks after the storming of the Bastille, he asked "whether one generation of men has a right to bind another." (TJ to Madison, September 6, 1789) He answers the question with the support of two analogies about the relation between the individual and society. The first analogy begins with the assertion that "no man can, by *natural right*, oblige [his successors] to the payment of debts contracted by him." It continues shakily in the form of an axiom: "what is true of every member of the society individually, is true of all of them collectively," and concludes that there is a "law of nature, that succeeding generations are not responsible for the preceding." The second analogy holds that society, like the individual, has a lifespan. When a majority of the members of a hypothetical generation have died, the generation itself may be considered dead and is no longer possessed of its natural right of majority rule.

Through these analogies Jefferson believed he had proved a natural law that "the earth belongs to the living." He then urged Madison, who had become a leader in the first Congress, to find opportunities to apply it to the United States and thus "exclude, at the threshold of our new government the contagious and ruinous errors of this quarter of the globe, which have armed despots with means not sanctioned by nature for binding in chains their fellow-men." Madison's response is remarkable for its failure even to mention natural rights and for its refutation of Jefferson's theory. It is impractical, indeed harmful, Madison replied, to require by law that all legislation go out of force after a generation, or to require positive reenactment in order to be retained. The generation theory in practice, Madison argued, was a guarantee of nothing but perpetual social disruption. No nation would stand for it. (Madison to TJ, February 4, 1790) Yet Jefferson, calling on nature to support his argument, was untroubled by the gap between theory and practice that Madison perceived.

Jefferson's most conspicuous problems in thinking with nature occur in his discussions of slavery and race, the torments of his life. His ideas were based on two pairs of contrasts. The first, which seems insignificant today, is the relation of American slavery to the international slave trade. The second, whose analytical clarity has presumably increased with distance from emancipation, is the relation between slavery and race.

The relation of the international trade to domestic slavery is complicated economically, but one can simplify it for present purposes. In Jefferson's day, the trade was a political stalking horse for the practice: whether one supported or opposed slavery, should the trade be ended today, the practice might be ended tomorrow. At the same time, the distinction between slavery and the trade provided an opportunity to level another charge against George III; hence Jefferson's accusation in the draft Declaration of Independence, deleted by the Continental Congress, that, in the slave trade, the king had "waged cruel war against human nature itself, violating it's most sacred rights of life and liberty." We notice in this clause "human nature" and "sacred rights." But "human nature" is what is inside us. It is not the same as an external natural law that condemns the slave trade or an external natural right not to be enslaved, both of which imply public action. That Jefferson's avoidance of "natural rights" is deliberate is confirmed by his labeling life and liberty "sacred."

Caleb Boyle. Thomas Jefferson at the Natural Bridge. Oil on canvas, ca. 1801. Kirby Collection of Historical Paintings, Lafayette College, Easton, Pennsylvania. *Boyle, about whom little is known, never drew Jefferson from life, nor is there evidence that he ever visited the Natural Bridge. Although his sources were the works of other artists, Boyle nonetheless succeeded in realizing the essence of the public man and promoter of "that most sublime of nature's works" in America, which Jefferson purchased, along with the 150 acres surrounding it, in 1774. Among the artists whom Jefferson apparently tried, but failed, to persuade to draw or paint the bridge were John Trumbull, Maria Cosway, and Charles Willson Peale. A quarter-century after Jefferson's death, the Hudson River School painter Frederick E. Church visited the Natural Bridge and subsequently succeeded in capturing at last its "sublime" quality (see page 184).*

Sacred is a word of emotion but, to Jefferson, not a foundation for political philosophy. Yet "human nature" and "sacred rights" were the way he characteristically approached natural rights language when he wrote directly about either slavery or the trade, whether in the draft clause of the Declaration or elsewhere. Although in his moral universe both slavery and the slave trade violated natural law and right, he avoided saying so explicitly, as if Jefferson the philosopher of freedom had to shield natural rights from Jefferson the owner of slaves.

The second pair of relations to consider is slavery and race. The difference between the two is conceptually obvious, but if all slaves are black and, in Virginia, nearly all blacks are slaves, was Jefferson able to separate slavery from race in his analysis? In *Notes on Virginia* he rather feebly attempted to isolate race by holding slavery constant when he compared the slavery of ancient Rome with that of America. But he demonstrated mainly that he was a poor comparative historian. He next attempted a natural science investigation of African Americans that, outside of Virginia, could easily have been refuted in his own time. In the end, we learn from the Declaration that all men have a right by nature to life and liberty, and from *Notes on Virginia* that, except for their moral sense, blacks were probably inferior to whites.

Notes on Virginia, indeed, contains two treatments of slavery. In one chapter Jefferson proposes legislation that would emancipate slaves on the condition they leave the country. In another, which implicitly extends the justification for colonizing freed slaves, he opens by suggesting a methodology for thinking with nature. He ends by breaking the bounds of nature thinking altogether.

"It is difficult to determine on the standard by which the manners of a nation may be tried, whether *catholic* or *particular*," Jefferson writes before describing the effects of slavery in Virginia. Revised, this sentence is a key to an important methodological problem in using nature: it is difficult to determine which understanding of nature should be applied to a subject, universal or particular. The same choices lay behind his options on weights and measures—a universal, decimalized system or a particular system, "the established habits" of America. In the *Notes on Virginia* he asks whether one should judge the effects of slavery according to universal nature, applicable everywhere, or according to particular nature, the situation of Virginia. Since he does not speak specifically to slavery in Virginia, Jefferson's distressing description and harsh judgment is logically based on the universal standard: slavery is incompatible with natural right.

Jefferson's judgment of slavery is in fact so severe—its effects on both slaves and masters —that he falls into nature language, really anti-nature language, that is utterly out of character. Considering that "God is just," he says, and "that his justice [on behalf of slaves] can not sleep forever," slaves may revolt, effecting an "exchange of situation" with their masters. And this, he exclaims in a phrase unique to a man who believed in natural religion, "may become probable by supernatural interference!" By the end of his treatment of the moral miasma that enveloped his life and seeped into his philosophy, nature is in rout. Abolitionists successfully appealed to Jefferson's natural rights doctrines in the decades after his death, but on slavery and race, nature failed the founder.

Why do we still study a man whose paths through nature could lead to such confusion or error, who could stumble without even being aware of it? It is because no other president has had the philosophic range and pretensions that Jefferson did, and nature language permeates, if it does not unite, his thought. We admire his curiosity, his energy, his style, his public service. We admire him for his invocation, his evocation, and at heart, his vocation of nature. We glimpse the true Jefferson in the White House in 1807, asking Caspar Wistar, a Philadelphia physician, to oversee the education of his grandson. The president took the occasion to critique contemporary medical practice and to argue for the "salutary efforts [of] nature" to restore us to health. At the end of the letter, he thanked his friend for the opportunity to write. Its composition, he said:

has permitted me, for a moment, to abstract myself from the dry & dreary waste of politics, into which I have been impressed by the times on which I happened, and to indulge in the rich fields of nature, where alone I should have served as a volunteer, if left to my natural inclinations & partialities. (TJ to Caspar Wistar, June 21, 1807)

Con-g-ss Embark'd on board the Ship Constitution of America bound to Conogocheque by way of Philadelphia.

Con-g-ss Embark'd on board the Ship Constitution of America bound to Conogocheque by way of Philadelphia.
Etching. [New York?], 1790. Prints and Photographs Division, Library of Congress.
To appease southern interests, Congress decided to move the capital permanently to a site not exceeding ten miles square
on the Potomac River "at some place between the mouths of the Eastern Branch and the Connogocheague." However, it was
to relocate temporarily to Philadelphia for a decade. This cartoon, in which a devil lures the Ship Constitution into rocky rapids,
is a cynical commentary on the profit opportunity for Philadelphia. As the ship nears its first stop in Philadelphia, three men in a dinghy

"the spirit of 1776, is not dead. it has only been slumbering."

TJ TO THOMAS LOMAX, MARCH 12, 1799

Drawn by G. Beck, Philadelphia.

George Town _and_ FEDERAL CITY, _or_ CITY _of_ Washington.

Published June 1ʃᵗ 1801 by Atkins & Nightingale, Nᵒ 143, Leadenhall Street, London, & Nᵒ 55, North Front Street, Philadelphia.

Engraved by T. Cartwright, London.

The Power of Opinion

Chapter 3

JEFFERSON'S HOMECOMING FROM PARIS was bittersweet. No sooner had he hit American soil than he received word of his appointment as secretary of state under President Washington:

on my way home I passed some days at Eppington in Chesterfield, the residence of my friend and connection, Mr. Eppes, and, while there, I recieved a letter from the President, Genl. Washington, by express, covering an appointment to be Secretary of State. I recieved it with real regret. my wish had been to return to Paris, where I had left my houshold establishment, as if there myself, and to see the end of the revolution, which, I then thought would be certainly and happily closed in less than a year. I then meant to return home, to withdraw from Political life, into which I had been impressed by the circumstances of the times, to sink into the bosom of my family and friends, and devote myself to studies more congenial to my mind. in my answer of Dec. 15. I expressed these dispositions candidly to the President, and my preference of a return to Paris; but assured him that if it was believed I could be more useful in the administration of the government, I would sacrifice my own inclinations without hesitation, and repair to that destination. this I left to his decision. (TJ, "Autobiography," 1821)

Jefferson lingered at Monticello before heading for New York, the seat of the government at that time. Warmly welcomed at home by his slaves and by his colleagues in the Virginia Assembly, he set about reacquainting himself with the political landscape and arranging for the wedding of his just seventeen-year-old daughter Patsy to her cousin Thomas Mann Randolph, Jr. Fortunately for Randolph, his discriminating father-in-law declared him to be a man of "genius, science and honorable mind." (TJ, "Autobiography," 1821)

The government Jefferson returned to was not the one he had left. When he arrived in New York on March 21, 1789, to take his post, Washington had been president for almost a year and the president's advisors—who would eventually become

---

T. Cartwright after George Beck. *George Town and Federal City, or City of Washington.* **Color aquatint. London, 1801. Prints and Photographs Division, Library of Congress.**

This rural view, focusing on a dirt road along the Potomac and revealing the serene port of Georgetown and sparsely inhabited landscape beyond, was based on an earlier design before work had begun on the earliest federal buildings in the new city of Washington. Jefferson was instrumental in creating a city plan for Washington, much of which had not yet been implemented when he took office as president in 1801.

the "cabinet"—included Alexander Hamilton in the Treasury, Edmund Randolph as attorney general, and Henry Knox in the War Department. Although they would be increasingly at odds, Jefferson and Hamilton formed an uncomfortable partnership on the issue of the Assumption Bill, by which Hamilton sought to have the central government repay the individual state debts incurred during the American Revolution. Anti-Federalists in Congress vehemently objected. Some states, including Virginia, had already paid a great share of their debt. These states resented having to compensate for the other states, like Massachusetts and South Carolina, which had paid less. Entangled in this controversy was the location of the capital. Southerners favored relocating the capital near the Potomac, farther from northern interests.

By the end of June 1790, agreement had been reached between Jefferson, Madison (who was then a leader of Congress), and Hamilton on a "bargain" to approve the assumption of state war debts by the federal government. The capital, it was agreed, would go to Philadelphia for ten years and then move permanently to Georgetown, on the Potomac River. Jefferson later referred to assumption as a bitter pill that southerners were forced to swallow. In his effort to preserve the Union, he felt he had been "duped" by Hamilton. The pot of partisan politics was beginning to boil.

Charles Willson Peale. *His Excel: G: Washington Esq.* Mezzotint engraving. Philadelphia, 1787. Prints and Photographs Division, Library of Congress.
George Washington had not yet assumed the presidency when the gifted portraitist Charles Willson Peale made this engraved likeness of him in 1787. Peale issued this elegant oval print of the former commander of the Continental Army at the culmination of the Constitutional Convention, over which Washington presided.

Charles Willson Peale. Thomas Jefferson. Oil on canvas. Philadelphia, 1791. Independence National Historical Park Collection.
This vibrant image painted from life by Charles Willson Peale shows Jefferson as he looked at age forty-eight, when serving as secretary of state in Washington's cabinet. Peale's letterbooks reveal that Jefferson sat for him in Philadelphia at least twice in December 1791.

The First Cabinet. Engraving after Alonzo Chappel. New York, 1874.
Prints and Photographs Division, Library of Congress.

Washington is seen here, far right, with the first executive council, as it was called during his presidency, including (from left): Henry Knox, secretary of war; Thomas Jefferson, secretary of state; Edmund Randolph, with back turned, attorney general; and Alexander Hamilton, secretary of the treasury. After a moderately cooperative beginning, Jefferson and Hamilton developed a contentious relationship.

Columb. Mag.

View of the FEDERAL EDIFICE *in* NEW YORK.

Attributed to Amos Doolittle. "View of the Federal Edifice in New York." Engraving from *The Columbian Magazine*, Philadelphia, August 1789. Rare Book and Special Collections Division, Library of Congress.

Doolittle's engraving depicts the scene of Washington's swearing in at Federal Hall in New York in April 1789. The balcony was festively decorated for the occasion. As secretary of state, Jefferson would have attended cabinet meetings in this building until the government relocated to Philadelphia in 1790.

William Birch. "High Street, from Ninth Street. Philadelphia." Hand-colored engraving from W. Birch & Son, *The City of Philadelphia in the State of Pennsylvania, North America as it appeared in the year 1800* **(Philadelphia, 1800). Rare Book and Special Collections Division, Library of Congress.**

When he served as secretary of state in Philadelphia, Jefferson rented a house from Thomas Leiper at 274 Market, or High, Street, depicted here. It was conveniently located just a few blocks away from the State House, President Washington's house, the American Philosophical Society, and Jefferson's own offices at Eighth and Market Streets. As was customary for Jefferson, he undertook a major and costly renovation of the premises. In addition to the exorbitant expense of remodeling, Jefferson had to foot the bill for the twenty-seven wagonloads of books, furniture, paintings, and papers delivered from previous residences and held in storage for him in New York until the house was ready.

By the summer of 1791, the rift between Jefferson and Hamilton had become more apparent. Jefferson believed his republican principles—particularly his trust in the people to rule themselves—were violated at every turn by the secretary of the treasury, whose aristocratic leanings provoked him to declare the common man "a great beast." Whereas Hamilton favored a strong central government with the wealthy in control of political power, Jefferson backed an agricultural economy that supported individual freedom. Soon the newspapers took on this battle. The Federalists, led by Hamilton and Adams, supported John Fenno's *Gazette of the United States.* Not to be outdone, Madison, with Jefferson's concordance, persuaded Philip Freneau to establish the rival *National Gazette.*

> **"nobody answers him, & his doctrine will therefore be taken for confessed. for god's sake, my dear Sir take up your pen, select the most striking heresies and cut him to pieces in the face of the public."**
>
> *TJ to James Madison, July 7, 1793 (writing about Hamilton)*

Throughout the decade, the battle of words raged on, from the most lofty declarations to gutter-level prose.

Despite the growing political discord, Jefferson threw himself into the planning of the national capital. His habit of being industrious seemed to take the edge off the burdens and disappointments of political life. Early in 1791, he drew a simple map of the federal city to be located on the Potomac River near Georgetown. He continued through his terms as vice president and president to lavish enormous energy on the details of the city, right down to suggesting that the road between the Capitol and the President's House, as it was called at the time, should be lined with Lombardy poplars.

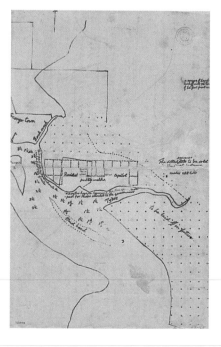

Thomas Jefferson. Plan for the city of Washington. Drawing, pen and ink. Philadelphia, January 31, 1791. Manuscript Division, Library of Congress.

Jefferson took a great interest in the Federal City, which relocated closer to his Virginia home in 1800. He submitted this simple plan for the Federal District in 1791, but the more grandiose design by Pierre L'Enfant was eventually adopted instead. Jefferson was the first U.S. president to spend his entire term of office in what is now Washington, D.C.

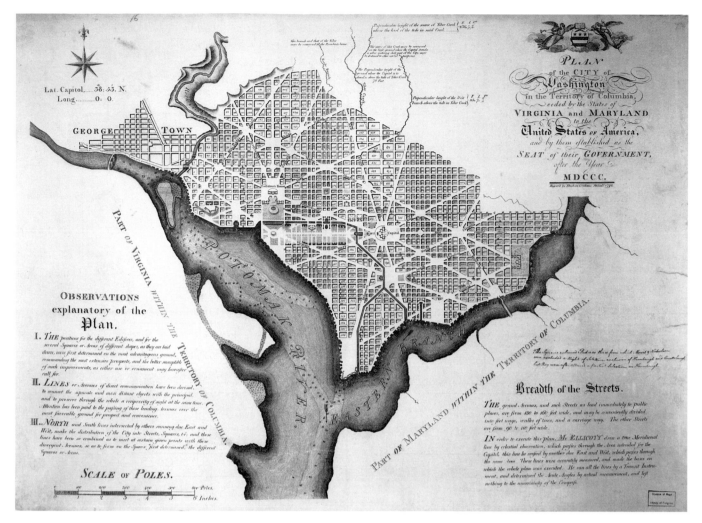

Thackara and Vallance after Ellicott from a drawing by Pierre L'Enfant. *Plan of the City of Washington.* **Engraving. Philadelphia, 1792. Geography and Map Division, Library of Congress.**

Pierre L'Enfant, a French engineer who came to America at age twenty-three, was selected by George Washington to prepare a plan for the new capital. Considered an achievement in city planning, the grid shows major avenues radiating north, south, east, and west from both the President's House and the Capitol. L'Enfant's original drawing, on which this engraving is based, is housed in the Library of Congress. In making a color facsimile of it for the two-hundredth anniversary of the plan, new photographic and electronic enhancement technology revealed faint editorial annotations in Jefferson's hand.

Nicholas King. Planting sketch for Pennsylvania Avenue, with King's letter to Thomas Munroe, Washington, D.C, March 12, 1803, forwarded by Munroe to Jefferson, March 14, 1803. Manuscript Division, Library of Congress.

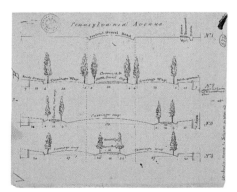

Thomas Munroe, superintendent of the city of Washington, wrote in his letter to Jefferson, "Dr. Thornton, Mr. King and myself have conversed on the manner of laying off the lines and planting the trees . . . The three modes illustrated by the enclosed sections were suggested . . . I mentioned the plan No. 3 as the one which I believed you had designed . . . I shall get the trees from Mount Vernon and Genl Masons Island . . . price twelve & a half cents each."

S. Smith after John Webber. "A View of the Habitations in Nootka Sound." Engraving from James Cook, *A Voyage to the Pacific Ocean . . . performed under the direction of Captains Cook, Clerke, and Gore . . . 1776, 1777, 1778, 1779, and 1789.* Atlas (London, 1784). Rare Book and Special Collections Division, Library of Congress.

While the Revolutionary War preoccupied the colonies, several European powers were already exploring uncharted areas of the North American continent. Sailing under the British flag, James Cook was charged with locating the western entrance to the Northwest Passage. The three-volume account of his final voyage—based posthumously on his journals—includes this view of the Nootka Sound, the scene of British conflict with Spain during Jefferson's term as secretary of state.

Thomas Jefferson to William Short, Philadelphia, January 3, 1793. Manuscript Division, Library of Congress.

This passionate letter to William Short, with Jefferson's famed lines— "but rather than it [French Revolution] should fail I would have seen half the earth desolated"—confirms that, although the Washington administration would not officially support the revolutionary government of France, Jefferson was hardly neutral in his personal attachment to its cause.

Anonymous. *The Providential Detection*. Etching, ca. 1800. Courtesy, American Antiquarian Society.

Jefferson's French sympathies are ridiculed in this political cartoon which shows the secretary of state kneeling at the "Altar to Gallic Despotism." He is about to fling a document named "Constitution & Independence. U.S.A." into the fire fed by the flames of radical writings, but, fortunately, the American eagle grabs the scroll in its talons, rescuing it from an evil fate. The letter "To Mazzei" shown falling from Jefferson's other hand refers to a famous April 24, 1796 letter from Jefferson to Philip Mazzei, interpreted by Jefferson's enemies as an attack on George Washington and John Adams.

Jefferson's principal duties as secretary of state were to protect the concerns of America's western frontier while maintaining American neutrality in foreign wars. While revolution raged in France, he sought to consolidate the United States's control over its own boundaries in the face of British, Spanish, and Native American intransigence on the northern, southern, and western borders. Britain's refusal to turn over her northwest posts, Spain's interference with American trade on the Mississippi, and both nations' commercial restrictions demanded Jefferson's diplomatic skill. A threatened war between Great Britain and Spain for control of the Nootka Sound on North America's West Coast was a harbinger of growing international crises.

The revolutionary spirit captured so well by Jefferson nearly two decades earlier in Philadelphia was infecting Europe. In 1793, France and England were at war. Britain was attempting to suppress the revolutionary government that had emerged in France. The American government insisted on a policy of neutrality, but Jefferson personally favored France. He had even chastised his own friend William Short because, "the tone of your letters had for some time given me pain, on account of the extreme warmth with which they censured the proceedings of the Jacobins of France." Jefferson asked, "was ever such a prize won with so little innocent blood?," and railed, "my own affections have been deeply wounded by some of the martyrs to this cause, but rather than it should have failed, I would have seen half the earth desolated. were there but an Adam & an Eve left in every country, & left free, it would be better than as it now is." A stunned Short was told to mend his ways. (TJ to Short, January 3, 1793)

Despite Jefferson's private affections for France and support of the revolutionary cause, in his official role as secretary of state he maintained a neutral stance. The strain this caused—another battle of the heart and the head—accelerated with the arrival of France's new minister to the United States, Edmond Genêt. Openly welcomed by the U.S., Genêt quickly violated the trust of the Washington administration by repeatedly attempting to violate American neutrality. Seeking to establish an alliance between the U.S. and his country in its war against Britain, Genêt threatened to interfere in domestic politics to achieve his goal. Jefferson described the key cabinet meeting on August 20, 1793, asking for Genêt's recall to France: "we met at the President's to examine by paragraphs the draught of a letter I had prepared to Gouverneur Morris, on the conduct of mr Genet. there was no difference of opinion on any part of it, except on this expression. 'an attempt to embroil both, to add still another nation to the enemies of his country, & to draw on both a reproach, which it is hoped will never stain the history of either, that of <u>liberty warring on herself</u>.'" (TJ, manuscript note, August 20, 1793) A lengthy debate between Jefferson and the rest of the cabinet—Hamilton, Randolph, and Knox—was finally resolved by President Washington who, "with a good deal of positiveness declared in favor of the expression, that he considered the pursuit of France to be that of liberty." Despite a few small victories, Jefferson's exasperation with Genêt was the culmination of a series of exhausting and frustrating episodes. He notified Washington of his desire to resign in late July, and was persuaded to stay through December. In January 1794, he returned to Monticello.

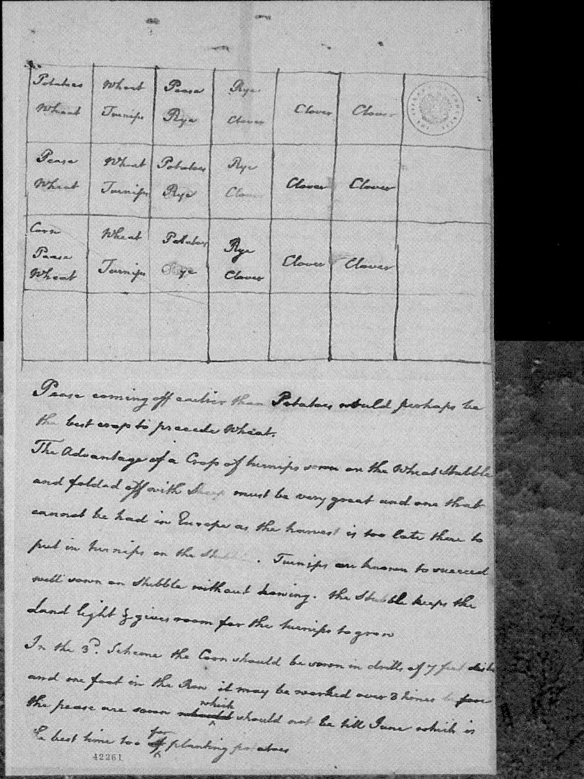

Potatoes Wheat	Wheat Turnips	Pease Rye	Rye Clover	Clover	Clover
Pease Wheat	Wheat Turnips	Potatoes Rye	Rye Clover	Clover	Clover
Corn Pease Wheat	Wheat Turnips	Potatoes Rye	Rye Clover	Clover	Clover

Pease coming off earlier than Potatoes, would perhaps be the best crop to precede Wheat.

The Advantage of a Crop of turnips sown on the Wheat Stubble and folded off with Sheep must be very great and one that cannot be had in Europe as the harvest is too late there to put in turnips on the Stubble. Turnips are known to succeed well sown on Stubble without having. the Stubble keeps the Land light & gives room for the turnips to grow

In the 3d. Scheme the Corn should be sown in drills of 7 feet distance and one foot in the Row it may be worked over 3 times before the pease are sown which should not be till June which is the best time to plant potatoes

42361

beam long ... 7 6
broad ... 3
thick where thickest ... 4½
height from ground to underside, behind 1-3
before 2-0
clevis hole from fore end ... 4 6

bar, length exclusive of wing ... 1- 10
breadth ... 1
thickness ... 2
wing, length exclusive of coulter point 1-0
breadth, including bar ... 0- 10

handle, height from ground 2- 9
length ... 5-0
rise 22 in 27
opening between ... 2- 0
breadth ... 3
thickness ... 0- 6
mould board, length 1- 11
breadth 9
height 1- 0
helve 3 6 3 4 2 6

rises 1 in 6
H 63 to shoulder

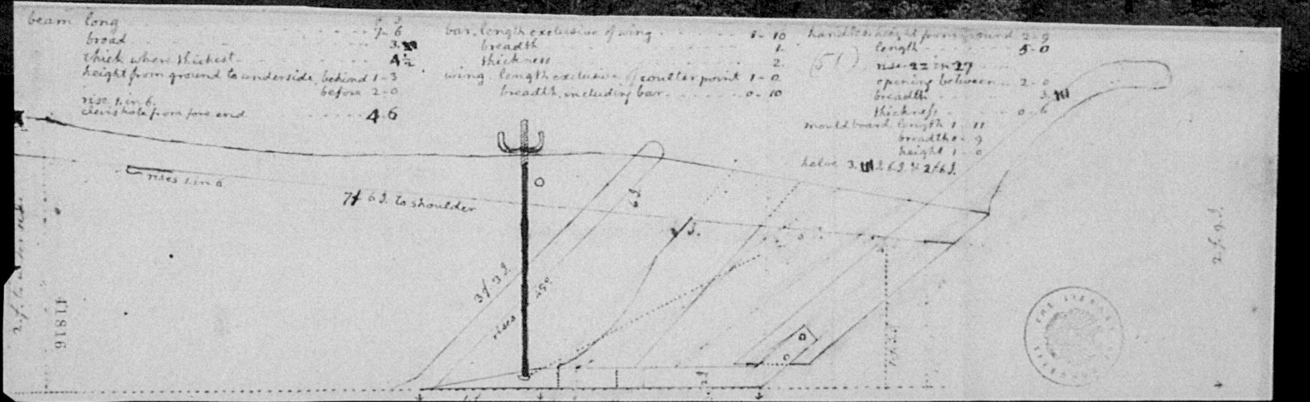

To say that Jefferson was relieved to be back at Monticello would be an understatement. In a letter to John Adams, he wrote:

the difference of my present & past situation is such as to leave me nothing to regret but that my retirement has been postponed four years too long. the principles on which I calculate the value of life are entirely in favor of my present course. I return to farming with an ardour which I scarcely knew in my youth, and which has got the better entirely of my love of study. instead of writing 10. or 12. letters a day, which I have been in the habit of doing as a thing of course, I put off answering my letters now, farmer-like, till a rainy day, & then find it sometimes postponed by other necessary occupations. (TJ to John Adams, April 25, 1794)

But, of course, relaxation for Jefferson meant hard labor of another kind. For the next four years he worked out a scientific method of farming his lands and developed a plow that would work without causing harmful erosion of the Piedmont hillsides. He was in desperate financial straits. The debt he inherited from his father-in-law's estate, as well as mismanagement of his own affairs, caused him to invent not only useful appliances for eighteenth-century life, but creative—though not always lucrative—business schemes as well. He tried to appease the Wayles's creditors by selling off and mortgaging large numbers of slaves and acres of land. To improve his financial fortunes, he devised a complex system of crop rotation, embarked on wine production, developed mill seats, and founded a slave-run nailery, which was the only business success he ever had. In the midst of all this activity, he began the long process of reconfiguring the house at Monticello, which was virtually torn down and rebuilt at double the size, incorporating many details of classical architecture that Jefferson had so admired in Europe. Although a frugal government unencumbered by debt was always a major concern of Jefferson's, his personal life was forever burdened by a lack of funds and an unrestrained appetite for the finest cultural and material goods.

> **"I return to farming with an ardour which I scarcely knew in my youth, and which has got the better entirely of my love of study . . . I put off answering my letters now, farmer-like, till a rainy day . . . ."**
>
> *TJ to John Adams, April 25, 1794*

(opposite) View of the west front of Monticello. Undated photograph. Monticello/Thomas Jefferson Memorial Foundation, Inc.

For Jefferson, Monticello (seen here in a recent photograph) was always a safe haven from public life. When he returned to his estate in 1794, he wrote, "I am then to be liberated from the hated occupations of politics, and to remain in the bosom of my family, my farm, and my books. I have my house to build, my fields to farm, and to watch for the happiness of those who labor for mine." (TJ to John Adams, April 25, 1794)

(opposite top) Thomas Jefferson. Crop rotation plan for Monticello. Undated. Manuscript Division, Library of Congress.

Jefferson's careful consideration of a workable method of crop rotation for Monticello proves that he took a scientific approach to farming. Crop rotation was not yet a widespread practice among landowners of his time. Throughout his life, Jefferson kept detailed books on farming and gardening, in which he recorded planting and harvesting as well as minute observations about the natural world.

(opposite bottom) Thomas Jefferson. Design for a Mouldboard Plow. Drawing, pen and ink. Charlottesville, Virginia, ca. 1794. Manuscript Division, Library of Congress.

Jefferson developed, with the help of his son-in-law Thomas Mann Randolph, who managed much of his land, a mouldboard plow that would work more effectively than a standard one on the hilly terrain near Monticello. This plow turned the furrow to the downhill side and thereby helped prevent soil erosion, a common problem in the Virginia Piedmont.

In other things the rules of proceeding are to be the same as in the
House, *Scob.* 39.

—⁂—

SEC. XIII.

EXAMINATION OF WITNESSES.

Common fame is a good ground for
the house to proceed by enquiry, and
even to accusation. *Resolution House
Commons* 1. *Car.* 1. 1625. *Rush.
L. Parl.* 115. 1. *Grey.* 16—22. 92.
3. *Grey.* 21. 23. 27. 45.*

Witnesses are not to be produced
but where the house has previously instituted an enquiry, 2 *Hats.* 102. nor
then are orders for their attendance
given blank, 3 *Grey.* 51. *the process is a sum-
mons from the house. 4 Hats. 255.258.*

When any person is examined before a committee, or at the bar of the
house, any member wishing to ask the
person a question, must address it
to the Speaker or Chairman, who re-
peats the question to the person, or
says to him ' you hear the questi-

* *as the heads of impeachment were seve- OR-
ally read against that. Clarendon in 1667. some member
in his place stated to the house ' that several persons had
undertaken to make that head good ', or ' that the member had
heard this from a certain great Lord ', or ' that this was too put-
-lic to stand in need of proof ', or, in one instance ' that the mem-
-ber did not doubt but it will be made out ? 2. St. tr. 558. 4 Hats. 137.*

on, answer it.' But if the propri-
ety of the question be objected to, the
Speaker directs the witness, counsel and parties, to withdraw ; for no
question can be moved or put, or debated while they are there. 2. *Hats.*
108. Sometimes the questions are
previously settled in writing before
the witness enters *ib.* 106. 107. 8.
Grey 64. The questions asked must be
entered in the Journals 3. *Grey*
81. But the testimony given in
answer before the house is never
written down ; but before a committee it must be, for the information of
the house who are not present to hear
it. 7. *Grey* 52. 334.

If either house have occasion for
the presence of a person in custody
of the other, they ask the other their
leave that he may be brought up to
them in custody. 3. *Hats.* 52.

A member, in his place, gives information to the house of what he
knows of any matter under hearing at
the bar. *Jour. H. of C. Jan.* 22. 1744
—5.

G   Either

"Sec. XIII. Examination of
Witnesses," from Thomas Jefferson,
*A Manual of Parliamentary Practice
For the Use of the Senate of the United
States* (Washington City, 1801).
Annotated in ink by Jefferson.
Rare Book and Special Collections
Division, Library of Congress.

*In his role as vice president, Jefferson hoped to
improve the procedures of Congress. However,
he found no book that could aid him in matters
of parliamentary practice, leaving him to write
his own based on the system of rules of the
British parliament. Ironically, although Jefferson
presided over the Senate, that chamber did
not officially incorporate the* Manual *into its
governing rules. It was the House of
Representatives that formally adopted it in
1837, except for those rules not consistent with
this body.*

Maybe it was fortuitous, then, that the siren call of public life roused Jefferson
from his mountain retreat once again in 1797. After Washington's farewell address,
both Jefferson and Adams were nominated to succeed him. At that time, by a quirk
of the Constitution, which was later resolved by the Twelfth Amendment, the candidate with the most electoral votes became president and the runner-up became
vice president. There was no real campaign and Jefferson anxiously awaited the
election results, writing to Madison that if the votes were tied, Adams ought to have
preference because he had "no confidence in myself for the undertaking."
(December 17, 1796) When Jefferson lost to his senior colleague by three votes, he
wrote Madison: "I am his junior in life, I was his junior in Congress, his junior in
the diplomatic line, and lately his junior in our civil government." (TJ to Madison,
January 1, 1797) He was also simply relieved to have what he called the "honorable
and easy office." He traveled to Philadelphia for the swearing in, met with Adams,
and dined with Washington. Back at Monticello, he confided in one letter, "a more
tranquil and unoffending station could not have been found for me," (TJ to
Benjamin Rush, January 22, 1797) and complaining in another that he had "a thousand visits of ceremony and some of sincerity." (to C. F. Volney, April 9, 1797)

Jefferson may have agreed with John Adams that the role of second fiddle was "the most insignificant office that ever the invention of man contrived or his imagination conceived." He managed to stay productive by collaborating with John Beckley, George Wythe, and Edmond Pendleton on *A Manual of Parliamentary Practice*, which is still a basis for procedural rules in the United States Senate. But, despite his cordial response to Adams's election, there was almost immediate friction between the lanky Virginia idealist and his northern chief executive, who had been dubbed "His Rotundity" by his detractors. Their dramatic physical incongruity made for splendidly cruel caricatures and political cartoons. In one such barb, Jefferson and his supporters, including the foreign born Albert Gallatin, were vilified for their French sympathies. In others, Jefferson was pictured as a corrupt slave owner, an atheist, and a coward for his unfortunate flight from the British during his term as governor in 1781. The Jeffersonian Republicans stirred the pot, attacking the Federalists as the party of Great Britain, calling Adams "the corrupt and despotic monarch of Braintree," and leaking information on Hamilton's affair with Maria Reynolds, the wife of a Treasury worker, and subsequent blackmail by her husband. The exposé was written by pamphleteer James Callender, who sometimes received financial help from Jefferson, but later created perhaps the greatest scandal of the then president's career. Jefferson conveyed sadness about the bitter divisiveness in a letter to Edward Rutledge, a colleague from the old Continental Congress:

> "I am his junior in life, I was his junior in Congress, his junior in the diplomatic line, and lately his junior in our civil government."
>
> *TJ to James Madison, January 1, 1797*

you & I have formerly seen warm debates and high political passions. but gentlemen of different politics would then speak to each other, & separate the business of the Senate from that of society. it is not so now. men who have been intimate all their lives cross the streets to avoid meeting, & turn their heads another way, lest they should be obliged to touch their hat. (TJ to Edward Rutledge, Philadelphia, June 24, 1797)

**"Stop the Wheels of Government."
Etching from *Porcupine's Political Censor*, Philadelphia, April 1796.
Rare Book and Special Collections Division, Library of Congress.**

Albert Gallatin was a Geneva-born congressman from Pennsylvania, who had criticized the Hamiltonian system, attacked the Jay Treaty, and like Jefferson, was considered a Francophile. This simple cartoon shows him poised, as if to make a pronouncement, beside a guillotine, a symbol of the French Revolution. It is interesting to note that another edition with this caricature shows the words "Stop de Wheels of Government" spewing from Gallatin's mouth— perhaps a Federalist slur on his accented English. Gallatin later became secretary of the treasury in Jefferson's administration.

"Stop the Wheels of Government".

Drawn & Engraved by W. Birch & Son.

Published by R. Campbell & Cᵒ. Nᵒ 30 Chesnut Street Philadᵃ. 1800.

HIGH STREET, From the Country Market-place PHILADELPHIA:

with the procession in commemoration of the Death of GENERAL GEORGE WASHINGTON, *December 26ᵗʰ 1799.*

He later tried to explain the party differences to John Wise of Virginia:

It is now well understood that two political Sects have arisen within the U.S; the one believing that the Executive is the branch of our Government which the most needs support; the other that like the analogous branch in the English Government, it is already too strong for the republican parts of the Constitution, and therefore in equivocal cases, they incline to the legislative powers; the former of these are called Federalists, sometimes Aristocrats or monocrats & sometimes Tories, after the corresponding Sect in the English government of exactly the same definition: the latter are stiled republicans, whigs, Jacobins, Anarchists, disorganisers &c.—these terms are in familiar use with most persons, ... (TJ to John Wise, February 12, 1798, transcript)

When George Washington died in December 1799, the only buffer between the warring factions disappeared and partisan battles accelerated. Matthew Lyon of Vermont and Roger Griswold of Connecticut actually came to blows on the floor of the House of Representatives. The unpopular Jay's Treaty, a Federalist-supported plan negotiated with Great Britain in 1794, led to repercussions with the French, which culminated in 1798 with the XYZ affair and the dissolution of the U.S. alliance with France. In its zeal to vanquish the military and naval threat posed by France, the Federalist government passed a number of bills that boosted national defense and placed restrictions on non-U.S. citizens. But perhaps the most insidious piece of legislation of that period was the Sedition Act of 1798, which effectively prohibited public criticism of the president or of the government of the United States. Designed by Federalists to curb the damaging prose from republican writers, such as John Beckley, James Callender, Madison, Monroe, and Matthew Lyon, the act—a blatant violation of the First Amendment—incited verbal violence. As partisan divisions escalated and the Republicans lost ground, Jefferson hung on to his mainstay in times of crisis   principles:

> **"It is now well understood that two political Sects have arisen within the U.S; the one believing that the Executive is the branch of our Government which the most needs support; the other that like the analogous branch in the English Government, it is already too strong for the republican parts of the Constitution, ..."**
>
> *TJ to John Wise, February 12, 1798*

. . . in every free & deliberating society, there must from the nature of man be opposite parties & violent dissensions & discords, and one of these for the most part must prevail over the other for a longer or shorter time. perhaps this party division is necessary to induce each to watch & delate to the people the proceedings of the other. but if on a temporary superiority of the one party, the other

(opposite) William and Thomas Birch. "High Street, From the Country Marketplace Philadelphia: with the procession in commemoration of the Death of General George Washington, December 26th, 1799." Hand-colored engraving from W. Birch & Son, *The City of Philadelphia . . . 1800* (Philadelphia, 1800). Rare Book and Special Collections Division, Library of Congress.
This engraved representation of a procession to commemorate the death of George Washington, who had died unexpectedly at Mount Vernon on December 14, 1799, shows a Philadelphia crowd dressed in mourning, bearing a hat and sword—presumably belonging to Washington—on a platform draped in black.

Congressional Pugilists. Etching. Philadelphia, 1798. Prints and Photographs Division, Library of Congress.

This marvelous, if crude, cartoon satirizes a fight that actually took place on the floor of Congress on February 15, 1798, between Vermont Representative Matthew Lyon and Roger Griswold of Connecticut. The setting is Congress Hall in Philadelphia, with Speaker Jonathan Dayton and Clerk John W. Condy (seated), Chaplain Ashbel Green (in profile on the left), and several other onlookers gathered around the warring pair. Griswold wields a cane while kicking his opponent. Lyon, with an enormous pair of tongs, is poised to strike back. The verse below reads, "He in a trice struck Lyon thrice / Upon his head, enrag'd sir, / Who seiz'd the tongs to ease his wrongs, / And Griswold thus engag'd, sir."

is to resort to a scission of the union, no federal government can ever exist. if to rid ourselves of the present rule of Massachusetts & Connecticut, we break the union, will the evil stop there? suppose the N. England states alone cut off, will our natures be changed? . . . an association of men who will not quarrel with one another is a thing which never yet existed, . . . a little patience and we shall see the reign of witches pass over, their spells dissolve, and the people recovering their true sight, restore their government to it's true principles. (TJ to John Taylor, June 4, 1798)

In an effort to fight the Sedition Act, Jefferson secretly drafted the Kentucky Resolutions and Madison the Virginia Resolutions, later interpreted as support of the states' rights doctrine: ". . . the several states composing the US. of America are not united on the principle of unlimited submission to their general government . . . reserving, each State to itself, the residuary mass of right to their own self-government," wrote Jefferson. It was this exultation of state over federal government that so alarmed the Federalists as the nation faced the future without the reassuring presence of George Washington. Having introduced the idea of a state's right to nullify federal law, Jefferson entered the fray of one of the dirtiest campaigns in political history. Always more comfortable disseminating his ideas through friends and fellow Republicans and remaining in the background, he urged Madison to rally Republican forces: "every man must lay his purse & his pen under contribution." (TJ to Madison, February 5, 1799)

The election of 1800, later trumpeted as the Second American Revolution by Jeffersonians, remains a testimony to the strength of character of party leaders Adams and Jefferson, and the civil respect for republican government among the national population. After a bruising campaign, the same constitutional quirk that brought Jefferson to the vice-presidency plunged the country into crisis and tested the national character. Adams was defeated, but Jefferson and Republican vice-presidential candidate Aaron Burr

> **"an association of men who will not quarrel with one another is a thing which never yet existed, . . . a little patience and we shall see the reign of witches pass over, their spells dissolve, and the people recovering their true sight, restore their government to it's true principles."**
>
> *TJ to John Taylor, June 4, 1798*

received the identical number of electoral votes. By constitutional law, the contest then had to go to the Federalist-controlled House of Representatives, where it would be decided by a vote of individual states.

With rumors of armed reprisal if the Federalists tampered with the election process, and mysterious fires having already destroyed some records of the Treasury, Vice President Jefferson personally presided over the initial meeting of both houses of Congress on February 11, 1801, in the newly occupied but unfinished U.S. Capitol, at which the tied electoral certificates were officially counted. The drama then moved to the House. Plots and counterplots, more suitable in espionage than in politics, flourished in the capital city. Staunch Republican John Beckley confided to Albert Gallatin on February 15, 1801: "The call of the Senate on 4th March—the manner of that call—the refusal to accept Latimers resignation in Delaware—the movements of A: Hamilton in New York—his overtures to Colo.

Burr, disdainfully rejected by the latter—the appointment of John Marshall—the deceptive letter written by the federalists in Congress in favor of Jefferson—all conduced to prove a settled Conspiracy, in which J. Adams has consented to act a part."

In the end, after six days and on the thirty-sixth ballot, the House of Representatives elected Jefferson. The deadlock was broken on February 17. Federalists in Vermont and Maryland abstained from the voting, putting those states in Jefferson's camp. Jefferson and his partisan political party, the Jeffersonian Republicans, had triumphed, and the man alluded to by John Beckley in a celebratory inaugural oration as the genius of liberty was now the third president of the United States.

Looking back on the turmoil, even Jefferson believed that Congress was literally forced to find a peaceful solution to the election crisis:

notwithstanding the suspected infidelity of the post, I must hazard this communication. the Minority in the H. of R. after seeing the impossibility of electing B. the certainty that a legislative usurpation would be resisted by arms, and a recourse to a Convention to reorganize & amend the government, held a consultation on this dilemma. whether it would be better for them to come over in a body, and go with the tide of the times, or by a negative conduct suffer the election to be made by a bare majority, keeping their body entire & unbroken, to act in phalanx on such ground of opposition as circumstances shall offer? (TJ to Madison, February 18, 1801)

As president, he fervently hoped to dig the country out of the mire of partisan politics which he believed was rooted in the intransigence of the high Federalist leaders:

the suspension of public opinion from the 11th. to the 17th. the alarm into which it threw all the patriotic part of the federalists, the danger of the dissolution of our union, & unknown consequences of that, brought over the great body of them to wish with anxiety & sollicitude for a choice to which they had before been strenuously opposed. in this state of mind, they separated from their Congressional leaders, and came over to us; and the manner in which the last ballot was given has drawn a fixed line of separation between them and their leaders . . . I am persuaded that week of ill-judged conduct here, has strengthened us more than years of prudent & conciliatory administration could have done. if we can once more get social intercourse restored to it's pristine harmony, I shall believe we have not lived in vain. and that it may, by rallying them to true republican principles, which few of them had thrown off, I sanguinely hope. (TJ to Thomas Lomax, February 25, 1801)

With Thomas Jefferson at the helm, the country set out to recapture the spirit that had driven thirteen states to declare independence in 1776. And, later, a Twelfth Amendment was added to the Constitution that specified electors should "name in their ballots the person voted for as President, and in distinct ballots the person voted for as Vice President."

recovered, they being due for property ſold and not conveyed, or ſecured by notes with ſufficient indorſers; yet the difficulty of enforcing payment is ſuch, they cannot be relied on for the punctual payment of the intereſt on the ſeveral loans from the ſtate of Maryland, of the ſums, due to individuals and the expences of the commiſſioners office.

We futher obſerve, that only 3 ſquares remain undivided, owing to the original proprietors not having agreed on their reſpective proportions therein; and that the diviſion of 33 ſquares has been agreed upon, but the papers reſpecting them not yet ſigned by the parties; and that the accounts with ſome of the original proprietors, for land appropriated to public uſe, have not been ſettled, owing to a difference of opinion between the commiſſioners and them, with reſpect to ſmall portions of land for which they claim payment.

Thomas Beall and John M. Gantt, the truſtees before named, have, at the requeſt of the Preſident of the United States, conveyed the building lots in the city of Waſhington, to Guſtavus Scott, William Thornton, and Alexander White, ſubject to the truſts remaining to be executed—Guſtavus Scott has ſince deceaſed. The ſaid truſtees have been required by the Preſident to convey the ſtreets and grounds appropriated to public uſe, to the commiſſioners, but have not complied.

Several acts of the Legiſlature of Maryland have veſted certain powers in the commiſſioners, which it may be proper to notice; particularly, an act paſſed 19th December, 1791, intituled, "An act concerning the territory of Columbia and city of Waſhington," a copy whereof is encloſed, marked H; and an act paſſed in December, 1793, being a further ſupplement to the act above mentioned. By the firſt paragraph of which, it is enacted, "That the certificates granted, or which may be granted by the ſaid commiſſioners, or any two of them, to purchaſers of lots in the ſaid city, with acknowledgement of the payment of the whole purchaſe money and intereſt, if any ſhall have ariſen thereon, and recorded agreeably to the directions of the act concerning the territory of Columbia and city of Waſhington, ſhall be ſufficient and effectual to veſt the legal eſtate in the purchaſers, their heirs and aſſigns, according to the import of ſuch certificate, without any deed or formal conveyance."

The ſecond paragraph of the laſt mentioned act, empowering the commiſſioners to reſell lots for default in payment of the firſt purchaſe money, has been before recited.

The commiſſioners having ſtated all the facts and obſervations, which appear to them neceſſary for the information of government, reſpecting the buſineſs committed to their charge; with the greateſt deference and reſpect ſubmit the ſame to the conſideration of the Preſident of the United States

WILLIAM THORNTON,
ALEX. WHITE,
W. CRANCH.

Commiſsimers Office,
28th Jan. 1801.

For Sale.

A Small tract of land containing 150 acres more or leſs. It is on the road to Frederic about five miles from George Town, and is a nigh and healthy ſituation. Terms are one third to be paid on poſſeſſion being given, the remainder in two yearly payments. Enquire of the printer, or at the Commiſſioners Office, City of Waſhington.

If not ſold within a month it will be rented on eaſy terms.

January, 28th, 1801.

Conrad & M'Munn

HAVE opened houſes of entertainment in the range of buildings formerly occupied by Mr Law, about two hundred paces from the Capitol, in New Jerſey avenue, leading from thence to the Eaſtern Branch. They are ſpacious and convenient, one of which is deſigned for ſtage paſſengers and travellers, the other for the accommodation of boarders. There is ſtableage ſufficient for 60 horſes——They hope to merit public patronage

City of Waſhington, Nov. 24, 1800. tf

LOTS FOR SALE,

In the City of WASHINGTON.

THE SUBSCRIBER offers for Sale a number of valuable Lots beautifully ſituated between the Capitol and the Eaſtern Branch Alſo a few Lots to be let on leaſe for ninety nine years in the vicinity of the Navy yard.

WILLIAM PROUT.

City of Waſhington December 12, 1800. tf

N B A few Tons of good Meadow Hay, one kiln of Bricks, and ſome Cord Wood.

W. P.

WASHINGTON CITY.

MONDAY, FEB. 23, 1801.

In House of Representatives of the United States.

Thurſday, February 19, 1801.

Ordered that the Committee appointed on the Seventeenth inſtant, to wait on the Preſident of the United States, and notify him that Thomas Jefferſon is elected Preſident of the United States, for the term commencing on the fourth day of March next, be authoriſed to notify the Preſident elect thereof.

The committee instructed on the 18th inst. to wait on the President elect, and notify him of his election,

REPORT—

That they have, according to order, performed that ſervice, and addreſſed the Preſident elect, in the following words to wit:

"The committee beg leave to expreſs "their wiſhes for the proſperity of your "adminiſtration; and their ſincere deſire "that it may promote your own happineſs "and the welfare of your country."

To which the Preſident elect, was pleaſed to make the following reply:

"I receive, gentlemen, with profound thankfulneſs, this teſtimony of confidence from the great repreſentative council of our nation. It fills up the meaſure of that grateful ſatisfaction, which had already been derived from the ſuffrages of my fellow-citizens themſelves, deſignating me as one of thoſe to whom they were willing to commit this charge, the moſt important of all others to them. In deciding between the candidates, whom their equal vote preſented to your choice, I am ſenſible that age has been reſpected, rather than more active and uſeful qualifications. I know the difficulties of the ſtation to which I am called, and feel and acknowledge my incompetence to them. But whatſoever of underſtanding, whatſoever of diligence, whatſoever of juſtice, or of affectionate concern for the happineſs of man, it has pleaſed providence to place within the compaſs of my faculties, ſhall be called forth for the diſcharge of the duties confided to me, and for procuring to my fellow citizens all the benefits which our conſtitution has placed under the guardianſhip of the general government. Guided by the wiſdom and patriotiſm of thoſe to whom it belongs to expreſs the legiſlative will of the nation, I will give to that will a faithful execution. I pray you to convey to the honorable body from which you are deputed the homage of my humble acknowledgements, and the ſentiments of zeal and fidelity, by which I ſhall endeavor to merit theſe proofs of confidence from the nation and its repreſentatives.

Accept yourſelves, gentlemen, my particular thanks for the obliging terms in which you have been pleaſed to communicate their will.

THOMAS JEFFERSON.

February 20, 1801.

Meſſrs. Pinckney, Tazewell, and Bayard.

HOUSE OF REPRESENTATIVES.

Friday, Feb. 20 1801.

The petitions of Mathias Shroyer and Margaret Culbertſon were preſented and referred to the Committee of claims.

A petition from ſundry perſons, reſiding on lands belonging to U. S. lying between Muſkingum and Scioto rivers, praying to be allowed a pre-emption to the lands on which the petitioners are ſettled on more favourable terms than thoſe heretofore granted by law.

Referred to Meſſrs. Dennis, M'Millan and Chriſtie.

A motion being made and ſeconded, that the houſe do come to the following reſolution, viz.

Reſolved that the Speaker of this houſe, in directing the Serjeant at Arms to order and expel from the gallery of this Houſe, Samuel Harriſon Smith, a citizen of the United States, has aſſumed a power not given him by the rules of this houſe, and deprived the ſaid Samuel Harriſon Smith of a right, which can only be forfeited by diſorderly behaviour.

MR. DAVIS. Mr. Speaker, my intention is to call for the Reſolution laid on the Table by me the other day, which relates to the conduct of the Speaker towards Mr. Smith: But before I call up the Reſolution I will remark that I have not introduced it with a view to afford myſelf an opportunity of venting invectives or perſonalities againſt the Speaker. The due reſpect to this Houſe forbids a conduct of that ſort. The number of days the Speaker has ſeen, compared with my own forbids it. I contend for principle; and thoſe who differ from me on this point, in opinion, may meet me on this ground and by a fair and diſpaſſionate argument diſcuſs the ſubject. If they chooſe to do ſo I ſhall be ſatisfied; it will be the moſt agreeable method to me.

But if Gentlemen are diſpoſed to introduce aſperity into the Debate, I am ready to repel it.

Reſolved unanimouſly that the Speaker be excuſed from deciding whether the ſaid motion is in order or not.

The queſtion was then taken, viz. "Is this motion in order?" and it paſſed in the negative, as follows, *Yeas* 49, *Nays* 54.

YEAS.

Meſſrs. Alſton, Bailey, Biſhop, R. Brown, Cabell, Chriſtie, Clay, Claiborne, Condit, Davis, Dawſon, Dent, Eggleſton, Elmendorf, Fowler, Gallatin, Gray, Gregg, Hanna, Heiſter, Holmes, Jackſon, Kitchell, Leib, Lyon, Linn, Livingſton, Macon, Muhlenberg, New, Nicholas Nicholſon, Randolph, Smilie, J. Smith, S. Smith, Spaight, Stanford, Stone, Sumper, Stuart, Taliaferro, Thompſon, A. Trigg, J. Trigg, Tazewell, Van Cortlandt, Varnum, R. Williams—49.

NOES.

Meſſrs. Baer, Bartlett, Bayard, Bird, J. Brown, Champlin, Cooper, Craik, Dana, J. Davenport, F. Davenport, Dennis, Dickſon, Edmond, Evans, Foſter, Freeman, Glen, Goode, C. Goodrich, E. Goodrich, Griſwold, Grove, Harper, Henderſon, Hill, Huger, Imlay, Kittera, H. Lee, S Lee, Lincoln, Mattoon, Morris, Otis, Page, Parker, Pinckney, Platt, Powell, J. Reed, N. Read, Rutledge, Shephard, J. C. Smith, Sheafe, Tenney, Thatcher, J. C. Thomas, R. Thomas, Wadſworth, Waln, L. Williams, Woods—54.

And ſo the ſaid motion was not in order.

A motion was then made and ſeconded that the houſe do come to the following reſolution, viz.

Reſolved that the power of the Speaker or chairman of the committee of the whole, ſhall not be conſtrued to extend (unleſs by conſent of the houſe, previouſly obtained, or in caſe of diſorderly behaviour) to the expulſion of any perſon, either from the lobby when introduced by any member of the houſe, or from the gallery, when the ſame is generally opened.

The previous queſtion was called for by five members viz. "ſhall the main queſtion to agree to the ſaid motion be now put?"

Whereupon the ſaid queſtion being under conſideration, Mr. Livingſton, having addreſsed the ſpeaker did in the opinion of the Speaker proceed to debate the main queſtion, and being thereupon called to order by the Speaker.

Whereupon an appeal was made to the houſe, from the deciſion of the Speaker, and on the queſtion of concurring with the Speaker in his ſaid deciſion, it was reſolved in the affirmative—Yeas 60, Nays 42. as follows:

Yea.—Meſſrs. Baer, Bartlett, Bayard, Bird, J. Brown, Champlin, Cooper, Craik, Dana, J. Davenport, F. Davenport, Dennis, Dent, Dickſon, Edmond, Evans, Foſter, Freeman, Glen, Goode, C. Goodrich, E. Goodrich, Gregg, Griſwold, Grove, Hanna, Harper, Henderſon, Hill, Huger, Imlay, Kitchell, Kittera, H. Lee, S. Lee, Lincoln, Mattoon, Morris, Otis, Page, Parker, Pinckney, Platt, Powell, J. Reed, N. Read, Rutledge, Shepard, J. Smith, J. C. Smith, Sheafe, Tenny, Thatcher, J. C. Thomas, R. Thomas, Varnum, Wadſworth, Waln, L. Williams, Woods. 62.

Nays.—Meſſrs. Alſton, Bailey, Biſhop, R. Brown, Cabell, Chriſtie, Clay, Claiborne, Condit, Davis, Dawſon Eggleſton, Elmendorf, Fowler, Gray, Heiſter, Holmes, Jackſon, Leib, Lyon, Linn, Livingſton, Macon, Muhlenberg, New, Nicholas, Nicholſon, Randolph, Smilie, S. Smith, Spaight, Stanford, Stone, Sumter, Stewart, Taliaferro, Thompſon, A. Trigg, J. Trigg, Tazewell, Van Cortlandt, R. Williams. 42.

The previous queſtion upon the ſaid motion being then taken, in the words following, viz. "Shall the main queſtion to agree to the ſame be now put?" It paſſed in the negative—Yeas 50—Nays 53; as follow:

YEAS.

Meſſrs. Alſton, Bailey, Biſhop, R. Brown, Cabell, Chriſtie, Clay, Claiborne, Condit, Davis, Dawſon, Dent, Eggleſton, Elmendorf, Fowler, Gallatin, Gray, Gregg, Hanna, Heiſter, Holmes, Jackſon, Kitchell, Leib, Lincoln, Lyon, Linn, Livingſton, Macon, Muhlenberg, New, Nicholas, Nicholſon, Randolph, Smilie, J. Smith, S. Smith, Spaight, Stanford, Stone, Sumter, Steuart, Taliaferro, Thompſon, A. Trigg, J. Trigg, Tazewell, Van Cortlandt, Varnum, R. Williams. Woods. 50.

NAYS.

Meſſrs. Baer, Bartlett, Bayard, Bird, J. Brown, Champlin, Cooper, Craik, Dana, J. Davenport, F. Davenport, Dennis, Dickſon, Edmond, Evans, Foſter, Freeman, Glen, Goode, C. Goodrich, E. Goodrich, Griſwold, Grove, Harper, Henderſon, Hill, Huger, Imlay, Kittera, H. Lee, S. Lee, Mattoon, Morris, Otis, Page, Parker, Pinckney, Platt, Powell, J. Reed, N. Read, Rutledge, Shepard, J. C. Smith, Sheafe, Tenney, Thatcher, J. C. Thomas, R. Thomas, Wadſworth, Waln, L. Williams.—53.

A meſſage was received from the Preſident of the U. States, as follows.

Gentlemen of the Senate, and
Gentlemen of the H. of Repreſentatives,

I tranſmit to Congreſs a report received this morning from Elias Boudinot, Eſq. director of the Mint, dated February 13, 1801, which will require the attention and deciſion of Congreſs before the cloſe of the ſeſſion.

JOHN ADAMS.

United States,
Feb. 20, 1801.

The meſſage and report were read, and ordered to lie on the table.

MR. MACON, from the committee of claims, made report on the petition of Charles Tomkins, in behalf of Arnold H. Dohrman and others; whereupon reſolved that the Preſident of the U. States, be authorized to iſſue a patent for the 13th townſhip in the 7th range to Arnold H. Dohrman or his legal repreſentatives, agreeable to a reſolution of Congreſs of October 1, 1787, and that a bill be brought in to that effect.

Reſolved that a committee be appointed to bring in a bill to revive and continue "An act declaring the conſent of Congreſs to an act of the ſtate of Maryland paſſed the 28th of December 1793, for the appointment of a Health-Officer.

Ordered that the committee of Reviſal and unfiniſhed buſineſs bring in ſaid bill.

MR. PINCKNEY, from the committee appointed for that purpoſe, reported that the committee had waited on the Preſident of the U. States, to inform him that Thomas Jefferſon is elected Preſident for four years, commencing on the 4th of March.

The houſe reſumed the conſideration of the amendments reported yeſterday from the committee of the whole to whom was committed the bill to amend the act to regulate the collection of duties on imports and tonnage, which were agreed to by the houſe, and the bill, after further amendment, was ordered to be engroſſed for a third reading tomorrow.

SATURDAY, FEB. 21, 1801.

A report was read in favour of continuing the MINT ESTABLISHMENT at Philadelphia till March 3, 1803, and agreed to, and a committee appointed to introduce a bill to that effect.—The houſe went into committee of the whole, Mr. Morris in the chair, on the ſedition bill.

The committee reported the bill without amendment, and on the queſtion of engroſſment for a third reading, it was decided in the negative, and of courſe the bill was loſt—The yeas and nays are as follow:

Yeas.—Meſſrs. Baer, Bartlett, Bayard, J. Brown, Champlin, Cooper, Craik, Dana, J. Davenport, F. Davenport, Dennis, Dickſon, Edmond, Evans, Foſter, Freeman, Glen, C. Goodrich, E. Goodrich, Griſwold, Grove, Harper, Henderſon, Hill, Imlay, Kittera, H. Lee, S. Lee, Mattoon, Morris, Otis, Page, Pinckney, Platt, Powell, J. Read, N. Read, Rutledge, Shepard, J. C. Smith, Sheafe, Tenney, Thatcher, J. C. Thomas, R. Thomas, Wadſworth, Waln, L. Williams, Woods.—49.

Nays.—Meſſrs. Alſton, Bailey, Biſhop, R. Brown, Cabell, Chriſtie, Clay, Claiborne, Condit, Davis, Dawſon, Dent, Eggleſton, Elmendorf, Fowler, Gallatin, Goode, Gray, Gregg, Hanna, Heiſter, Holmes, Huger, Jackſon, Kitchell, Leib, Lincoln, Lyon, Linn, Livingſton, Macon, Muhlenburg, New, Nicholas, Nicholſon, Parker, Randolph, Smilie, J. Smith, S. Smith, Spaight, Stanford, Stone, Sumter, Stewart, Talliaferro, Thompſon, A. Trigg, J. Trigg, Tazewell, Van Cortlandt, Varnum, R. Williams.—53.

The houſe went into a committee of the whole on the bill from the Senate in relation to the Territory of Columbia, and after conſidering the ſame, reported progreſs and aſked leave to ſit again.

Isaac Jefferson. Daguerreotype #2041, ca. 1840s. Tracy W. McGregor Library, Special Collections Department, University of Virginia Library.

Isaac Jefferson was born in 1775, the third son of trusted Monticello slaves, George, the foreman of labor, and Ursula, a household servant. Isaac was trained as a blacksmith and was taken by Jefferson to Philadelphia in the 1790s to learn tinsmithing. Back at Monticello, he worked in those two trades and also as the most efficient nailer, according to Jefferson, in the Mulberry Row nailery. Isaac Jefferson provided lively details of life at Monticello, describing a benevolent and inventive master, in an interview in 1847 when he was living in retirement in Petersburg, Virginia. Some historians have connected his report that fellow slave Madison Hemings became "a fine fiddle player" with the fact that Thomas Jefferson also played the violin.

Thomas Jefferson and the Boundaries of American Civilization

by Annette Gordon-Reed

FOR THE FORESEEABLE FUTURE it is Thomas Jefferson's fate to be portrayed as the embodiment of the deepest contradiction in the political and social life of the United States. In this country the quest for a sound democratic society has often run counter to the desire among large segments of the population to maintain white supremacy. Complicating matters further, the Judeo-Christian ethic, with its counsel against open expressions of hatred, has made it difficult for some white Americans to confront the depth of their ambivalence about sharing the blessings of American liberty with the descendants of those who arrived on these shores as enslaved men and women.

Jefferson's life and writings bring this conflict into sharp relief. The principal author of the American Declaration of Independence, the world-renowned proponent of the rights of man, the first leader of an organized American political party (one that billed itself as the representative of the "common man" against the agencies of powerful interests in society), Jefferson also owned slaves and voiced his suspicions about the innate inferiority of those he kept in bondage. From the height of noble aspirations to the depth of the most dispiriting reality, the study of Jefferson offers up a tantalizing and exasperating expression of the origins and development of American civilization.

Still, it is quite a thing to be seen as a symbol. The humanity of one subjected to this treatment inevitably shrinks underneath the shroud of others' expectations and hopes. Because of the role Jefferson played in the creation of the American nation—in ways both good and bad—his life seems naturally fit for symbolic treatment. Yet, it has been clear for some time now that the role has ill-served our third president, and us.

At the dawn of the 1960s, Merrill Peterson observed that Jefferson the man was often "lost in the vastness" of attempts to present him as the human exemplar of many, sometimes contradictory, ideals and philosophies. Over three decades later, Gordon Wood created the perfect image for the mind's eye when he wrote in *Jeffersonian Legacies* of "Jefferson standing for America and carrying the moral character of the country on his back." Who could bear such a burden without faltering?

For modern observers, the crucial point at which Jefferson faltered, over and over again throughout the course of his long life, was on the question of slavery and race. This has been of particular moment for those alive during the latter half of the twentieth century when America underwent what is called the Second American Revolution, aimed at bringing black Americans into full citizenship. During that era, Jefferson's words were offered up as part of the unfinished promise of democracy in the United States. From his cell in the Birmingham City jail Martin Luther King, Jr., wrote of "the pen of Jefferson" etching "the majestic words of the Declaration of Independence . . . across the pages of history." Later, in his "I Have a Dream" oration on the steps of the Lincoln Memorial during the March on Washington, Jefferson was on his mind again. King offered his hope that the country would "rise up and live out the true meaning of its creed: We hold these truths to be self-evident: that all men are created equal." While King's sentiment was without question deeply felt, it was also a brilliant display of strategy. Whatever had happened in the past, blacks would not give up on the American ideal. They were not the enemies of American civilization. Instead they wanted to be a part of the development of a truly moral one—guided, in part, by the words of a white slaveholder from Virginia.

District of Ohio, which will con-
Cincinnati on the first day of April.

t the spring election the voters of
ship will be called upon to vote
ber of Constitutional Convention,
stees, Clerk, Treasurer, Assessor,
f the Peace and three Constables.
rporation there will be to elect a
ecorder, three Councilmen and one
Trustee.

o-morrow the personal property of
aker, deceased, will be offered for
ction by the administrator, Thomas
ick. The advertisement which de-
e property may be found in another
We looked over the property on
and found it to average well. The
good and cattle fair.

ner Wetmore will answer us one
we will promise him never again
in "agricultural matters." Ques-
make a goose lay eggs, do you sub-
rn under?—*Watchman.*

l, you goosey! By sub-soiling the
ade to grow which feeds the goose,
e may "accumulate much grease"
ggs to her heart's content. The
is always the best. Now you are
agricultural matters forever and
Good!!

mmissioners' Meeting.

mmissioners met in regular session
y last. On that day it was
l, That from and after the 10th day
, 1873, the court-room shall not be
any other purpose than holding of
nventions or political meetings.

aths of one mill on the dollar was
be levied on the entire taxable
of the county for building and re-
f bridges.

was granted on the petition of M,
e for a road leading from his stone
ear the old infirmary farm to the
under special statute concerning
arries, swamps, low lands, &c.

orders on the county treasury were

ntations and petitions were pre-
king for the building of bridges—
s Crooked creek near the Kern's
se, Pee Pee township; near Joseph
ion; across Kelly's run near Mrs.
eaver; across the canal in Waver-
st street, and one across the Scioto
Sharonville. The Commissioners
to meet March 31, and make per-
ection of the places for the bridges.

ve the farmers of Pike county
r advice of two weeks ago to take
of their cattle, especially those
oung, this cold, changeable, pinch-
h of March? We hope so. In a
o after that article was written we
to visit Reuben Slavens', in Union
and he remarked that he was con-
t it paid to house fattening cattle.
enced feeding 16 steers on the first
vember and continued to feed them
en field till January 8—68 days—
put them in a rough building with
fed them 40 days. In the 68 days
d on the average 94 pounds; dur-
4days 96 pounds. They averaged

Let all the Republicans of the township be present. R. M. VINCENT, Ad. Com.

Life Among the Lowly.

NUMBER I.

MADISON HEMINGS.

I never knew of but one white man who bore the name of Hemings; he was an Englishman and my greatgrandfather. He was captain of an English trading vessel which sailed between England and Williamsburg, Va., then quite a port. My grandmother was a fullblooded African, and possibly a native of that country. She was the property of John Wales, a Welchman. Capt. Hemings happened to be in the port of Williamsburg at the time my grandmother was born, and acknowledging her fatherhood he tried to purchase her of Mr. Wales, who would not part with the child, though he was offered an extraordinarily large price for her. She was named Elizabeth Hemings. Being thwarted in the purchase, and determining to own his flesh and blood he resolved to take the child by force or stealth, but the knowledge of his intention coming to John Wales' ears, through leaky fellow servants of the mother, she and the child were taken into the "great house" under their master's immediate care. I have been informed that it was not the extra value of that child over other slave children that induced Mr. Wales to refuse to sell it, for slave masters then, as in later days, had no compunctions of conscience which restrained them from parting mother and child of however tender age, but he was restrained by the fact that just about that time amalgamation began, and the child was so great a curiosity that its owner desired to raise it himself that he might see its outcome. Capt. Hemings soon afterwards sailed from Williamsburg, never to return. Such is the story that comes down to me.

Elizabeth Hemings grew to womanhood in the family of John Wales, whose wife dying she (Elizabeth) was taken by the widower Wales as his concubine, by whom she had six children—three sons and three daughters, viz: Robert, James, Peter, Critty, Sally and Thena. These children went by the name of Hemings.

Williamsburg was the capital of Virginia, and of course it was an aristocratic place, where the "bloods" of the Colony and the new State most did congregate. Thomas Jefferson, the author of the Declaration of Independence, was educated at William and Mary College, which had its seat at Williamsburg. He afterwards studied law with Geo. Wythe, and practiced law at the bar of the general court of the Colony. He was afterwards elected a member of the provincial legislature from Albemarle county. Thos. Jefferson was a visitor at the "great house" of John Wales, who had children about his own age. He formed the acquaintance of his daughter Martha (I believe that was her name, though I am not positively sure,) and an intimacy sprang up between them which ripened into love, and they were married. They afterwards went to live at his country seat, Monticello, and in course of time had born to them a daughter whom they named Martha. About the time she was born my mother, the second daughter of John Wales and Elizabeth Hemings was born. On the death of John Wales, my grandmother, his concubine, and her children by him fell to Martha, Thomas Jefferson's wife, and consequently became the property of Thomas Jefferson, who in the course of time became famous, and was appointed minister to France during our revolutionary troubles, or soon after independence was gained. About the time of the appointment and before he was ready to leave the country his wife died, and as soon after her interment as he could attend to and arrange his domestic affairs in accordance with the changed circumstances of his family in consequence of this misfortune (I think not more than three weeks

stewards and overseers. He always had mechanics at work for him, such as carpenters, blacksmiths, shoemakers, coopers, &c. It was his mechanics he seemed mostly to direct, and in their operations he took great interest. Almost every day of his latter years he might have been seen among them. He occupied much of the time in his office engaged in correspondence and reading and writing. His general temperament was smooth and even; he was very undemonstrative. He was uniformly kind to all about him. He was not in the habit of showing partiality or fatherly affection to us children. We were the only children of his by a slave woman. He was affectionate toward his white grandchildren, of whom he had fourteen, twelve of whom lived to manhood and womanhood. His daughter Martha married Thomas Mann Randolph by whom she had thirteen children. Two died in infancy. The names of the living were Ann, Thomas Jefferson, Ellen, Cornelia, Virginia, Mary, James, Benj. Franklin, Lewis Madison, Septemia and Geo. Wythe. Thos. Jefferson Randolph was Chairman of the Democratic National Convention in Baltimore last spring which nominated Horace Greeley for the Presidency, and Geo. Wythe Randolph was Jeff. Davis' first Secretary of War in the late "unpleasantness."

Maria married John Epps, and raised one son—Francis.

My father generally enjoyed excellent health. I never knew him to have but one spell of sickness, and that was caused by a visit to the Warm Springs in 1818. Till within three weeks of his death he was hale and hearty, and at the age of 83 years he walked erect and with stately tread. I am now 68, and I well remember that he was a much smarter man physically, even at that age, than I am.

When I was fourteen years old I was put to the carpenter trade under the charge of John Hemings, the youngest son of my grandmother. His father's name was Nelson, who was an Englishman. She had seven children by white men and seven by colored men—fourteen in all. My brothers, sister Harriet and myself were used alike. They were put to some mechanical trade at the age of fourteen. Till then we were permitted to stay about the "great house," and only required to do such light work as going on errands. Harriet learned to spin and to weave in a little factory on the home plantation. We were free from the dread of having to be slaves all our lives long, and were measurably happy. We were always permitted to be with our mother, who was well used. It was her duty, all her life which I can remember, up to the time of father's death, to take care of his chamber and wardrobe, look after us children and do such light work as sewing, &c.

Provision was made in the will of our father that we should be free when we arrived at the age of 21 years. We had all passed that period when he died but Eston, and he was given the remainder of his time shortly after. He and I rented a house and took mother to live with us, till her death, which event occurred in 1835.

In 1831 I married Mary McCoy. Her grandmother was a slave, and lived with her master, Stephen Hughes, near Charlottesville, as his wife. She was manumitted by him, which made their children free born. Mary McCoy's mother was his daughter. I was about 23 and she 22 years of age when we married. We lived and labored together in Virginia till 1836, when we voluntarily left and came to Ohio. We settled in Pebble township, Pike county. We lived there four or five years, and during my stay in that county I worked at my trade on and off for about four years. Joseph Sewell was my first employer. I built for him what is now known as Bizzleport No. 2, in Waverly. I afterwards worked for George Wolfe, Senior, and did the carpenter work of the brick building now owned by John J. Kellison, in which the Pike County Republican is printed. I worked for and with Micajah Hinson. I found him to be a very clever

will strike hard in the very pla
where an effective blow has lo
been needed. Then, all saloon kee
ers are made responsible by bo
for damages, and in all cases mu
give a bond of $1,000 before ope
ing their saloons. In several wa
have laws been made stronger,
technical breeding sections havi
the legal cobwebs swept away, a
made as clear as they are intend
to be forcible in checking this ev

The Finest Speech Ever Made.

The West Minster Review pr
nounced Abraham Lincoln's Getty
burg speech the finest that ever f
from human lips. It was short, a
we give it below:

Four score and seven years a
our fathers brought forth upon th
continent a new nation, conceived
liberty and dedicated to the prop
sition that all men are created equ
Now we are engaged in a great ci
il war, testing whether that natio
or any nation so conceived or ded
cated, can long endure. We a
now on a great battlefield of th
war. We are met to dedicate
portion of it as the final restir
place of those who here gave the
lives that the nation might live.
is altogether fitted and proper th
we should do this.

But in a large sense we cann
consecrate, we cannot hallow th
ground. The brave men, livir
and dead, who struggled here ha
consecrated it far above our pow
to add or detract. The world wi
little note nor long remember wh
we say here. It is for us, the li
ing, rather to be dedicated to tl
great task remaining before us-
that from those honored dead w
take increased devotion to the cau
for which they here gave the fu
measure of devotion—that we we
highly resolved that the dead sha
not have died in vain—that the n
tion shall, under God, have a ne
birth of freedom, and that the go
ernment of the people, by the pe
ple, shall not perish from the eart

Thirteen years ago, this winte
Lewis Mason and Samuel Barn
caught a large gray fox, near Lov
ell, in Washington county, th
State; they tied him with a rop
first having placed a leather stra
around his neck. This rope M
Fox gnawed off and made his e
cape. This winter the same pa
ties recaptured the fox, and, strang
to state, he had on his neck th
same identical strap which the
placed there thirteen years before
They slaughtered their game, th
time, to make sure of him.

Madison Hemings, "Life Among the Lowly. Number 1." Interview in *Pike County (Ohio) Republican*, March 13, 1873. Ohio Historical Society.

Madison Hemings's explosive claim that he was the son of Thomas Jefferson and Sally Hemings and that there were four other children of the relationship—"We were the only children of his by a slave woman"—was long ridiculed and vehemently denied by Jefferson's white descendants and by many prominent historians. Madison Hemings's statement was corroborated by another former Monticello slave, Israel Jefferson, nine months later.

The deep irony, of course, is that the man whose words King invoked on both occasions did not have the confidence that blacks could be a part of the American civilization. In his other famous text, *Notes on the State of Virginia*, responding to questions by a French diplomat, Jefferson sets forth his most complete and revealing discourse on the subjects of slavery, race, and the role he thought both would play in American society. The book contains some of the most insightful and condemnatory passages about American slavery ever written. It also reveals Jefferson's primitive beliefs about the differences between blacks and whites, as well as his lack of faith that the two races could ever rise above the circumstances of their initial engagement on this continent. There could be no long term peaceful co-existence between blacks and whites. He wrote:

Deep rooted prejudices entertained by the whites, ten thousand recollections, by the blacks, of the injuries they have sustained, new provocations: the real distinctions which nature has made, and many other circumstances will divide us into parties, and produce convulsions which will probably never end but in the extermination of the one or the other race. ("Query XIV," Notes on the State of Virginia*)*

These words appear venomous to all those who presently embrace this country's multicultural heritage and future. So much so that it has been suggested by Conor Cruise O'Brien that the man who wrote them should be stricken from the canon of American heroes. The matter is not so simple. We take it for granted, at least in our public discourse, that the issue of black citizenship in the United States has been settled. Yet, the long and deep struggle for acceptance of black peoples' equal humanity is evidence that Jefferson's remarks, although impolitic, hit the proverbial nail on the head.

We can never forget that it took a civil war to end slavery. Even after that, it has taken a virtual army of legal and legislative initiatives to mandate de jure racial equality. The matter still has not been resolved. White Americans are born into natural citizenship. Black Americans' citizenship rights must be supported by an extensive network of laws and programs of social engineering that are vulnerable to ever-shifting political winds. What is seen as evidence of Jefferson's blind-

ness then is, in truth, more suitably described as a clear-eyed assessment of the basic problem the country has always faced. Even as we enter the twenty-first century the fundamental question remains: can a racial minority (that remains a visible minority) ever attain true and full citizenship in the United States?

It is true that, during Jefferson's time, there were whites who answered yes to that question. Paul Finkelman has written in *Jeffersonian Legacies* that Jefferson's status as the "author of the Declaration of Independence and a leader of the American enlightenment" means that he must be judged not on "whether he was the best of the worst of his generation, but whether he was the leader of the best; not whether he responded as a southerner and a planter, but whether he was able to transcend his economic interests and his sectional background to implement the ideals he articulated." Jefferson, he wrote, "fails" the test.

This view is problematic at best because the central premise rests upon a non-sequitur, and unfairly stacks the deck. It is simply not true that we can (should) expect a person who is extraordinary on several fronts to be extraordinary on all fronts. If one has been able to figure out some things in life, must one figure out everything or risk extreme opprobrium for being merely average in some regards? Talent is unusual. That is why we recognize it. When a person rises above the average, we have no right to punish the individual for not extending his exceptionalism into areas beyond his capabilities.

There were, no doubt, whites in Jefferson's time who were more racially enlightened. But it is an undisputable fact that racial enlightenment in slaveholding Virginia was in short supply. Jefferson should not be held to an unrealistically high standard because he displayed certain talents that have led us to see him symbolically. The Jefferson of our memory is judged not on the basis of his own character, but rather on our estimations of what that character means to us. Is there any way to come to grips with the man whose legacy is so indelibly stamped onto the American psyche? Can we ever come to see him as a human being in all his majesty and with all his faults, giving each portion its just—and only its just—due?

At this point in our history, the thing most urgently need-

View of Monticello from Mulberry Row. Photograph by L. Fosso. Monticello/Thomas Jefferson Memorial Foundation, Inc.
At one time there were at least seventeen structures on Mulberry Row, including workshops and cabins for both slaves and free workmen. Although Jefferson could not afford to free his slaves, accounts suggest that he was a benevolent master.

ed is to try to rescue Jefferson from the prison of symbolism—to the extent that it can be done. This undertaking requires a start from first principles. For the most part, talk about Jefferson and slavery, or Jefferson and race, is carried out on an abstract level. That is precisely why the expectation that he be extraordinary on all fronts is so appealing. Divorced from the need to think about the reality of Jefferson's day-to-day existence from the time of his birth until his death, it is easy to forget the contending emotional, social, and intellectual forces that went into shaping who he really was.

If we see Jefferson as a human being, we understand that it is extremely rare for an individual to totally escape the external forces that helped to mold his or her personality. For this reason, it is important that Jefferson was born into the class of southern planters. It is also important to consider that he lived from birth to death within the confines of a slave society that actively promoted, supported, and defended white supremacy. The doctrine would have suffused every waking moment. He managed to fight through this enough to understand that slavery was a moral wrong, which was more

than most of his Virginia cohort managed to do. He could not, however, become even more extraordinary and eschew the belief in white supremacy that was an integral part of his cultural and social milieu. Less than total success is not the same thing as failure.

When we, at the beginning of a new century, congratulate ourselves on our own enlightenment, and take the measure of Jefferson and find him wanting in character, we fail to properly acknowledge those people and circumstances that made it easy for us to be enlightened. We did not get to this place without enormous help. Our currently more progressive racial climate is the product of decades of concerted efforts by thousands of ordinary citizens, lawyers, artists, politicians, and religious figures. A world war that killed millions, brought to light a racially based holocaust, and changed the balance of power among nations helped to transform our understanding of the corrosive aspect of America's racial landscape.

Jefferson during his time had the benefit of no similar supports. That some of his mentors and friends—his old law teacher George Wythe, the physician Benjamin Rush—were able to develop sensibilities about race that were ahead of their time is no answer. Those individuals who opposed slavery more vigorously than Jefferson cannot be automatically placed within the ranks of the racially sensitive because it is clear that not all abolitionists were non-racist. The writings and actions of a few outstanding individuals cannot be compared to the force of world-wide influences that have helped set our current understanding about race.

None of the individuals who could be cited as having transcended the racial attitudes of their time also became lawyers, justices of the peace, legislators, drafters of the Declaration of Independence, governors of Virginia, ambassadors to France, secretaries of state, vice-presidents and presidents of the United States, as well as all the other roles Jefferson played in his life. There is such a thing as expecting too much from one individual. The burden of expectations robs Jefferson of humanity and prevents us from appreciating the real value that remains even when we acknowledge his deficiencies.

Ironically, the very thing that scholars thought might destroy Jefferson may yet be his salvation in modern times. If we are concerned about having lost touch with Jefferson the man, the story of his relationship with Sally Hemings brings his humanity to the forefront with crashing force, and not for the reason most typically cited. It is a cliché—a somewhat thoughtless one—to say that the knowledge that Jefferson had children with Sally Hemings makes him seem more human because it shows that he was capable of making a mistake. The real significance of the Hemings story is that it will force historians to take a deeper and more sophisticated look at Jefferson's complicated family life. The story of Jefferson's political career has often overshadowed aspects of his life at Monticello. The personal character has been extrapolated from the public character as defined by Jefferson's life as a politician and from his contributions to the "republic of letters." That is why the relationship with Hemings seemed so implausible to many. Jefferson's theoretical musings about miscegenation were taken too literally, when it should have been clear that it is common for individuals to hold and express intellectual positions for public consumption that they are not so emotionally wedded to in private.

In this regard, consider one of the last important documents Jefferson ever wrote: his will—throughout the ages the repository of individuals' final attempts to settle all accounts, financial, moral, and spiritual. Jefferson freed five slaves in his will. Two of them were his sons with Sally Hemings, Madison and Eston. Their older siblings, Beverley, a male, and Harriet had left Monticello several years before, escaping into whiteness without formal emancipation. The other three slaves freed were trusted men who were also relatives of Jefferson's mistress and children.

Slaves freed in Virginia were required to leave the state within one year after their emancipation unless the master sought special permission from the legislature to allow them to remain. Jefferson made his request to the legislature in a codicil to his will giving freedom to his sons and their relatives. He justified the men's continued residence in Virginia by explaining that they should be allowed to stay because that was where "their families and connexions" were. What better explanation for why the descendants of slaves, along with white settlers and immigrants, have the right to live in America and build its civilization?

Jefferson's writings up until that moment indicate that he could not make the leap from his private understandings about the way the world worked and his beliefs about the likely course of the American journey. If there was a place in America for his mixed race children, why wasn't there a place for the millions of other similarly situated individuals? This, of course, invites the over-used charge of Jeffersonian hypocrisy. We can continue to play that one note. Or, perhaps we can move on to think in a different way about this extraordinary man who could never fully come to grips with a subject that bedevils us to this very day. Jefferson succeeded grandly in some parts of his life, and failed miserably in others, as we all do. One hopes the next century, in which Jefferson will be as much in the forefront as he was in the last, will bring a more considered understanding of what we can reasonably expect of him. When we do this, we may also have a better sense of what we, with the knowledge gleaned during the 174 years since his death, should demand from ourselves.

4

as bitter & bloody persecutions. during the throes & convulsions of the antient world, during the agonising spasms of infuriated man, seeking thro' blood & slaughter his long-lost liberty, it was not wonderful that the agitation of the billows should reach even this distant & peaceful shore; that this should be more felt & feared by some & less by others; & should divide opinions as to measures of safety. but every difference of opinion, is not a difference of principle. we have called by different names brethren of the same principle. we are all republicans: we are all federalists. if there be any among us who would wish to dissolve this Union, or to change it's republican form, let them stand undisturbed as monuments of the safety with which error of opinion may be tolerated, where reason is left free to combat it. I know indeed that some honest men fear that a republican government cannot be strong; that this government is not strong enough. but would the honest patriot, in the full tide of successful experiment, abandon a government which has so far kept us free and firm, on the theoretic & visionary fear, that this government, the world's best hope, may, by possibility, want energy to preserve itself? I trust not. I believe this, on the contrary the strongest government on earth. I believe it the only one where every man, at the call of the law, would fly to the standard of the law, and would meet invasions of the public order as his own personal concern. some times it is said that man cannot be trusted with the government of himself. can he then be trusted with the government of others? or have we found angels in the form of kings, to govern him? Let history answer this question.

Let us then, with courage & confidence, pursue our own federal & republican principles; our attachment to union & representative government. kindly separated by nature & a wide ocean from the exterminating havoc of one quarter of the globe; too high-minded to endure the degradations of the others; possessing a chosen country, with room enough for our descendants to the thousandth & thousandth generation, enjoying the most favourable temperatures of climate, entertaining a due sense of our equal right to the use of our own faculties, to the acquisitions of our own industry, to honour & confidence from our fellow citizens, resulting not from birth, but from our actions & their sense of them, enlightened by a benign religion, professed indeed & practised in various forms, yet all of them inculcating honesty, truth, temperance, gratitude & the love of man, acknoleging and adoring an overruling providence, which by all it's dispensations proves that it delights in the happiness of man here, & his greater happiness hereafter; with all these blessings, what more is

CHAPTER 4: A SECOND REVOLUTION

"we are all republicans: we are all federalists."

JEFFERSON'S FIRST INAUGURAL ADDRESS, MARCH 4, 1801

A PHILOSOPHIC COCK

Tis not a set of features or Complexion
Or tincture of a Skin that I admire

A Second Revolution

JEFFERSON'S INAUGURAL ON MARCH 4, 1801 was an understated affair, yet it sent a resounding message to the American people. There was little of the pomp displayed at Adams's swearing in. A somberly dressed Jefferson, accompanied by a small escort of horsemen, walked from his Washington boarding house to the Senate chamber to take the oath of office. In the unfinished Capitol building, before hundreds of spectators, the once-reluctant statesman became America's third president. It was a quiet affair, but spoke volumes about the strength of the relatively new nation. When tested, the Union would hold. A peaceful transfer of power—considered impossible in large republican nations had occurred. Never a public speaker, Jefferson delivered one of the nation's most memorable inaugural addresses in a voice barely audible to his audience:

James Akin. *A Philosophic Cock.* Hand-colored aquatint. Newburyport, Massachusetts, ca. 1804. Courtesy, American Antiquarian Society.
Jefferson's Federalist foes had a field day with reports of his alleged affair with Sally Hemings, a slave at Monticello. Jefferson, portrayed here as the cock or rooster, courts Hemings, the hen. The cock was also a symbol of revolutionary France, which Jefferson's critics thought he unduly favored. The quotation at upper right reads, "Tis not a set of features or complexion / Or tincture of a Skin that I admire."

Let us then, fellow citizens, unite with one heart & one mind; let us restore to social intercourse that harmony and affection without which liberty, & even life itself, are but dreary things. And let us reflect that having banished from our land that religious intolerance under which mankind so long bled & suffered, we have yet gained little if we countenance a political intolerance, as despotic, as wicked, & capable of as bitter & bloody persecutions . . . but every difference of opinion, is not a difference of principle. We have called by different names brethren of the same principle. We are all republicans: we are all federalists.

Jefferson's call for party cooperation has reverberated through the centuries and has served to rally national unity in times of crises. Years after his presidency, Jefferson looked back on the election of 1800 as a revolution in government:

they contain the true principles of the revolution of 1800. for that was as real a revolution in the principles of our government as that of '76. was in it's form; not effected indeed by the sword, as

Rembrandt Peale. Thomas Jefferson. Oil on canvas. Washington, D.C., 1805. Collection of The New-York Historical Society.

Rembrandt Peale, a son of the famous portrait painter Charles Willson Peale, was only twenty-six years old when he executed this accomplished image of President Jefferson in 1805. Jefferson, then sixty-one years old and about to begin his second term, sat for Peale on the 23rd, 24th, and 31st of January that year. On March 3, 1805, the eve of Jefferson's second inaugural, this painting was exhibited at the Peale Museum in Philadelphia. It remained in the museum's collection until the mid-nineteenth century.

that, but by the rational and peaceable instrument of reform, the suffrage of the people. the nation declared it's will by dismissing functionaries of one principle, and electing those of another, in the two branches, executive and legislative, submitted to their election. (TJ to Judge Spencer Roane, September 6, 1819)

Two weeks after the ceremony, Jefferson moved into the still unfinished President's House.

Despite Jefferson's conciliatory speech, all was not totally peaceful in the capital. In the month before Jefferson's triumphal inauguration, President Adams, determined to leave a Federalist judiciary in power, had completed a series of appointments of federal judges and magistrates, including Chief Justice John Marshall. Jefferson called these appointments an "outrage in decency," and the soon-to-be secretary of state, James Madison, wrote to Jefferson before the inaugural: "The conduct of Mr. A. is not such as was to have been wished or perhaps expected. Instead of smoothing the path for his successor, he plays into the hands of those who are endeavoring to strew it with as many difficulties as possible; and with this view does not manifest a very squeamish regard to the Const:n. Will not his appts.

William Thornton. Sketch of the President's House/Executive Offices, south elevation (detail). Ink drawing, 1793–1805. Prints and Photographs Division, Library of Congress.

When the government moved from Philadelphia to Washington in 1801, the President's House, designed by James Hoban, was under construction. John and Abigail Adams braved four uncomfortable months in the unfinished residence, but Jefferson was the first inhabitant of the finished building—although construction continued while he lived there—and was instrumental in making several important architectural modifications. This sketch shows the President's House. The low structures masked by trees at either side of the President's House may be service buildings, which Jefferson thought should be single-story and concealed by trees, so as not to be too obtrusive.

Benjamin Henry Latrobe. *View of the East front of the President's House with the addition of the North and South Porticos.* Drawing, pencil, ink, and watercolor. Washington, D.C., 1807. Prints and Photographs Division, Library of Congress.

President Jefferson appointed Latrobe surveyor of the public buildings of the United States in 1803. Aided by Latrobe, Jefferson made several changes to Hoban's design for the President's House, transforming it from a simple rectangular edifice to the more elegant porticoed building it is today. Despite these improvements, when Charles William Janson, author of A Stranger in America *(1807), visited it during Jefferson's time, he was not impressed: "The ground around it, instead of being laid out in a suitable style, remains in its ancient rude state, so that, in a dark night, instead of finding your way to the house, you may, perchance, fall into a pit, or stumble over a heap of rubbish."*

William Birch. *The Capitol in 1800.* **Watercolor. Washington, D.C., 1800. Prints and Photographs Division, Library of Congress**.

Enamel painter and engraver William Birch also became well-known for his watercolors. His view of the Capitol in 1800 shows workmen and carriages in front of the north, or Senate, wing of the original building. Jefferson was inaugurated here in 1801, despite the fact that the building was not yet finished.

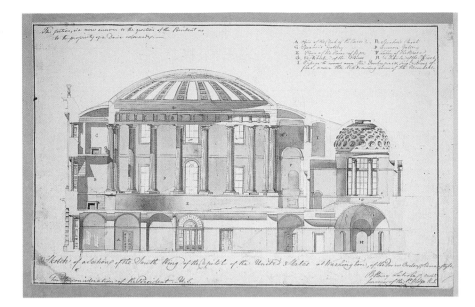

(above) Benjamin Henry Latrobe.
Sketch of a Section of the South Wing
of the Capitol of the United States at
Washington, of the Doric Order, Roman,
[ ] For the consideration of the
President, U.S. Longitudinal sectional
elevation drawing, pencil, ink, and
watercolor. Newcastle, Delaware, or
Philadelphia, 1804. Prints and
Photographs Division, Library of
Congress.

*Latrobe directed the design and construction of
the Capitol from 1803–1811, and again in
1815–1817, after it was destroyed by the British
in 1814. The south wing, which would house
the Hall of Representatives, was of particular
concern to Jefferson, who suggested to Latrobe
the incorporation of Roman Doric capitals. The
architect prepared this sketch in response to the
president's wishes, but disagreed with him on
using Roman architecture as a model, preferring
Greek ornament. He eventually won Jefferson
over on this point, and the Corinthian columns
in the vestibule in the House of Representatives
are now the oldest* in situ *Greek-inspired
columns in America.*

(below) Benjamin Henry Latrobe.
To Thomas Jefferson Pres. U.S.
Perspective drawing, pencil, ink, and
watercolor. Philadelphia, 1806. Prints
and Photographs Division, Library
of Congress.

*Inscribed "To Thomas Jefferson Pres. U.S.,
B.H. Latrobe. 1806," this watercolor sketch
reveals alterations and improvements to William
Thornton's award-winning design for the
U.S. Capitol. By pushing Thornton's pedimented
portico forward, and placing a colonnade behind it
and a wide staircase in front of it, Latrobe's design
invited the public to enter a great domed "Hall
of the People." The Capitol as we know it
was influenced by Charles Bullfinch and Thomas
U. Walter, as well as Latrobe.*

to offices, not vacant actually at the time, even if afterwards vacated by acceptances of the translations, be null?" (Madison to TJ, February 28, 1801)

Jefferson chose to eliminate as many judiciary positions as he could and replace some, though by no means all, Federalist office holders with Republicans. In reducing the number of appointments to the court of the District of Columbia, he denied a commission to William Marbury, a Federalist appointee. This ultimately led to the famous pivotal Supreme Court case, *Marbury* v. *Madison*. Marbury brought a suit in the Supreme Court to compel Secretary of State Madison to give him his commission. Adams-appointee Chief Justice Marshall ruled that the section of the Judiciary Act that would enable the court to issue a writ in favor of Marbury was unconstitutional; in other words, although Marbury was entitled to his commission, the Supreme Court could not force Madison to grant it to him. Although Madison won the suit, Marshall emerged victorious as well, by establishing the concept of judicial review, which allows the Supreme Court the power to declare acts of Congress unconstitutional.

> " . . . for that was as real a revolution in the principles of our government as that of '76 was in it's form; not effected indeed by the sword, as that, but by the rational and peaceable instrument of reform . . . . "
>
> *TJ to Judge Spencer Roane, September 6, 1819*

Jefferson's cabinet set out to change other Federalist programs as well. Fortunately, the commander-in-chief was a better manager of the national debt than of his personal finances. Appointing Albert Gallatin secretary of the treasury, he charged him with curbing national spending and balancing the federal budget. Gallatin's reduction of funds for military and naval forces helped accomplish this goal. Ironically, as Jefferson was cutting warships from the national fleet, he soon needed them in a war with Tripoli, one of the Barbary states in northern Africa. That the U.S. had an agreement to pay annual tribute to stop the attacks on American vessels incensed the president: "I am an enemy to all these douceurs, tributes & humiliations . . . I know that nothing will stop the eternal increase of demand from these pirates but the presence of an armed force, and it

Nathaniel Currier. *August 1804, Bombardment of Tripoli.* **Hand-colored lithograph. New York, © 1846. Prints and Photographs Division, Library of Congress.**

One of the first problems that Jefferson tackled as president was the Barbary pirates' repeated raids on American ships. Although the American government made yearly payments of tribute, friction persisted. Jefferson had already sent U.S. vessels to the Mediterranean to protect U.S. interests when Tripoli declared war in 1801. The city was later bombarded, as depicted in this lithograph, by the American navy in August 1804.

BOMBARDMENT OF TRIPOLI.

WASHINGTON CITY.

Friday, March, 6, 1801.

APPOINTMENTS BY AUTHORITY.

JAMES MADISON, jun. Esq. of Virginia, Secretary of State.

HENRY DEARBORN, Esq. of the District of Maine, Secretary of War.

LEVI LINCOLN, Esq. of Massachusetts, Attorney General of the United States, and

ROBERT R. LIVINGSTON, Esq. of New-York, Minister Plenipotentiary to the French Republic.

The Senate concurred *unanimously* in the above appointments. After which, a committee, consisting of Mr. Nicholas and Mr. Baldwin, were instructed to wait upon the President, to know whether he had any further communications to make. Having waited upon him, they made report that the President had no further communication to make. Whereupon the Senate adjourned.

GENERAL DEARBORN has arrived in this city.

Commodore TRUXTON also arrived last evening.

At an early hour on Wednesday the City of Washington presented a spectacle of uncommon animation, occasioned by the addition to its usual population of a large body of citizens from the adjacent districts. A discharge from the company of Washington artillery ushered in the day; and about 10 o'clock the ALEXANDRIA company of riflemen, with the company of artillery, paraded in front of the President's lodgings.

At 12 o'clock THOMAS JEFFERSON, attended by a number of his fellow citizens, among whom were many members of Congress, repaired to the Capitol. His dress was, as usual, that of a plain citizen, without any distinctive badge of office.

He entered the Capitol under a discharge from the artillery.

On his entry into the Senate chamber, where were assembled the Senate, and the members of the House of Representatives, the members rose, and Mr. Burr left the chair of the Senate, which Mr. Jefferson took.

After a few moments of silence, Mr. Jefferson rose, and delivered his address before the largest concourse of citizens ever assembled here. Having seated himself for a short period he again rose, and approached the clerk's table, when the oath of office was administered by the Chief Justice; after which he returned to his lodgings, accompanied by the Vice-president, Chief Justice, and the heads of departments; where he was waited upon by a number of distinguished citizens.

As soon as he withdrew, a discharge of artillery was made. The remainder of the day was devoted to purposes of festivity, and at night there was a pretty general illumination.

Neither Mr. ADAMS, nor THEODORE SEDGWICK, Speaker of the House of Representatives, were present at the Inaugural Ceremony; both those gentlemen having left the city at day light on that morning.

The Address of THOMAS JEFFERSON, President of the United States, which was issued on Wednesday at an early hour from the office of the National Intelligencer, is of such a character as to reward all the curiosity the expectation of it may have excited.

The manner in which it was delivered was plain, dignified, and unostentatious; the style is chaste, appropriate, and eloquent; the principles are pure, explicit, and comprehensive.

It is the Address of the Chief Magistrate of a People, who have shewn themselves amidst the storm of war and the calm of peace equally competent to protect their rights and establish their common happiness; and who in the enjoyment of foreign unlimited power, have betrayed neither the intoxications of prosperity, or the depressions of fear.

will be more economical & more honorable to use the same means at once for suppressing their insolencies." (TJ to James Madison, August 28, 1801)

Jefferson had already dispatched a fleet to the Mediterranean under Commodore Richard Dale in response to threats when Tripoli declared war. In 1804, Stephen Decatur led a rousing commando action during what came to be known as the Barbary Wars. In a surprise attack, he and his men boarded the USS *Philadelphia*, which Tripoli had taken possession of, dispatched the Tripolitan crew, and burned the vessel. This young naval officer became a national hero in a "small war" that took four years to win.

In the tangle of principles and politics Jefferson struggled to hang on to the ideals that enabled him to write the Declaration of Independence and the Virginia Statute for Religious Freedom. When the Danbury Baptist Association wrote to the president in late 1801 expressing the hope that his attitude toward religious freedom would come to prevail even in New England, Jefferson replied in a now-famous letter: "Believing with you that religion is a matter which lies solely between man & his god . . . <u>their</u> legislature should make no law respecting an establishment of religion, or

"To Messrs. Nehemiah Dodge, Ephraim Robbins, & Stephen S. Nelson" **[Thomas Jefferson to the Danbury Baptist Association], Washington, D.C., January 1, 1802. Manuscript Division, Library of Congress.**
This hand-written draft of Jefferson's famous letter to the Danbury Baptist Association affirms his belief that "religion is a matter which lies solely between man & his god," and includes the celebrated phrase "a wall of separation between church and state," which he first called "a wall of eternal separation." It is interesting to note that Jefferson deleted the sentences circled here regarding executive proclamation of religious devotion, explaining in the margin that he feared offending some of his "republican friends in the eastern states," who cherished their ritual days of fasting and thanksgiving.

prohibiting the free exercise thereof; thus building a wall of separation between church and state." (TJ to Danbury Baptists, January 1, 1802)

Although Jefferson attended church services while president, even at times in the chambers of the House of Representatives, his critics continued to condemn his deism and sectarian approach to education. Jefferson was concerned enough about such criticism to defend his views in his second inaugural address: "In matters of Religion, I have considered that it's free exercise is placed by the constitution independant of the powers of the general government. I have therefore undertaken, on no occasion to prescribe the religious exercises suited to it: but have left them, as the constitution found them, under the direction & discipline of state or church authorities acknoleged by the several religious societies." (TJ, Second Inaugural Address, March 4, 1805)

The attacks on the new president did not stop with his beliefs. One of the oldest American scandals to make the history books—and which still resurfaces in today's newspapers—is Jefferson's relationship with his slave, Sally Hemings. What made the scandal all the more intriguing was that it was first reported by James Callender, a newsman of dubious integrity, whom Jefferson had previously supported in his efforts to discredit Federalists in the Republican press. In early 1802, Callender turned on the president when Jefferson refused to reward him with the position of postmaster of Richmond in return for past labors on behalf of the Republican cause. Callender felt that payback for his slanderous prose was justified because the columns had led to his imprisonment for sedition by Federalist officials. Jefferson would go only so far, soliciting funds to repay Callender's fines, but refusing him a post. Callender, a new partner in the Richmond *Recorder,* used his pen in revenge. A series of exposés about Jefferson's long history of inappropriate behavior—his supposed affair with Elizabeth Walker, a neighbor's wife, the Sally Hemings situation, and his attempt to repay a debt to a friend with depreciated money—became fuel for the Federalist cause. Jefferson condemned his former ally's "base ingratitude" and wondered "what use the tories will endeavor to make of their new friend." (TJ to James Monroe, July 15, 1802) The president remained characteristically silent— a sure sign of guilt to his enemies and an equally emphatic gesture of innocence to his friends—except to admit his rejected offer of love in 1768 to Elizabeth Walker. In a letter of July 1, 1805, to Robert Smith, secretary of the navy, he confessed:

The inclosed copy of a letter to Mr. Lincoln will so fully explain it's own object, that I need say nothing further in that way. I communicate it to particular friends because I wish to stand with them on the ground of truth, neither better nor worse than that makes me. You will perceive that I plead guilty to one of their charges, that when young and single I offered love to a handsome lady. I acknolege its incorrectness. It is the only one founded in truth among all their allegations against me.

> **"You will perceive that I plead guilty to one of their charges, that when young and single I offered love to a handsome lady. I acknolege its incorrectness. It is the only one founded in truth among all their allegations against me."**
>
> *TJ to Robert Smith, July 1, 1805*

It is doubtful that many people were satisfied by the few public explanations of Jefferson's private life. Jeffersonian Republicans did their best to master the "spin," and the Federalists gained little ground from such low ploys, but after these incidents Jefferson's view of the press never recovered: "our newspapers, for the most part, present only the caricatures of disaffected minds . . . ." (TJ to Marc Pictet, February 5, 1803) Always an advocate for freedom of the press, he was suddenly wary of a free press that had no respect for the truth.

Happily for Jefferson, his first term is best remembered by his almost accidental acquisition of the entire Louisiana Territory in 1803—a purchase that doubled the size of the United States and assured U.S. traders access to the Mississippi and western lands. This huge and critical area of North America—extending from Canada to the Gulf of Mexico and from the Mississippi River to the Rocky Mountains— had been claimed by Spain for centuries. With news that Spain would cede this Louisiana territory to France, a more powerful and threatening nation, Jefferson

William Satchwell Leney after Elkanah Tisdale. "Infant Liberty nursed by Mother Mob." Engraving from *The Echo* (New York, 1807). Rare Book and Special Collections Division, Library of Congress.

Published in The Echo, *a satirical periodical intended to stem the torrent of Jacobinism in America, this cartoon shows the infant Liberty being fed neat liquor by her slovenly wet-nurse, while Jefferson's Republican supporters attack a government building. Verses that originally were published with the image mock Jefferson's principles of liberty and equality, implying that they lead to oppression not freedom.*

Aaron Arrowsmith. *A Map Exhibiting all the New Discoveries in the Interior Parts of North America.* **London, 1802. Geography and Map Division, Library of Congress.**

The original 1795 edition of this map by British surveyor Arrowsmith incorporated information from surveys by Peter Fidler in the Northwest (1792), Samuel Hearne's explorations west of the Hudson Bay, from Alexander Mackenzie's journey to the Arctic Ocean (1789), and from George Vancouver's chart of the Northwest coast and the "River Oregan." In addition, Arrowsmith relied heavily on Indian sources. The 1802 edition, seen here, supports the notion that the Pacific Ocean could be conveniently reached by the Missouri River. Jefferson was convinced this was true; however, Lewis and Clark later found out otherwise. Still, in Jefferson's time, this was considered the most valuable map to explorers of the newly acquired American territory.

knew he must take action to protect American interests and maintain access through New Orleans to critical shipping routes along the Mississippi River. Robert Livingston, the American minister to France, was instructed to question the French about the possibility of buying New Orleans and the Floridas. To emphasize his determination, Jefferson later dispatched James Monroe to France with more pointed instructions to effect the purchase. He urged Monroe to accept this critical appointment:

the agitation of the public mind on occasion of the late suspension of our right of deposit at N. Orleans is extreme. in the Western country it is natural and grounded on honest motives. in the seaports it proceeds from a desire for war which increases the mercantile lottery; in the federalists generally & especially those of Congress the object is to force us into war if possible, in order to derange our finances, or if this cannot be done, to attach the Western country to them, as their best friends, and thus get again into power . . . something sensible therefore was become necessary; and indeed our object of purchasing N. Orleans & the Floridas is a measure liable to assume so many shapes, that no instructions could be squared to fit them. it was essential then to send a Minister extraordinary, to be joined with the ordinary one, with discretionary powers . . . you possessed the unlimited confidence of the administration & of the Western people . . . all eyes, all hopes are now fixed on you . . . for on the event of this mission depends the future destinies of this republic. (TJ to James Monroe, January 13, 1803)

> ## "all eyes, all hopes are now fixed on you . . . for on the event of this mission depends the future destinies of this republic."
>
> *TJ to James Monroe, January 13, 1803*

Monroe had the good fortune to arrive in France on the heels of the French army's devastating defeat in Santo Domingo by rebellious former slaves who had rallied under Toussaint L'Ouverture. The timing was perfect. Jefferson had wisely refrained from committing his country to war for New Orleans and had waited for diplomacy to work its magic. The wait had been worth it, but success was not so much due to diplomatic skill as to Napoleon's need to recover from his disastrous campaign in the Western Hemisphere and the likelihood of war with Britain. The French leader saw an opportunity to recover financial losses and bolster the

American buffer against Great Britain. Not only was he willing to sell New Orleans and the Floridas, but the whole of Louisiana. A treaty was signed. The only obstacle to completing the transaction was the Constitution. Jefferson drafted several amendments, including one drawing on the opinions of Madison:

Louisiana, as ceded by France to the US. is made a part of the US. ~~it's white inhabitants shall be citizens, and stand, as to their rights & obligations, on the same footing with other citizens of the US. in analogous situations. Save only~~ But ~~that~~ as to the portion thereof lying North of an East & West line drawn through the mouth of Arkansa river, no new state shall be established, nor any grants of land made, other than to Indians in exchange for equivalent portions of land occupied by them, until authorized by ~~further~~ subsequent ~~an~~ amendment to the Constitution. ~~shall be made for these purposes.~~ (July 1803)

Fearing Federalist opposition to the purchase and a retraction of the offer from Napoleon, Jefferson changed his mind about the amendment and chose to skirt the constitutional issue. He asked Congress to ratify the treaty, and they obliged on October 20, 1803. The purchase did come at a cost internationally. Napoleon redirected his military efforts at another adversary—Great Britain—and that meant added pressure on neutral countries such as the United States.

Constantine Brumidi. *Cession of Louisiana*. Fresco. U.S. Capitol, Washington, D.C., 1875. Courtesy, Architect of the Capitol.

In this later reconstruction of negotiations for purchase of the Louisiana territory from France in 1803, James Monroe and Robert Livingston are shown with Charles Maurice de Talleyrand-Périgord, Napoleon's foreign minister. Acquisition of the territory raised a host of issues—among them, assimilation of the area's French citizens, relations with Native Americans, and the spread of slavery—but it also excited Jefferson's imagination and fulfilled his desire for expansion.

LE SOLDAT DU CHENE,

AN OSAGE CHIEF.

PUBLISHED BY F. W. GREENOUGH, PHILAD.ª

Drawn Printed & Coloured at I.T.Bowen's Lithographic Establishment Nº. 94 Walnut St:

Entered according to act of Congress in the Year 1838 by F.W.Greenough, in the Clerks Office of the District Court of the Eastern District of Penn.ª

Even before the Louisiana Purchase, Jefferson was in awe of the West and commissioned Meriwether Lewis and William Clark to lead a covert expedition in what was then Spanish territory. Described as a "literary expedition," and approved by Congress after a confidential appeal by the president, the Lewis and Clark Expedition successfully crossed the Rocky Mountains to the Pacific Ocean, mapped and explored the Northwest, and secured the help of Native Americans. A tragic outcome of Jefferson's presidency was the expulsion from their homelands of people whom Jefferson had described as "breathing an ardent love of liberty and independance." (TJ, Second Inaugural Address, March 4, 1805)

With high approval ratings, Jefferson ended his first term as president. Before the next election, the Twelfth Amendment was ratified, preventing a repeat of the 1800 deadlock by providing separate votes for president and vice-president. The Republicans had already jettisoned the unpredictable Aaron Burr from the ticket before Burr fatally wounded Alexander Hamilton in a duel, choosing George Clinton instead. The Federalists turned to Charles Cotesworth Pinckney to oppose Jefferson. Their meager hopes were dashed by a landslide victory, with Jefferson and Clinton winning 162 electoral votes to Pinckney's fourteen.

Jefferson knew that the challenges of his second term were different from those of his first: "The former one was an exposition of the principles on which I thought it my duty to administer the government. the second then should naturally be a Compte rendu, or a statement of facts, shewing that I have conformed to those principles. the former was <u>promise</u>: this is <u>performance</u>." (TJ, "Notes on a Draught for a second Inaugural Address," before March 4, 1805) Jefferson's performance in the second term was not what he would have hoped, but there were a few successes of which he was proud. Midway through the second term he accomplished what he had begun thirty years earlier in opposing the importation of slaves from foreign territories. The United States Constitution

> "The object of your mission is to explore the Missouri river, & such principal stream of it, as, by it's course and communication with the waters of the Pacific ocean may offer the most direct & practicable water communication across this continent, for the purposes of commerce."
>
> *TJ to Meriwether Lewis, June 20, 1803*

had forbidden Congress to end "the Migration or Importation of such Persons as any of the States now existing shall think proper to admit" prior to 1808. In his Sixth Annual Message to Congress on December 2, 1806, Jefferson called on Congress to abolish the importation of slaves from outside the United States at the earliest possible moment, which quickly complied with his request:

I congratulate you, fellow-citizens, on the approach of the period at which you may interpose your authority constitutionally, to withdraw the citizens of the United states from all further participation in those violations of human rights which have been so long continued on the unoffending inhabitants of Africa, & which the morality, the reputation, & the best interests of our country have long been eager to proscribe. although no law you may pass can take prohibitory effect till the first day of the year 1808, yet the intervening period is not too long to prevent by timely notice, expeditions which cannot be compleated before that day.

Education was another area in which Jefferson hoped the government would intervene. In his plea to Congress for the establishment of a national university, he appeared to exceed the generally narrow limits he placed on federal power:

education is here placed among the articles of public care; not that it would be proposed to take it's ordinary branches out of the hands of private enterprise, which manages so much better all the concerns to which it is equal; but a public institution can alone supply those sciences, which, tho' rarely called for, are yet necessary to compleat the circle, all the parts of which contribute to the improvement of the country, & some of them to it's preservation. The subject is now proposed for the consideration of Congress, because, if approved by the time the state legislatures shall have deliberated on this extension of the federal trusts, and the laws shall be passed, & other arrangements made for their execution, the necessary funds will be on hand, & without employment. I suppose an amendment of the constitution, by consent of the states, necessary; because the objects now recommended are not among those enumerated in the constitution, and to which it permits the public monies to be applied. (TJ, Draft of Sixth Annual Address to Congress, December 2, 1806)

> **" . . . a public institution can alone supply those sciences, which, tho' rarely called for, are yet necessary to compleat the circle, all the parts of which contribute to the improvement of the country, & some of them to it's preservation."**
>
> *TJ, Sixth Annual Address to Congress*

Domestic politics continued to play a critical role in Jefferson's major foreign policy decisions. The major world powers—France, Spain, Russia, and Great Britain—were still threats to be kept in check. In the midst of his concerns about protecting U.S. interests, a conspiracy led by former vice president Aaron Burr threatened to upset the Union. Burr had lost his bid for governor of New York in 1804 and then

G. Parker after John Vanderlyn. "Aaron Burr." Engraving from Matthew L. Davis, *Memoirs of Aaron Burr*
(New York, 1836). Rare Book and Special Collections Division, Library of Congress.
Although Burr served as Jefferson's vice president, he was probably—aside from Alexander Hamilton—his most powerful political
enemy. He was accused in 1807 of plotting a separatist conspiracy, but pleaded innocent to the charge and was acquitted for lack of
evidence. By mid-1808 he had exiled himself to Europe, where he engaged in various schemes to overthrow Jefferson, unite France
and Great Britain against the U.S., and return Canada to France. He came back to the U.S. in 1812 and opened a law practice in
New York. This engraving was published about the time of his death in 1836.

killed the primary opponent to his election, Alexander Hamilton. He nonetheless served out his term as vice president, and before he left Washington in 1805, he had begun to plan an armed Western foray. He met with U.S. Army General James Wilkinson, whom later confirmed rumors held to be employed by the Spanish and a seasoned conspirator. With encouragement from the British ambassador Anthony Merry, but no known help, Burr engineered a military expedition against the Spanish Southwest. Future president Andrew Jackson was one of the people he persuaded to be involved. It is unclear if Burr intended to separate the Louisiana territory from the United States and declare himself ruler, or to seize Mexico from the Spanish. Jackson believed that the Spanish territory was the only target. Wilkinson, concerned for his own future and doubtful of Burr's success, revealed the scheme to Jefferson, without implicating himself.

The trauma of the Burr Conspiracy clouded Jefferson's second term and culminated in a series of trials in 1807. Long disappointed in his former second-in-command, Jefferson hoped to see Burr convicted for treason. With Chief Justice Marshall presiding, a sitting president under subpoena to testify, and a former vice president as the defendant, the trials became a battle ground between the executive and judicial branches of government. Marshall, consistent in his efforts throughout Jefferson's terms of trying to establish the power of the judiciary, refused to permit most of the evidence that the prosecution had assembled because it did not meet the Constitution's strict definition of treason. The federal attorneys had no choice but to adhere to such laws, and Burr was acquitted. Still a fugitive from justice in Ohio, he sailed for England in June 1808 and moved on to Paris in early 1810, consistently and fruitlessly looking for support for his ambitions in the Southwest.

Jefferson recovered enough from the Burr incident to redirect his efforts on the international front. He hoped to be the first president to make a ministerial appointment to Russia but met opposition from President-elect Madison and a reluctant Senate. Jefferson had only corresponded briefly with Tsar Alexander but believed Russia could be an important ally in preserving the rights of neutrals. On April 19, 1806, he wrote:

Having taken no part in the past or existing troubles of Europe, we have no part to act in it's pacification. but as principles may there be settled in which we have a deep interest, it is a great happiness for us that they are placed under the protection of an Umpire, who looking beyond the narrow bounds of an individual nation, will take under the cover of his equity the rights of the absent & unrepresented . . . it is only by a happy concurrence of good characters, & good occasions that a step can now & then be taken to advance the wellbeing of nations. if the present occasion be good, I am sure your Majesty's character will not be wanting to avail the world of it. by monuments of such good offices, may your life become an epoch in the history of the condition of man, and may he who called it into being for the good of the human family give it length of days & success, & have it always in his holy keeping.

After the adjournment of Congress in 1808, Jefferson directed his confidant William Short to go to Russia as America's first minister. Short's long dalliance in France en route to Moscow prevented him from reaching Russia before the Senate unanimously refused to approve his post.

"The President of the United States of America." Subpoena served on Thomas Jefferson, June 12, 1807. Manuscript Division, Library of Congress.

Aaron Burr was tried for treason in federal court in Richmond, Virginia. In preparing his defense, Burr subpoenaed Jefferson, who was then serving his second term as president. This was the first time a sitting president was subpoenaed, and Jefferson failed to comply fully with the demands of this document, citing presidential privilege. Burr was eventually acquitted, a verdict which many historians attribute to Chief Justice Marshall's strict interpretation of the treason clause in the U.S. Constitution.

Irwin John Bevan. *The "Chesapeake" and the "Leopard," 21st June 1807.* **Watercolor, ca. early twentieth century. Courtesy of The Mariners' Museum, Newport News, Virginia.**

After the British ship Leopard *fired on the U.S. frigate* Chesapeake *in June 1807, Congress imposed an embargo in December on the export of American goods to Britain. This policy backfired, however, by setting the two nations on the road to war. The incident was reconstructed in this watercolor made by artist and naval historian Irwin Bevan(1852-1940), probably for a projected history of the U.S. Navy.*

The foreign situation had reached the boiling point well before Short was commissioned and American neutrality was on shaky ground. During their war with each other, which had resumed in 1803, superpowers Britain and France openly disregarded the rights of American vessels. England, in desperate need of sailors because hers often deserted to America, seized crewmen from American ships and forcibly enlisted them into British naval service. This practice of capture and impressment came to a head in 1807, when the United States frigate *Chesapeake* was stopped by the British warship *Leopard*. This incident, in which the American ship was fired on and forced to surrender four of its men, brought the United States to the brink of war with Britain. When Britain and France both threatened to take ships trading with its enemy, Jefferson persuaded Congress to implement the Embargo Act in December 1807. Based on the assumption that deprivation of American goods from foreign ports would force France and Britain to make concessions to the United States, the embargo, though relatively well supported except in New England, became a domestic disaster. France and Britain thought they could find alternate sources for American goods, but American merchants and farmers suffered devastating losses without the income from international trade.

The embargo law, far from settling the foreign crisis, led to Jefferson's public embarrassment and humiliation. The Federalists seized the opportunity to ridicule the president and proclaimed the federal legislation to enforce the embargo uncon-

Peter Pencil [pseudonym]. *Intercourse or Impartial Dealings.* Etching and stipple printed with sepia ink, 1809.
By permission of the Houghton Library, Harvard University.

Jefferson is the victim in this remarkable cartoon published in 1809. George III wields a club at the president and "pulls on his coat," slang for being robbed. The English king exclaims, "Well Tommy! I brought you at last to close Quarters," while Napoleon, his hand shaking coins from Jefferson's purse, demands, "I want de Money and must ave it!" but in fact suggests by his earlier words that he is in collusion with Jefferson against the British. Although Jefferson's Embargo Act was a response to both countries' violation of American neutrality, it proved to be a disastrous policy for him and damaged his reputation in his second term as president.

Peter Pencill [pseudonym; sic]. *Non Intercourse or Dignified Retirement.* **Etching and stipple printed with sepia ink, 1809. By permission of the Houghton Library, Harvard University.**

Here Jefferson, in ragged clothes, has "stript myself rather than submit to London or Parisian Fashion!" This is a mocking reference to the less restrictive Non-Intercourse Act, which replaced Jefferson's unpopular Embargo Act, just after his retirement from office in 1809. The Non-Intercourse Act allowed indirect trading with Britain and France and promised a repeal of all commercial restrictions to either if it would remove its own restrictions. The cartoonist implies that the Act favored Napoleon. In the background, George III of England appears to be negotiating a monetary transaction with a Spaniard before the British and Spanish flags.

Inscribed "Thos Jefferson The Pride of America, Retired March 4, 1809," this engraving, based on the portrait by Charles de Saint-Mémin, shows the former president in heavenly clouds, with Minerva, Goddess of Wisdom above him, and Fame below. Two days after he left office, Gimbrede sent Jefferson "a Little Sketch in Cameo" as a token of his esteem. Jefferson responded that it added "to the consolation he receives from the testimony of the worthy that the purity of his intentions, at least, has atoned for whatever error he may have involuntarily committed." (TJ to Gimbrede, March 7, 1809) This engraving is probably the published version of that cameo given by Gimbrede and Jefferson's reply shows that he still felt the sting of criticism heaped upon him in his final term in office.

stitutional. Finally, with support from both political parties, Congress repealed the Act to take effect after Jefferson left office in March 1809. The Non-Intercourse Act, which was less restrictive of international trade, was welcomed in its place.

Although he was offered the Republican nomination again in 1808, Jefferson declined. He was more than ready for the retirement he had sought several times earlier in his political career. Grief over the death of his younger daughter Mary in 1804 had weakened his spirit and resolve in his second term as president. Jefferson's relief at being delivered from the office he had once called "a splendid misery" is palpable in this letter to an old friend:

never did prisoner released from his chains, feel such relief as I shall on shaking off the shackles of power. nature intended me for the tranquill pursuits of science, by rendering them my supreme delight. but the enormities of the times in which I have lived, have forced me to . . . commit myself on the boisterous ocean of political passions. I thank god for the opportunity of retiring from them without censure, and carrying with me the most consoling proofs of public approbation. (TJ to Pierre du Pont de Nemours, March 2, 1809)

Now a free man, Jefferson prepared to move his household back to Virginia and, with characteristic charm, penned farewells to friends:

Th: Jefferson presents his respectful salutations to mrs. Smith, and sends her the Geranium she expressed a willingness to receive. it is in very bad condition, having been neglected latterly, as not intended to be removed. he cannot give it his parting blessing more effectually than by consigning it to the nourishing hand of mrs. Smith. if plants have sensibility, as the analogy of their organisation with ours seems to indicate, it cannot but be proudly sensible of her fostering attentions. of his regrets at parting with the society of Washington, a very sensible portion attaches to mrs. Smith, whose friendship he has particularly valued. her promise to visit Monticello is some consolation; and he can assure her she will be received with open arms and hearts by the whole family. (TJ to Mrs. Samuel H. Smith, March 6, 1809)

It is telling that though he spent the rest of his years at Monticello—little more than a day's journey from the capital—Jefferson never again returned to Washington.

> " . . . never did prisoner released from his chains, feel such relief as I shall on shaking off the shackles of power. nature intended me for the tranquill pursuits of science . . . . "
>
> *TJ to Pierre du Pont de Nemours, March 2, 1809*

THOS JEFFERSON THE PRIDE OF AMERICA

L. Prang & Co. after Albert Bierstadt. *Sunset: California Scenery.* **Chromolithograph.**
Boston, 1868. Prints and Photographs Division, Library of Congress.
When this color lithograph was published in the 1860s, the West had already captured the imagination of the American public and
westward expansion—under the label of Manifest Destiny—was in full spate. While he never traveled west of the Appalachians,
Jefferson envisioned the grandeur and potential of the landscape depicted so beautifully here.

"I considered as a great public acquisition the commencement of a settlement on that point of the Western coast of America, & looked forward with gratification to the time when its descendants should have spread themselves thro' the whole length of that coast, covering it with free and independant Americans."

TJ TO JOHN JACOB ASTOR, MAY 24, 1812

Tab. 18.

PEHRISKA-RUHPA.

Mandan Krieger in Anzug des Hundetanzes.   Guerrier Mennitarri costumé pour la Danse du Chien.

MENNITARRI WARRIOR IN THE COSTUME OF THE DOG DANSE.

Chapter 5 | Empire for Liberty

René Rollet after Johann Karl Bodmer. "Pehriska-Ruhpa, Moennitarri Warrior in the Costume of the Dog Danse." Hand-colored copperplate engraving from Prince Maximilian Alexander Philipp von Wied-Neuwied, *Reise in das innere Nord-America in den Jahren 1832 bis 1834*. (Koblenz, 1839–1841). Rare Book and Special Collections Division, Library of Congress.

Karl Bodmer, the young Swiss who accompanied naturalist Prince Maximilian of Wied-Neuwied on his expedition up the Missouri River in 1832–34, was the most accomplished artist to paint Plains Indians. During the bitter winter of 1833–34 at Fort Clark, Maximilian and Bodmer studied the small, little-known Mandan tribe which had been so hospitable to Lewis and Clark nearly three decades earlier, as well as their close neighbors the Hidatsa (the better-known tribal name for the warrior depicted here). Although western Indians were rarely illustrated during Jefferson's lifetime, the 1830s saw the publication of three great portfolios of Indian portraits and scenes, of which this was one.

THROUGHOUT HIS LIFE, JEFFERSON THOUGHT LARGE. His informed imagination allowed him to visualize possibilities that most men of his time would not even consider. Despite scant evidence in the eighteenth century of what lay beyond his Virginia home, Jefferson saw the West as fertile ground in which to plant the seeds of republican government. After the United States declared independence from Britain in 1776, there were several attempts to explore the unknown western territory that made up the North American continent. Jefferson was at the heart of several of these expeditions. From his childhood, the land west of the Appalachians had beckoned. His own father was a member of a land company that owned thousands of acres west of the mountains, and a fellow Virginian, Thomas Walker, had crossed the Cumberland Gap in 1750. Walker later set out to find the Missouri River, but was thwarted by the outbreak of the French and Indian War. Despite the enormous difficulty and risk of westward exploration, Jefferson felt it was key to securing the land between the Atlantic and Pacific Oceans and ultimately establishing the principles of political liberty throughout the Western Hemisphere.

When Jefferson took office in 1801, even his enlightened mind could not grasp what actually lay west of the Mississippi. Donald Jackson, the noted Lewis and Clark scholar, provides a wonderful image of Jefferson's beliefs at that time, which is repeated in Stephen Ambrose's popular 1996 account of the expedition, *Undaunted Courage*:

That the Blue Ridge Mountains of Virginia might be the highest on the continent; that the mammoth, the giant ground sloth, and other prehistoric creatures would be found along the upper

Missouri; that a mountain of pure salt a mile long lay somewhere on the Great Plains; that volcanoes might still be erupting in the Badlands of the upper Missouri; that all the great rivers of the West—the Missouri, Columbia, Colorado, and Rio Grande—rose from a single 'height of land' and flowed off in their several directions to the seas of the hemisphere. Most important, he believed there might be a water connection, linked by a low portage across the mountains, that would lead to the Pacific. (Donald Jackson, Thomas Jefferson and the Stony Mountains: Exploring the West from Monticello, *1981)*

The promise of the West, only glimpsed through books in his extensive library, became an obsession of the Republican president.

Jefferson's reputation, diplomatic skills, and plain good luck enabled him to build an "empire for liberty." The author of the Declaration of Independence wasted no time in writing Revolutionary War general George Rogers Clark, after the Treaty of Paris was signed in 1783, to assess his interest in exploring the West. He was concerned by reports of a British team who possessed a "very large sum of money in England for exploring the country from the Missisipi to California. they pretend it is only to promote knolege. I am afraid they have thoughts of colonising into that quarter. some of us have been talking here in a feeble way of making the attempt to search that country . . . how would you like to lead such a party?" (December 4, 1783) Clark had his own business to attend to. He declined Jefferson's offer, but not before offering him some advice: "Large parties will never answer the purpose[.] they will allarm the Indian Nations they pass through[.] Three or four young Men well qualified for the Task might perhaps compleat your wishes at a very Trifling Expence . . . ." (February 8, 1784)

Jefferson's hopes were derailed, but only temporarily. A few years later, while living in Paris, he learned of a French "scientific expedition" to the Pacific Northwest. Further investigation confirmed his suspicions. The French were there as fur traders, and such commerce was a prelude to colonization. Jefferson's response to such a threat was to support John Ledyard's fantastic goal of exploring the American West via Siberia. In his autobiography, Jefferson presents this account:

In 1786, while at Paris I became acquainted with John Ledyard of Connecticut, a man of genius, of some science, and of fearless courage, & enterprize. he had accompanied Capt. Cook in his voyage to the Pacific, had distinguished himself on several occasions by an unrivalled intrepidity, and published an account of that voyage with details unfavorable to Cook's deportment towards the savages, and lessening our regrets at his fate. Ledyard had come to Paris in the hope of forming a company to engage in the fur trade of the Western coast of America. he was disappointed in this, and being out of business, and of a roaming, restless character, I suggested to him the enterprize of exploring the Western part of our continent, by passing thro' St. Petersburg to Kamschatka, and procuring a passage thence in some of the Russian vessels to Nootka sound, whence he might make his way across the Continent to America; . . . he eagerly embraced the proposition . . . .

This elaborate scheme was not one of the most successful that Jefferson encouraged. Ledyard only made it as far as Siberia, where he was turned back by order of Catherine the Great.

Thomas Jefferson to James Madison, Monticello, April 27, 1809. Manuscript Division, Library of Congress.

Jefferson wrote this letter to Madison after the latter assumed the presidency in 1809. It is possible that by reaffirming his faith in the United States as an "empire for liberty," Jefferson hoped to encourage his successor to continue his policy of expansionism. During his own presidency, Jefferson had focused on the West; however, as this letter shows, he also envisioned expanding U.S. borders both to the south, with the hope of eventually incorporating Cuba, and to the north, in order to include British North America, or Canada.

May 17.

In 1786. while at Paris I became acquainted with John Ledyard of Connecticut, a man of genius, of some science, and of fearless courage, & enterprise. he had accompanied Capt. Cook in his voyage to the Pacific, had distinguished himself on several occasions by an unrivalled intrepidity, and published an account of that voyage with details unfavorable to Cook's deportment towards the savages, and lessening our regrets at his fate. Ledyard had come to Paris in the hope of forming a company to engage in the fur trade of the Western coast of America. he was disappointed in this, and being out of business, and of a roaming, restless character, I suggested to him the enterprise of exploring the Western part of our continent, by passing thro' St. Petersburg to Kamschatka, and procuring a passage thence in some of the Russian vessels to Nootka sound, whence he might make his way across the continent to America; and I undertook to have the permission of the Empress of Russia solicited. he eagerly embraced the proposition, and M. de Simoulin, the Russian Ambassador, and more particularly Baron Grimm the special correspondent of the Empress, solicited her permission for him to pass thro' her dominion to the Western coast of America. and here I must correct a material error which I have committed in another place to the prejudice of the Empress, in writing some Notes of the life of Capt Lewis, prefixed to his expedition to the Pacific, I stated that the Empress gave the permission asked, & afterwards retracted it. this idea, after a lapse of 26. years, had so insinuated itself into my mind, that I committed it to paper without the least suspicion of error. yet I find, on recurring to my letters of that date that the Empress refused permission at once, considering the enterprise as entirely chimerical. but Ledyard would not relinquish it, persuading himself that by proceeding to St. Petersburg he could satisfy the Empress of it's practicability, and obtain her permission. he went accordingly, but she was absent on a visit to some distant part of her dominions,* and he pursued his course to within 200. miles of Kamschatka, where he was overtaken by an arrest from the Empress, brought

39116   * the Crimea.

In 1793, Jefferson wrote the instructions for another effort to explore the West, this time overland to the Pacific. Its stated purpose was to find "the shortest & most convenient route of communication between the US. & the Pacific ocean." (TJ's instructions to Michaux, January 23, 1793) French botanist André Michaux led this mission, which would require skillful maneuvering past Spanish-held land to the Missouri River. Sponsored by subscribers from the American Philosophical Society in Philadelphia, Michaux was counseled by Jefferson to "take notice of the country you pass through, it's general face, soil, rivers, mountains, it's productions animal, vegetable, & mineral so far as they may be new to us & may also be useful or very curious . . . ." (Instructions to Michaux). Unfortunately, Michaux was engaged by the French ambassador Genêt to involve Americans in a scheme to overthrow the Spanish government in Louisiana. Although the political plot never materialized and Michaux never traveled very far west, he did collect a number of botanical specimens.

> **". . . they pretend it is only to promote knolege. I am afraid they have thoughts of colonising into that quarter. some of us have been talking here in a feeble way of making the attempt to search that country. . . how would you like to lead such a party?"**
>
> *TJ to George Rogers Clark, December 4, 1783*

(opposite) **Charles Balthazar Julien Fevret de Saint-Mémin. Meriwether Lewis. Watercolor, 1807. Collection of The New-York Historical Society.**

Born near Charlottesville, Virginia, not far from Jefferson's Monticello, Lewis served as a captain in the U.S. Army and participated in a number of Indian campaigns before becoming secretary to President Jefferson. Many of Jefferson's colleagues criticized his selection of Lewis as the leader of the proposed westward expedition, citing his lack of formal academic training and his worrisome reputation as a risk-taker. In a letter to Benjamin Rush, Jefferson explained his choice: "Capt. Lewis is brave, prudent, habituated to the woods, & familiar with Indian manners & character. he is not regularly educated, but he possesses a great mass of accurate observation on all the subjects of nature which present themselves." Lewis is shown wearing the otter and ermine skin mantle given to him by Chief Cameahwait of the Shoshone tribe. Lewis later presented it to the Peale Museum in Philadelphia.

(above) **Charles Willson Peale. William Clark. Oil on canvas, 1810. Independence National Historical Park.**

William Clark distinguished himself as co-leader with Meriwether Lewis of the famous overland expedition to the Pacific. Born in Virginia, he had served as an army officer prior to his frontier experience with Lewis. His observations of nature, journals, and maps greatly assisted in further exploration of the American West. After the success of the Lewis and Clark expedition, he was appointed superintendent of Indian affairs—a position he held about the time this portrait was made—and eventually became governor of the Missouri Territory.

"Washington City. Monday, July 4. Official." From the *National Intelligencer and Washington Advertiser,* **Washington City, July 4, 1803. Serial and Government Publications Division, Library of Congress.**

This is an announcement of the signing of the treaty authorizing the Louisiana Purchase, a high point of Jefferson's presidency, which more than doubled the size of the nation. The total cost of the transaction was $15 million for 825,000 square miles.

A decade later, as president of the United States, Jefferson was finally able to put the power of government behind his zeal for expansion. Certainly, the famous Lewis and Clark expedition is one of the great achievements of his presidency, but it was not the only successful mission of Jefferson's administration. Explorations by Thomas Freeman and Peter Custis, as well as Zebulon Pike, proved valuable as well. Still, the Lewis and Clark assignment was a stroke of genius on Jefferson's part. With knowledge that the weak nation of Spain was going to cede New Orleans to the all-powerful republic of France, the western landscape took on a new meaning for the president. On January 18, 1803, before the Louisiana Purchase treaty was even proposed, however, he had sent a secret message to Congress asking it to approve an expedition up the Missouri River to the Pacific Ocean. The cost, including $696 for Indian presents, was estimated at exactly twenty-five hundred dollars.

> **"In all your intercourse with the natives treat them in the most friendly & conciliatory manner which their own conduct will admit."**
>
> *TJ to Meriwether Lewis, June 20, 1803*

The mission was depicted solely as a scientific pursuit by Jefferson as he sought passports from France, Spain, and Great Britain. Jefferson had chosen his secretary and fellow Virginian Meriwether Lewis to lead the team, and Lewis asked William Clark, a frontiersman and younger brother of George Rogers Clark, to be co-leader. While Meriwether Lewis gathered provisions and prepared for his departure, after spending several months under the tutelage of his learned employer, studying up on his maps, instrumentation, and botany, news of the Louisiana Purchase reached Washington and was published in the *National Intelligencer* on July 4, 1803. The final transfer of Louisiana to the United States was recognized in a ceremony in St. Louis on March 10, 1804, attended no doubt by Lewis and Clark before their Corps of Discovery began its ambitious ascent of the Missouri River.

Jefferson's instructions to Lewis emphasized the commercial, scientific, and diplomatic aspects of the venture. Not only was Lewis to find the Missouri River's "course & communication with the waters of the Pacific ocean" but he was also to produce accurate maps, ascertain trading possibilities, establish friendly relations with Native Americans, obtain scientific examples of plants, minerals, and fauna, and record Native American vocabularies. Native American culture was of particular interest to Jefferson. Lewis was instructed:

In all your intercourse with the natives treat them in the most friendly & conciliatory manner which their own conduct will admit. allay all jealousies as to the object of your journey, satisfy them of it's innocence, make them acquainted with the position, extent, character, peaceable & commercial dispositions of the US, of our wish to be neighborly, friendly & useful to them, & of our dispositions to a commercial intercourse with them; confer with them on the points most convenient as mutual emporiums, & the articles of most desirable interchange for them & us." (TJ to Meriwether Lewis, June 20, 1803)

Thomas Jefferson to Meriwether Lewis, Washington, D.C., June 20, 1803. Manuscript Division, Library of Congress.

Based on advice from his eminent colleagues at the American Philosophical Society, as well as his cabinet members and other political colleagues, Jefferson prepared detailed instructions for Lewis and Clark. His priority was that they find the "most direct & practicable water communication across this continent, for the purposes of commerce." In addition, he instructed them to collect as many specimens of plant and animal life as possible.

While Jefferson's political policies with respect to Native Americans have come under fire, he idealized Indian peoples from an early age, writing to the marquis de Chastellux on June 7, 1785, "I believe the Indian then to be in body & mind equal to the whiteman." He had an intense curiosity about native languages and hoped that linguistic analysis of them would provide a key to understanding the origins of native culture. Over the course of thirty years, Jefferson identified more than fifty Indian vocabularies keyed to an identical set of words. Those collected by Lewis and Clark, and later given to Jefferson, were unfortunately among items stolen and destroyed in the move from Washington back to Monticello:

I have now been thirty years availing myself of every possible opportunity of procuring Indian vocabularies to the same set of words: my opportunities were probably better than will ever occur again to any person having the same desire. I had collected about 50, and had digested most of them in collateral columns and meant to have printed them the last year of my stay in Washington. but not having yet digested Captain Lewis's collection, nor having leisure then to do it, I put it off till I should return home. the whole, as well digest as originals were packed in a trunk of stationary & sent round by water with about 30. other packages of my effects from Washington, and while ascending James river, this package, on account of it's weight & presumed precious contents, was singled out & stolen. the thief being disappointed on opening it, threw into the river all it's contents of which he thought he could make no use. among these were the whole of the vocabularies. (TJ to Benjamin Smith Barton, September 21, 1809)

(overleaf) Jean Lattré. *Carte des Etats-Unis de L'Amérique.* Engraved map. Paris, 1784. Geography and Map Division, Library of Congress.
This map, made for Benjamin Franklin in 1784 during his term as minister to France, predates the acquisition of the Louisiana territory by almost twenty years, but it gives a sense of the native settlements spread throughout the land that Jefferson acquired and of the number of native populations that he hoped to relocate in his quest for an "empire for liberty."

PRINCIPAUX EVENEMENS
Militaires entre
LES AMÉRICAINS ET LES ANGLOIS.

Massachuset.

1775.
18. Avril. Les Anglois tirent sur la Milice Américaine à Lexington, 1r hommes tués ou blessés.

19. les Anglois tirent sur la Milice Améric. à Concord, les Améric. rendent le feu, font des prisonniers et bloquent Boston par terre.

Juin. 16. les Américains prennent Bunker's hill, et s'y retranchent 17 les Anglois attaquent ce Poste et prennent les retranchemens.

Mars. 2. les Américains canonent et bombardent Boston et
1776. les Vaisseaux Anglois.

le 5 les Anglois abandonnent Boston, se retirent au Fort William
le 17. partent pour Halifax.

Virginie.

1775. le 25. Avril. le Gouvern.r Danmore fait enlever les poudres du Magazin de la province.

les Américains prennent les armes pour se les faire restituer et forcent un magazin du Roi.

Juin. Danmore se retire sur un Vaisseau et va ravager son Gouvernem.t partout ou il peut aborder. Il incendie 2 le 18 octobre Falmouth, et Norfolk le 1r Janvier 1776.

Canada.

1775. le 20 Allen Américain part de Bennington pour prendre Ticonderago.
Avril.

May. 19 emporte le Fort d'assault. le 22 prend le Fort Gyown-point; et celui de Rénesborough.

Septemb. Arnold part de Boston, va s'embarquer à Newbury, est porté à l'embouchure du Kennebec, remonte ce fleuve jusqu'à sa source, traverse les montagnes qui séparent

Novemb. la Nouvelle Angl.e du Canada, entre le 3. Novemb. dans les parties habitées du Canada, arrive le 9. devant Quebec et le 15 là Ville est bloquée par terre.

Dans le même tems Montgomery part de Boston, prend la route des Lacs, traverse le Lac Champlain sur les Bateaux préparés par Allen à Crown-Point, parvient à la rivière Sorel, prend les Forts S.t Jean et Chambly, bat les Anglois sous Carleton, ensuite sous Maclean, assiège Montréal qui se rend le 2.

Décemb. Arrive le 7 devant Quebec et fait avec Arnold le Siège de cette Ville.

le 31 les Américains donnent l'assaut par quatre endroits sans Succès.

1776. le 6 May. les Améric. ne recevant pas de secours, quittent leur Camp devant Quebec, évacuent Montréal et se rendent à Ticonderago.

New York.

Septemb. le 15 les Anglois sous Howe, débarq.t à l'Isle de Manahatan.
les Américains évacuent New York.
le 20. un tiers de la Ville est incendié.

Octob. le 12. les Anglois s'embarquent à Turtlebay, prennent terre à Frog's neck.
le 18. se rembarquent, prennent terre à Pell's point.
le 21 campent au dessus de New Rochelle.
Washington fait suivre à son Armée une direction conforme à la marche des Anglois, il les harcelle par des détachemens et les retarde.
le 28. Il prend une forte position aux White-Plains.
les Anglois marchent aux Américains. à les suivre.

Novemb. le 1r. les Amér. se r.t.n vers NorthCastle. Le 6. les Angl. renon.t
le 13. ils vont Camper sur les hauteurs de Fordham.
le 15. ils prennent le Fort Washington, et le 18. le Fort Lee.
ils prennent leurs Quartiers d'Hyver depuis Brunswik, jusque sur la rive orientale de la Delaware.
les Américains prennent leurs Quartiers sur la rive occidentale.
le 28. Clinton prend Rhode-Island.

Décemb. le 26. les Américains s'emparent des postes Anglois, à Trenton, et à Monmouth.

New-York

1777. 2 Janvier Les Anglois marchent aux Améric.s postés à Trenton Creek, Combat; Avantage aux Américains.
le 3. les Américains se portent à Prince-Town, battent des détachemens Anglois, et vont prendre leurs Quartiers à Moretown.
les Anglois retournent à Brunswik.

Février. les Anglois harcelés par les Américains se retirent vers Brunswik
les Américains redeviennent maitres du New Jersey.

Mars. le 23 les Anglois détruisent des Magazins à Peck's hill.

Avril. le 26. à Danbury.

Juin. le 13 les Anglois marchent aux Américains postés à Mordecai's Gap, et n'osant les attaquer reviennent à Brunswik. Ils quittent Brunswik et vont camper à Amboy.

Juillet. le 25 quittent le New Jersey.
Ils s'embarquent à Staten-Island pour se rendre à la Chesapeak.

Carte des Etats-Unis de l'Amerique, suivant le Traité de Paix de 1783, dédiée et présentée à S. Excellence Mr. Benjamin Franklin. Par Lattré, 1784.

Virginie

1777. Aoust. le 24. les Anglois sous Howe débarquent à l'embouchure de l'Elk. Wasington y étoit pour les harceler, il se porte sur la rive gauche de la Brandywine.

Septemb. le 11. les Anglois passent la riviere, Combat. Washington se retire à Chester, puis sur la Suilkill, Howe passe la Suilkill et va à Philadelphie qu'il trouve évacuée.

Octobre. le 4. les Américains attaquent les Angl. à German-Town.
le 22. les Anglois attaquent le Fort Red-bank, ensuite le F. Mifflin sans succès.
le 25. la Fayette bat un détachement Anglois supérieur au sien.
Howe hyverne à Philadelphie, et Washingt. à Walley-forge.

York-County

1777. Juin. le 16. les Angl. sous Burgoyne s'embarq. à St. John.
le 30. prennent terre à Crown-Point.

Juillet. le 5. entré dans Ticonderoga évacué.

Aoust. le 30. arrivent au Fort Edward. le 13 passent la riviere Hudson, occupent les hauteurs de Saratoga.

Septemb. des corps Améric. se placent entre Ticonderoga et Sarratoga.

Octob. le 7. Burgoyne attaq. les Améric. sous Gates, et est batu.
le 10. Burgoyne se retire sous Saratoga, il est enveloppé par les Améric. le 16. il rend son armée aux Américains.
les Américains reprennent Ticonderoga.

Pensylvanie

1778. la Fayette prend poste à Barenhill à 4 m. de Philadelphie.

Juin. l'Armée Angl. marche pour envelopper ce détachement. Howe avoit promis aux Dames de la Ville de les faire souper, avec ce jeune Guerrier. la Fayette se retire sans perdre un homme, quoiqu'au milieu de l'Armée Angl. le 18 les Anglois évacuent Philadelphie. les Améric. les suiv. et les harcelent le 28. Combat à Monmouth-Court-house.
le 30. les Angl. arrivent à Sandy-hook.

Juillet. le 5. les Anglois s'embarquent pour New-York.

Georgie

Novemb. le 27 les Angl. sous Camp-bell s'embarq. à Sandy-hook.

Decemb. pour la Georgie. le 23. jettent l'encre à l'Isle Toby, sur prennent les Améric. en divers endroits. Combat près Savanah où les Américains ont l'avantage. le 29 les Angl. prennent Savanah et sont maîtres de la Georgie.

New-York

1779. Mars. le 30. les Anglois sous Waughan s'embarq. sur la riviere North: une part. débarque à l'Est près Wer-Plank. l'autre près Stony-point. le 31 les armées évacuent Stony-point. les Angl. prennent le Fort la Fayette.

Juin. le 16. les Améric. reprenn. Stony-point puis le quittent.

Connecticut

Pillages, Destruct. incend. par les Angl. sous Tryon.

Georgie et Caroline merid.

1779. les Angl. sous Prevost mênent de la Floride, prennent Sunbury. surprenn. les Améric. près Briars-Creek.

Juin. le 12 ils arrivé devant Charles Town, Somm. la Ville de se rendre, elle refuse, le 13 se retir. aux Isles St. James et St. John.
le 20. les Améric. sous Lyncoln attaq. les Angl. à Stono-ferry.
le 24. les Anglois se retirent à Port-Royal.

Septemb. le 9. d'Estaing jette l'ancre à l'Isle Tybée. le 16 les troupes sont débarquées et les Améric. se joignent aux François.

Octobre. le 5 le Siege de Savanah est commencé. le 9 assaut donné sans succès. Siège abandonné.
le 18 les François s'embarquent, et les Américains retournent en Caroline.

Caroline merid.

1780. Fevrier. les Anglois sous Clinton débarquent à North-Edisto, prennent St. John. et St. James.

Mars. le 20. l'Escadre Angl. entre dans le Port de Charles Town. Clinton arrive sur le Col de Charles Town.

Avril. le 1. Clinton Campe près des ouvrages de la Ville. le 8 Cornwallis arrive, acheve le Blocus. le 10 la Ville sommée de se rendre. le Siège continué, les Angl. prennent le F. Moultrie.

May. le 11 la Ville se rend.

Juillet. Lord Rawdon poste à Camden, est obligé de faire replier sur cette place des détachemens.
les Améric. sous Gates, s'avancent vers Lynch-creek.
les Améric. sous Sumpter, essayent de couper la communication entre Charles Town et l'Armée de Rawdon.

Aoust. Rawdon se retire à Camden, Cornwallis marche à son sec.
le 19. Cornwallis et Gates se rencontre près Ragley. Combat opiniâtre.

Massachuset

Juillet. le 13. arrivée des Troupes Françoises, à Rode-Island.
Clinton et Arbuthnot réunis pour aller attaquer les Troupes et l'Escadre Françoises, apprennent que les Américains sous Washington s'avancent vers New-York, abandonnent leur projet et rentre à New-York.

New-Jersey

les Anglois sous Knuphausen march. pour surprendre les postes avancés de Washington, ne réussissent pas, Dévastent le pays, brulent Springfield.

Virginie

1781. les Anglois sous Arnold déserteur, ravagent les côtes de la
Janvier. Chesepeak. et des grandes rivieres de Virginie, les Anglois sous Philips ravagent l'interieur. Petite Escadre franç. envoyée pour arreter ces devastations, prend le Romulus de 44. Canons.

Mars. l'Escadre de Ternay qui portoit des Troupes de Terre, à la Chesapeak rencontre la Flotte Angloise. Combat opiniâtre. l'Escadre franç. retourne à Rode-Island, et l'Angl. devant la Chesapeak.
les Anglois sous Cornwallis multiplient leurs dévastations et destructions, dans la Virginie, jusqu'au mois d'Aoust.

Avril. le 2 l'Armée Franç. sous Newport marche vers le sud. et arrive

Juin. le 6 à Philadelby. l'Prince-town près de N. Windsor vient camper le même jour le F. près de l'Armée Françoise.

Aoust. le 29 les Armées alliées se mettent en marche separ. sur la même ligne. et se concentrent à peu de distance. après avoir feint de vouloir à N. York, à Sandy hook ceux Staten Island, elles se portent en Virginie.

Septemb. Le 28 elles arrivent à York et Glocester. Les Franç. ayant fait 262 lieues.

Octobre. Le 6 on ouvre la tranchée, chaque Armée opère separém. Le 9 les batteries des deux Couronnes ouvrent le feu. Le 14. les Batterie Françoises avancées,
le 15. les Franç. enlevent livré à l'assaut n 2 redouttes du côté de l'York.
Le 17 Cornwallis demande à capituler.
Le 18 l'Armée Angl. rend prisonniere et livre York et Glocester.

Despite his respect for Indian culture, Jefferson remained convinced that the native population needed either to be civilized or removed to land that lay beyond the boundaries of United States settlements.

Having dispatched Lewis and Clark's Corps of Discovery on the United States government's first and now most celebrated trans-Mississippi expedition, Jefferson turned his attention to geographic areas on the cusp of American settlement. In 1805, army Lieutenant Zebulon Pike was sent by General James Wilkinson of the Burr conspiracy up the Mississippi to find the source of the river, which Pike mistakenly identified as Leech Lake in present-day Minnesota. Although unsuccessful in this task, Pike's explorations, his meetings with Native Americans and British trading agents, and his efforts to obtain Native American permission to build military posts, supported the United States's claims to land still in dispute and provided valuable cartographic information.

The lower Mississippi Valley and its western tributaries, such as the Red and Arkansas Rivers, also intrigued Jefferson. Correspondence and long reports from Indian agent Dr. John Sibley and naturalists George Hunter and William Dunbar confirmed Jefferson in his desire to support a scientific mission up the Red River. In 1806, astronomer and surveyor Thomas Freeman and botanist Peter Custis set out on the assignment. Custis was a student of noted scientist Benjamin Smith Barton of Philadelphia, but more importantly, he was a relative of former president Washington. Unfortunately, Freeman's and Custis's progress was brought to a halt by Spanish troops in 1806. Still, Jefferson stuck to his grand vision of an empire that would span the continent. His unabashed quests for acquiring more territory from the Spanish in West Florida and the Red River Valley soon became targets of political critics.

Undaunted by Spanish opposition and Federalist opponents, Jefferson approved the 1806 expedition of frontier soldier and veteran explorer Zebulon Pike, again dispatched by Wilkinson, this time to accumulate geographical knowledge about the region between the Arkansas and Red Rivers. The territory bordered on that controlled by the Spanish, who had already sent armed parties to intercept Lewis and Clark, and when he strayed off course, Pike came dangerously close to the Spanish stronghold of Santa Fe. Pike's second venture was tainted by conspiratorial overtones. Not only was the son of James Wilkinson, a major player in the Burr conspiracy, second in command of the expedition, but the territory itself, perhaps coincidentally, was marked for inclusion in Burr's new Western empire. Pike was successful in following the Arkansas River to the Colorado Mountains, where he saw the mountain later named Pike's Peak, but Spanish soldiers captured his party on the return trip. Pike's maps and notes were confiscated before his release in Mexico, but he was able to recreate a detailed report from memory. He was later killed in the War of 1812.

M. E. D. Brown after Titian Ramsay Peale. "American Buffaloe." Colored engraving from Thomas Doughty, *Cabinet of Natural History and American Rural Sports* (Philadelphia, 1832). Rare Book and Special Collections Division, Library of Congress.

Titian Ramsay Peale, an artist and son of the famous portraitist Charles Willson Peale, accompanied the western expedition led by Major Stephen H. Long in 1820. This engraved print from Peale's original sketch became a classic and much-copied image of the American West. Views such as this one served to document the landscape and people Long encountered.

David Edwin after Charles Willson Peale. "Lieut. Z. M. Pike." Frontispiece engraving from Zebulon Pike, *An Account of expeditions to the sources of the Arkansas, Kansas, La Platte, and Pierre Juan Rivers* **(Philadelphia, 1810). Rare Book and Special Collections Division, Library of Congress.**

Zebulon Montgomery Pike is best known for two Western expeditions, one to search for the source of the Mississippi River in 1805, and another in 1806 to the Southwest, where he discovered and named Grand Peak, which would later come to bear his name. Based on his observations, he cautioned against establishing U.S. settlements in the Great Plains, and suggested the Southwest as a more suitable and profitable territory. These comments later served to fuel American expansionism in that area.

M. A. Rooker after Jonathan Carver. "The falls of St. Anthony in the River Mississippi, near 2400 Miles from its entrance into the Gulf of Mexico." Engraving from Carver, *Travels Through the Interior Parts of North-America* (London, 1781). Rare Book and Special Collections Division, Library of Congress.

Jonathan Carver led the first overland expedition in an effort to find the Northwest Passage in 1766. He headed west to the Falls of St. Anthony (in present-day Minnesota), making maps and observations, but got no further than the Sioux settlements on the Minnesota River. He later published an account of his journey, in which this engraving appeared. Although Carver found no Northwest Passage, his journal and maps proved invaluable to Lewis and Clark, Pike, and Long in their respective western travels.

The PRAIRIE DOG sickened at the sting of the HORNET
or a Diplomatic Puppet exhibiting his Deceptions!

Lewis and Clark had better luck. Their triumphant return in the fall of 1806 was accompanied by great fanfare. It was a publicist's dream. Along with detailed journals, cartographic notes, scientific data and specimens, they also brought the promise of great wealth in the western territory. President Jefferson wasted no time in sending a letter from Lewis with details of the expedition to Samuel H. Smith, who published a summary in the October 27, 1806 *National Intelligencer*. In a bit of hyperbole, Lewis had reported that the explorers had found a valuable source of furs and a "short, direct course for them to the Eastern coast of China." In his sixth annual message to Congress, Jefferson elaborated on the entire western achievement:

> "Very useful additions have also been made to our knolege of the Missisipi by Lieut. Pike, . . . those of Messrs. Lewis, Clarke, & Freeman will require further time to be digested . . . ."
>
> *TJ, manuscript message to Congress, December 2, 1806*

Very useful additions have also been made to our knolege of the Missisipi by Lieut. Pike, who has ascended it to it's source & whose journal & map, giving the details of his journey, will shortly be ready for communication to both houses of Congress. those of Messrs. Lewis, Clarke, & Freeman will require further time to be digested & prepared. these important surveys, in addition to those before possessed, furnish materials for commencing an accurate map of the Missisipi & it's Western waters. some principal rivers however remain still to be explored, towards which the authorization of Congress, by moderate appropriations, will be requisite. (TJ, manuscript message to Congress, December 2, 1806)

(opposite) Nicholas King. Map for the Lewis and Clark expedition (detail). Manuscript map, 1803. Geography and Map Division, Library of Congress.
Among the Library of Congress's materials documenting the expedition of Lewis and Clark is this map compiled by Nicholas King at the request of Jefferson and Albert Gallatin. Drawn from the best cartographic sources of the time, the map was carried by Lewis and Clark for much of their journey. The annotations made in brown ink by Lewis reflect new information gained from their own observations and from the reports of fur traders and Native Americans.

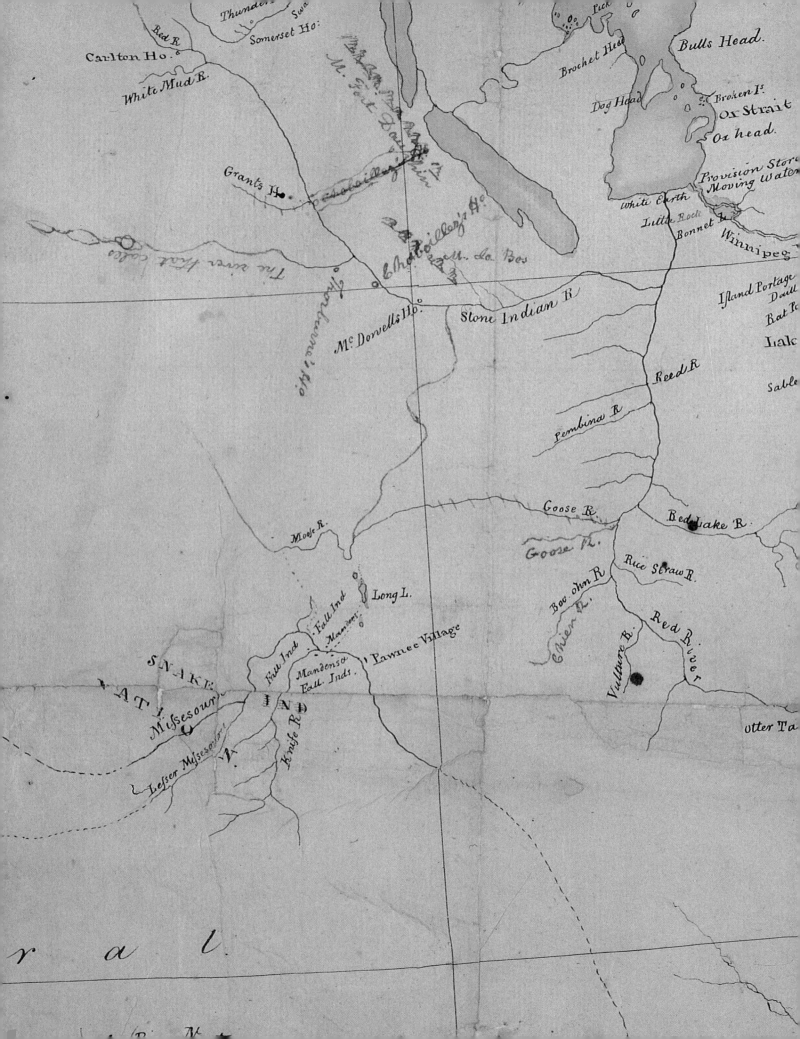

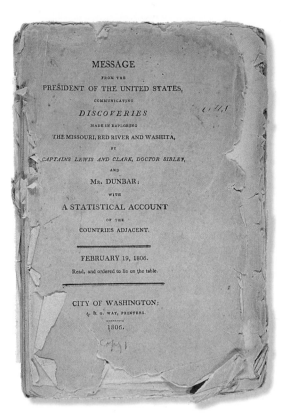

MESSAGE
FROM THE
PRESIDENT OF THE UNITED STATES,
COMMUNICATING
DISCOVERIES
MADE IN EXPLORING
THE MISSOURI, RED RIVER AND WASHITA,
BY
CAPTAINS LEWIS AND CLARK, DOCTOR SIBLEY,
AND
Mr. DUNBAR;
WITH
A STATISTICAL ACCOUNT
OF THE
COUNTRIES ADJACENT.

FEBRUARY 19, 1806.
Read, and ordered to lie on the table.

CITY OF WASHINGTON;
A. & G. WAY, PRINTERS.
1806.

Thomas Jefferson. *Message from the President of the United States* **(City of Washington, February 19, 1806). Rare Book and Special Collections Division, Library of Congress.**

In the spring of 1805, as the Corps of Discovery headed west from Fort Mandan in present-day North Dakota on the final leg of a journey across mountains to the Pacific, a shipment of plant, animal, and mineral specimens, journals, and maps was heading back east to the president. Thrilled by the results of the expedition thus far, Jefferson reported them to Congress, along with the achievements of several other expeditions up to that point. This is Jefferson's copy of his printed report.

Jefferson, the ultimate armchair traveler, had become the champion of continental exploration and chief proponent of the "empire for liberty." Whatever plans he had originally had for turning the Louisiana territory into a vast reserve for Native Americans had died. The nineteenth-century concept of Manifest Destiny was a cleverly disguised and painstakingly plotted Jeffersonian policy.

Jefferson was well aware that his policies had changed the fate of the native residents of the western territory. But his humanitarian concerns were weaker than his political ones. In his second inaugural address of March 4, 1805, he captured the sad history of the people he hoped to "civilize":

The Aboriginal inhabitants of these countries I have regarded with the commiseration their history inspires. endowed with the faculties & the rights of men, breathing an ardent love of liberty and independance, & occupying a country which left them no desire but to be undisturbed, the stream of overflowing population from other regions directed itself on these shores. without power to divert, or habits to contend against it, they have been overwhelmed by the current, or driven before it. now reduced within limits too narrow for the hunter-state, humanity enjoins us to teach them agriculture & the domestic arts; to encourage them to that industry which alone can enable them to maintain their place in existence, & to prepare them in time for that state of society which to bodily comforts adds the improvement of the mind & morals. we have therefore liberally furnished them with the implements of husbandry & houshold use; we have placed among them instructors in the arts of first necessity; and they are covered with the Aegis of the law against aggressors from among ourselves. (TJ, Draft of Second Inaugural Address, before March 4, 1805)

In a typically Jeffersonian paradox, the empire for liberty was not liberty for all.

"Captains Lewis & Clark holding a Council with the Indians" and "Captain Lewis shooting an Indian." Engravings from Patrick Gass, *A Journal of the Voyages and Travels of a Corps of Discovery, Under the Command of Capt. Lewis and Capt. Clarke* **(Philadelphia, 1812). Rare Book and Special Collections Division, Library of Congress.**

Upon the return of the Corps of Discovery, publication of the official account of the journey became one of the highest priorities of Lewis and Jefferson. Lewis consulted botanists, artists, mathematicians, and others to help him analyze and present his and Clark's data in a lavish multi-volume work. But it was Sergeant Patrick Gass, an expedition member, whose account of the voyage was the first to be published, in 1807 (the illustrations made for publisher Matthew Carey's 1810 and 1812 editions were based on actual incidents described by Gass). Despite the urgings of others, Lewis never carried out the publication of his journals. They did not appear until 1814, after Lewis had committed suicide and Clark had turned the journals over to Nicholas Biddle.

Captains Lewis & Clark holding a Council with the Indians   Page 17

Page. 245.

Captain Lewis shooting an Indian.

(opposite) Gilbert Stuart. Thomas Jefferson. Oil on wood. Washington, D.C., 1805. Monticello/Thomas Jefferson Memorial Foundation, Inc./National Portrait Gallery, Smithsonian Institution.

Although Jefferson sat for this portrait in 1805 when he was sixty-two, it was not shipped by the painter to Monticello until 1821, sixteen years after its execution. Gilbert Stuart habitually refused to finish portraits of his more famous subjects so he could retain them as sources for creating numerous replicas—a profitable enterprise. Of the four recorded replicas of this original portrait, the one commissioned by John Doggitt some time after 1816 has been most frequently copied and became the official image of Jefferson on both stamps and currency in 1867. The original Doggitt portrait was destroyed in the 1851 fire in the Library of Congress.

Even after he left office, Jefferson continued to show interest in U.S. expansion. Sheltered at Monticello, but not detached from the affairs of state, he encouraged his successor, James Madison, to continue his expansionist policy: "we should then have only to include the North in our confederacy, which would be of course in the first war, and we should have such an empire for liberty as she has never surveyed since the creation: & I am persuaded no constitution was ever before so well calculated as ours for extensive empire & self government." (TJ to Madison, April 27, 1809) On the eve of the War of 1812, Jefferson voiced his support for John Jacob Astor's establishment of a trading settlement in the Pacific Northwest at the mouth of the Columbia River, which he hoped would spread the rights of self-government along the whole length of the Pacific shore. However, the war's bitter reality temporarily curbed Jefferson's dreams of a northern extension of the American nation.

While the Pacific coast marked the westernmost limit of Jefferson's zeal for exploration, his influence as the author of the Declaration of Independence exceeded natural boundaries. With time, the writing of the Declaration took on almost mythic proportions and Jefferson's leading role made him an icon of revolutionaries throughout the Western Hemisphere. The task that had been relegated to him as the junior member of the Virginia delegation in 1776 became Jefferson's defining moment, the root of his fame, and ultimately his identity.

Thomas Jefferson to John Jacob Astor, Monticello, May 24, 1812. Manuscript Division, Library of Congress.

Astor sought to guarantee his position as a leader in the fur trading industry by establishing a trading post, Astoria, at the mouth of the Columbia River in 1811. Although Jefferson had been aware of Astor's plans for this settlement for some time, he mistakenly remembers in this letter having proposed the Pacific establishment himself. He was happy to see an American settled in the enviably profitable territory, and such a settlement seemed to support his vision of a loose confederation of independent nations. Ultimately, Astor's plans were curtailed by the War of 1812.

So it was in keeping with this role that Jefferson lent support to republican efforts throughout Europe and the Americas. His claim that "this ball of liberty, I believe most piously, is now so well in motion that it will roll round the globe" (TJ to Tench Coxe, June 1, 1795) proved to be true, first in France during the Revolution and later in Poland and Greece. Jefferson maintained a firm friendship with Thaddeus Kosciuszko, whose rebellion in Poland was unsuccessful. Adamantios Koraës of Greece later found his literary and revolutionary efforts endorsed by the Declaration author as well.

Jefferson settled permanently in Virginia after his retirement from office, but his mind traveled far afield. He had always kept watch on South America. As minister to France he had met with several agents of Brazil who, he reported, "consider the North American revolution as a precedent for them" and "look to the United States as most likely to give them honest support." (TJ to John Jay, May 4, 1787) Later in his life, while revolutions raged in South America, Jefferson told John Adams that, "I feared from the beginning that these people were not yet sufficiently enlightened for self-government." (TJ to Adams, January 22, 1821) Still, his recognition of emerging powers in that region had great influence on the future path of American foreign policy.

Triumph of Liberty
Dedicated to its Defenders in America

P. C. Verger after J[oh]n F[ranc]is Renault. *Triumph of Liberty. Dedicated to its Defenders in America.* **Engraving. Paris and New York, 1798. The Library Company of Philadelphia.**

In this allegory of liberty flourishing and monarchy in decline, Jeffersonian ideals are affirmed. Here, the goddess Minerva, symbolic of America, stands in a wooded grove, bearing a shield with the arms of the U.S. and a flag adorned with stars. She pours libations on an altar fire. Three female figures—Plenty, Justice, and Peace—stand beside her. Behind them is an obelisk inscribed with the names of some of the heroes of the American Revolution. Above all, Liberty, from her column adorned with "The American Constitution" and a little Genius of Liberty holding the "Declaration of American Independence," holds out a crown of oak to honor her followers. In the left foreground, a venerable deity tames the maimed hydra of despotism. Cowering at right are the deposed monarchs and their supporters. Renault and Verger initially collaborated on an allegory of French revolution but changed the inscribed references to suit an American audience. A copy of the French allegorical print is in the Library of Congress collections.

In March of 1822 President Monroe officially recognized the new governments of Buenos Aires, Chile, Peru, Mexico, and Columbia, setting the stage for a confrontation with European colonial powers. On September 7, 1822, Brazil declared its independence from Portugal. Expressing his hopes for the new nation and for the region as a whole, Jefferson wrote to Monroe:

altho' we have no right to intermeddle with the form of govmt of other nations yet it is lawful to wish to see no emperors nor kings in our hemisphere, and that Brazil as well as Mexico will homologize with us—" (TJ to James Monroe, December 1, 1822)

It was precisely such sentiments which were codified in Monroe's famous Doctrine of 1823, which stated that the United States would not tolerate interference in North or South America by European nations. Surely such a message had Jefferson's guiding and reassuring hand behind it.

> **"altho' we have no right to intermeddle with the form of govmt of other nations yet it is lawful to wish to see no emperors nor kings in our hemisphere, ..."**
>
> *TJ to James Monroe, December 1, 1822*

Today Jeffersonian principles are cited by people exploring political freedoms as far away and as disparate from Jefferson's America as China and the former Soviet Union. However, Jefferson did not live long enough to enjoy the satisfaction of knowing that his "empire for liberty" would spread through the Americas and shake the foundations of monarchical and totalitarian government around the world.

(opposite) Michel Sokolnicki after Thaddeus Kosciuszko. *Thomas Jefferson A Philosepher a Patriote and a Friend*. Colored aquatint. Paris, 1798 or 1799. Prints and Photographs Division, Library of Congress.

Kosciuszko, one of the heroes of the American Revolution, made the original of this image while in Philadelphia during Jefferson's term as vice president. The two became close friends. Kosciuszko took his Jefferson portrait with him to Paris, where he entrusted it to his compatriot and friend Sokolnicki to make an aquatint copy. Kosciuszko then returned to his country to organize the fight for a reunited Polish state. The whereabouts of the original portrait is not known.

Thomas Jefferson

A Philosopher a Patriote and a Friend

Dessiné par son Ami Tadée Kosciuszko

Et Gravé par Mr Sokolnicki

Liberty to Learn

by Peter S. Onuf

PUBLIC EDUCATION WAS A CENTRAL concern of Thomas Jefferson's career. Jefferson understood the American Revolution in generational terms, as the liberation of the "living generation" from the despotic rule of its predecessors. (TJ to James Madison, September 6, 1789) Aristocracy, the dominion of privileged families whose estates were preserved across the generations through the legal devices of primogeniture and entail, had to be uprooted and destroyed if republican citizens were to enjoy the genuine equality that made government by consent possible.

It was natural for parents to provide for their children, passing on property they had inherited and enlarged through their own productive efforts. But when the founders of great families sought to buttress their superior position through unequal legal privilege and political power, their solicitude for their children—and children's children—became unnatural and destructive. The state should play no part in securing the preeminence of the privileged few over the mass of citizens, for such inequality inevitably would weaken and destroy the commonwealth. The state should instead treat all of its children equally, teaching them to be conscious of their equal rights as individuals and of their collective rights as a generation that would one day govern itself.

Conceiving of the Revolution as a moment when Americans suddenly became conscious of themselves as a people and grasped the "self-evident principles" that justified their claims to independence and self-government, Jefferson saw public education as the essential means of preserving republican government. The patriotic movement against British tyranny that culminated in resistance and revolution had been a sustained exercise in popular political education.

Yet for Jefferson and other anxious revolutionaries, the end of British rule was not a sufficient guarantee of republicanism, for ambitious individuals would always seek to use public authority to advance selfish private purposes while everyone else, absorbed in their own private pursuits, looked the other way. Public education thus would serve to sustain the revolutionary spirit, the patriots' consciousness of themselves as a free people, bound together by the fraternal ties so eloquently articulated in Jefferson's Declaration of Independence.

Jefferson and his fellow patriots urged the "sons of liberty" to overthrow George III, a tyrannical father figure who had shown himself "unfit to be the ruler of a free people." (Declaration as adopted by Congress, July 4, 1776) The British king was the antitype of the good republican father, always solicitous of his children's welfare. As Jefferson had written in his famous pre-revolutionary pamphlet, *A Summary View of the Rights of British America* (1774), "kings are the servants, not the proprietors of the people." Because political authority was a kind of trust, its continuing exercise was conditional on the fulfilment of its original purpose: the people's welfare and happiness. It was finally up to the people themselves, after "a long train of abuses & usurpations," to judge whether the king had violated his trust, for they were the ultimate source of all legitimate authority. (Declaration, July 4, 1776) But deposing the king and instituting a republican form of government were not sufficient safeguards of popular rights.

Jefferson understood that every generation began its career in a dependent, child-like condition, necessarily reliant on its predecessors for nurture and development. His own generation of patriots had come of age in the hard school of familial betrayal. George III had disowned the Americans, treating them as foreigners, not as free-born Britons, his own legitimate children. His most unnatural crime was to divide one people into two, turning the British—"these unfeeling brethren"—against the Americans. The royal father betrayed his trust by elevating some of his "children" over the rest, denying the colonists their birthright. In George III's betrayal—and in the fratricidal betrayal of their British "brethren"—Jefferson thus conjured up a compelling narrative about the fall of once enlightened Britons from a golden age of peace and prosperity. Had the British king not been "deaf to the voice of justice & of consanguinity," he exclaimed, "we might have been a free & a great people together." (TJ's "original Rough draught" of the Declaration) Instead, George III sought to destroy the Americans' liberty and property in order to raise up a cor-

patriot juggernaut, and growing numbers of loyalists and neutrals thereafter reflected the revolutionaries' poor performance on the battlefield. Lack of enthusiasm for the war effort, insufficient public virtue, and an unwillingness to make necessary sacrifices all suggested that the people's education was not yet complete, that it was not enough to subscribe to the "self-evident truths" of Jefferson's Declaration. Ignorant and credulous Americans were all too vulnerable to the seductive wiles of would-be aristocrats happy to pose as popular leaders. If the people had shown great political maturity in the moment of national crisis, they also revealed a distressing tendency to revert to child-like ignorance and indifference.

With other educational reformers, such as Benjamin Rush and Noah Webster, Jefferson saw publicly-sponsored education as the great engine of republican enlightenment.

Henry Schenck Tanner. "University of Virginia." Engraving after an 1824 drawing. Detail from *Map of the State of Virginia* by Herman Böÿe. Philadelphia, 1825. Geography and Map Division, Library of Congress.

Construction of the neoclassical pavilions, colonnades, and rotunda designed by Jefferson was still underway when this view was drawn. The new university campus is framed and "enlightened" symbolically by the emerging rays of the sun and a rainbow following a storm.

rupt and subservient aristocracy, a sorry colonial caricature of the metropolitan social order.

The notion that the British king and his wicked ministers were solely responsible for all of America's afflictions was an attractive one, but not one that thoughtful revolutionaries could long sustain. Before the imperial conflict turned to war in April 1775, many native-born Americans had resisted the

Constitutional machinery might check and balance dangerous powerful interests and dangerous ambitions, but a vigilant electorate alone could keep the republican experiment on track. Jefferson proposed his famous three-tier education system in 1779, when he served as chair of a committee to revise Virginia's laws to make them compatible with the new republican dispensation. Unable to take a significant role in writing the new state constitution in 1776 because of responsibilities in Congress (most notably drafting the Declaration), Jefferson saw the revisal of the laws as his opportunity to reinforce and complete Virginia's republican revolution. Of the 126 bills reported by the committee, he considered four most crucial: those abolishing primogeniture and entail, his celebrated bill for religious freedom (passed in 1786), and a "Bill for the More General Diffusion of Knowledge" (never adopted). Together, Jefferson recalled in his "Autobiography" (1821), these bills were designed to form "a system by which every fibre would be eradicated of antient or future aristocracy; and a foundation laid for a government truly republican." Without legal provisions for keeping landed estates intact (entail) and "for making one member of every family rich, and the rest poor" (primogeniture), aristocracy could not take root in Virginia; freedom of conscience meant that taxpayers would no longer have to support the established "religion of the rich." But it was only through education that citizens of the commonwealth would be "enabled to understand their rights, to maintain them, and to exercise with intelligence their parts in self-government." To preempt an aristocratic revival, the "Bill for the More General Diffusion of Knowledge" proclaimed, Virginians must "know ambition under all its shapes." Under Jefferson's proposal, young Virginians—boys and girls alike—would be entitled to three years of primary schooling; a select group of worthy boys would receive scholarships to pursue advanced studies, including Latin and Greek, at grammar schools scattered across the state; and, finally, one student each year would rise to the apex of this educational pyramid with state support to attend the College of William and Mary.

Though Jefferson failed to gain passage of his general education bill, the final crucial element and capstone of his state-building project, he remained ever optimistic. The thrust of his proposal was broadly political, after all, and the citizenry could be aroused and enlightened by other means at a time when wary taxpayers considered a comprehensive public school system much too ambitious and expensive. Indeed, it was a nice irony that vigilant legislators in Virginia

and other states manifested a characteristically Jeffersonian hostility to "energetic" (big) government in voting down school bills. It was yet another irony that anti-partisan politicians such as Jefferson should have developed rudimentary party organizations and propaganda machinery to disseminate their views and educate the public. Jeffersonian Republicans' faith in the people's wisdom—and in their own ability to shape public opinion—was sorely tested in the 1790s, particularly when the Quasi-War with France and widespread prosperity boosted the popularity of the Adams administration. But the electoral cycle provided the most immediate and compelling sites for sustaining—or redeeming—the republican revolution by educating and mobilizing voters. As long as the future of the republic remained in doubt, as it did until Jefferson's election in the "revolution of 1800," provision for schooling the rising generation would have to wait. And when the Republicans finally did ascend to power, the rapid decline and ultimate disgrace of the Federalists made popular political education seem less urgent.

Yet Jefferson never lost interest in public education. During his retirement, he campaigned vigorously for a state university, the top tier of the comprehensive system he had been advocating throughout his career. Following the recommendation of a commission headed by Jefferson, the general assembly voted to site the University of Virginia in Charlottesville, a few short miles away from Monticello. Jefferson set forth the new institution's rationale in the commission's report: "to form the statesmen, legislators and judges, on whom public prosperity and individual happiness . . . so much depend." The University could only fulfill its role, however, with the implementation of a comprehensive scheme of primary and secondary education that would enable "every citizen" to "understand his duties" and "know his rights." (Report of the Commissioners for the University of Virginia, August 4, 1818)

Though Jefferson acknowledged the value of literacy and numeracy for the business of everyday life, his interest in basic education was animated by his concern for sustaining the republic. He pinned his hopes for primary schools on a thorough-going reform of Virginia's constitution that would devolve authority on neighborhoods or "wards," thus bypassing recalcitrant state legislators reluctant to invest in the rising generation. "In government, as well as in every other business of life," he wrote an advocate of constitutional reform in 1816, "it is by division and subdivision of duties alone, that all matters, great and small, can be managed to perfection." (TJ to Samuel Kercheval, July 12, 1816) Jefferson had long been a critic of Virginia's oligarchical system of county government, in which local voters played virtually no role. The commonwealth's republican promise would only be fulfilled, he told trusted lieutenant Joseph C. Cabell, by instituting a "gradation of authorities," from "the elementary republics of the wards, the county republics, the State republics, and the republic of the Union." At the ward or township level, the chief responsibility of voters would be to run the local schools: "if it is believed that these . . . schools will be better managed" by functionaries of the state government "than by the parents within each ward, it is a belief against all experience." (TJ to Joseph C. Cabell, February 2, 1816)

The educational benefits of local schools redounded both to neighborhood parents and children. Sharing "in the direction of his ward-republic," the once passive citizen who was only called into action "at an election one day in the year" would now feel that he was a "participator . . . every day." (TJ to Cabell) Political participation was itself educational, teaching citizens to look beyond their immediate circumstances toward a larger public interest. But episodic voting in state or national elections too often played into the hands of self-aggrandizing elites who could frame the issues—and inflame popular passions—to promote their own interests. Jefferson's "gradation of authorities" would avert such dangers by establishing a hierarchy of republican governments that would link the most humble voter to the nation as a whole. By the continuous exercise of authority within his appropriate sphere, however modest and circumscribed, the republican citizen would form ever stronger attachments to the "federal and republican principles" Jefferson articulated in his First Inaugural Address (March 4, 1801) and therefore to the union. A nation that could appeal to such strong popular loyalties would be, as he said then, "the strongest Government on earth." Or, as he put it to Cabell in 1816, the citizen who actively participated "in the government of affairs"—even the management of a small village school—"will let the heart be torn out of his body sooner than his power be wrested from him by a Caesar or a Bonaparte."

The key figure in Jefferson's scheme for republican renewal was not therefore simply an idealized, public-spirited voter, but rather a father or "parent." Indeed, the parent's solicitude for his children forced him to look beyond his immediate circumstances, to the time when the rising generation would come into its patrimony. Jefferson's scheme of "division and subdivision" thus did not end with the isolated, self-regarding individual, but rather with the head of a family who followed the dictates of nature in providing for the future welfare of his children. For Enlightenment thinkers like Jefferson this altruism or moral sense was the fundamental building block of a just republican social order. When parents acted together in their neighborhoods to provide for all their children, they would learn to think less of their own families' fortunes and more of the welfare of the whole younger generation. Private interest and the public good were therefore not antithetical terms; on the contrary, man was by nature altruistic and sociable, always capable of seeing himself as part of a larger whole. The challenge was to construct a constitutional order of ascending levels of political association—little republics, beginning with the family itself, that were imbedded within ever larger republics—and so give full scope to these civic impulses, thus transforming family feeling into true patriotism.

Jefferson's ward system would encourage the good republican father to provide not only for his own children but for the children of his neighbors. In seeing these children as a generation that would one day come into its collective estate and govern the commonwealth, republican fathers would come to recognize themselves as a generation, responsible for

Jane Braddick Peticolas. ***View of the West Front of Monticello and Garden.*** **Watercolor, 1825. Monticello/Thomas Jefferson Memorial Foundation, Inc.**

In this rare view of Monticello from Jefferson's time, we see three of his grandchildren: George Wythe Randolph is shown rolling a hoop, while his sisters Mary and Cornelia Randolph stand together on the lawn. Jefferson took great delight in having his family together at Monticello. It was one of the true pleasures of his retirement. One of his granddaughters remembered, "Our grandfather seemed to read our hearts, to see our invisible wishes, to be our good genius, to wave the fairy wand, to brighten our young lives by his goodness and his gifts." (Ellen Coolidge in Sarah N. Randolph, The Domestic Life of Thomas Jefferson, *1871)*

University of Virginia.
Photograph by Jackson Smith.
Courtesy of University of Virginia.

This contemporary photograph of the University of Virginia shows the Lawn and Rotunda much as Jefferson left them almost two centuries ago. The campus is a fitting memorial to classical principles of architecture and to Jeffersonian ideals.

their country's future welfare. Every man's affectionate regard for his own family was thus the font of a more capacious public virtue. When the American revolutionaries proclaimed the sovereignty of the people, they hoped to realign patriarchal impulses with a just and natural republican social order. The abolition of aristocratic privilege was the necessary precondition for the reign of good republican fathers. Not only would all the children of the commonwealth be treated as equals "endowed by their creator with inalienable rights," but the fathers collectively would cede their self-governing authority to the rising generation. The genius of republicanism was as much epitomized by the self-restraint of fathers who did not attempt to rule from beyond the grave—as did the founders of great aristocratic families—as by the more familiar doctrine that governments derived "their just powers from the consent of the governed."

Jefferson's educational ideas grew out of his fundamental premise that good republican fathers should prepare the next generation for the duties and responsibilities of self-government. The role of mentor or teacher was one that Jefferson embraced enthusiastically in his own personal life. After the death of his father when he was fourteen years old, William Small at the College of William and Mary and law teacher George Wythe served as mentors—or father-substitutes—for the young Jefferson. In later years, Jefferson performed a similar role for a series of young men, exercising the sort of disinterested form of paternal authority—the temporary government of children in their own best interest—that the perpetuation of the republic required. The mentor figure showed that family feeling need not take the selfish and destructive forms so characteristic of aristocratic society. A republican commonwealth would prosper and endure when the generation of the fathers thought of all its children, the generation that would one day take its place, in such disinterested terms.

Thomas Jefferson may have enjoyed only limited success as an educational reformer but a narrow focus on schools does not do justice to his republican vision. The American Revolution was itself a great experiment in popular political education. When Jefferson and his fellow patriots accused George III of failing to discharge his responsibilities as the American people's political father, they fashioned a new conception of legitimate authority and therefore of an enlightened, vigilant citizenry capable of giving—or withholding—its consent to government.

By emphasizing the temporary, contingent character of authority, the revolutionaries took the familiar idea of political rule as a kind of trust or stewardship in a radical new direction. The master fiction of a monarchical regime was that the king-father and his line were immortal while the people, his children, remained in a perpetual state of dependency. In Jefferson's republic, by contrast, paternal authority was diffused through the whole living generation, but was only temporary. Conscious of their own mortality, republican fathers recognized the importance of preparing the next generation to govern itself—and to provide, in turn, for succeeding generations. Political participation was the chief spur to popular enlightenment, for liberty—the consciousness of rights and responsibilities—would inspire a republican citizenry to learn. This was the animating principle of Jefferson's scheme for ward republics. Jefferson believed that his wards would give full scope to the natural impulses of republican fathers to promote the welfare of their own and their neighbors' children and that provision for schools was sure to follow.

Jefferson eloquently articulated the fundamental transformation of generational relations that characterized the new American nation. The widespread establishment of tax-supported public schools would not take place for several generations, but private schools and academies catering to enterprising and ambitious young people of all classes flourished in every part of the country. Meanwhile, the democratization of the electorate and emergence of party organizations made ordinary citizens conscious of their political power. Under these dynamic circumstances, the aristocratic ethos of the old monarchical regime rapidly gave way to a new democratic way of life in which republican sons came into their own and "the earth belong[ed] to the living." (TJ to James Madison, September 6, 1789) Jefferson undoubtedly would have found many of the results of this great transformation disturbing and distasteful. But it was the logical expression and consequence of the republican principles he had so memorably set forth in the Declaration of Independence.

could the dead feel any interest in Monu-
-ments or other remembrances of them, when, as
Anacreon says ΟΛΙΓΗ ΔΕ ΚΕΙΣΟΜΕΣΘΑ
            ΚΟΝΙΣ, ΟΣΤΕΩΝ ΛΥΘΕΝΤΩΝ
the following would be to my Manes the most
gratifying.
On the grave
        a plain die or cube of 3.f without any
mouldings, surmounted by an Obelisk
of 6.f. height, each of a single stone:
on the faces of the Obelisk the following
inscription, & not a word more

            Here was buried
              Thomas Jefferson
    Author of the Declaration of American Independance
          of the Statute of Virginia for religious freedom
      & Father of the University of Virginia.

because by these, as testimonials that I have lived, I wish most to
be remembered.   to be of the coarse stone of which
my columns are made, that no one might be tempted
hereafter to destroy it for the value of the materials.
my bust by Ciracchi, with the pedestal and truncated
column on which it stands, might be given to the University
if they would place it in the Dome room of the Rotunda.
on the Die, might be engraved
                of the Obelisk
            Born Apr. 2. 1743. O.S.
            Died _____

Thomas Jefferson. Design and instructions for his tombstone and epitaph.
Ink on paper. Undated. Manuscript Division, Library of Congress.
In his last years Jefferson prepared for his death. He drew this design for his tombstone—a simple obelisk—and composed a short
epitaph, wishing to be remembered for only three of his many significant contributions: writing the Declaration of Independence and
the Statute of Virginia for Religious Freedom, and founding the University of Virginia.

"Here was buried
Thomas Jefferson
Author of the Declaration
of American Independance
of the Statute of Virginia
for religious freedom
& Father of the University
of Virginia."

Tacitus (upper book)

(Latin text, largely obscured)

senatu ab Arruntio & Ateio, an ob moderandas Ti-
beris exundationes verterentur flumina & lacus
quos augeret. Auditæque municipiorum & colo-
rum legationes; orantibus Florentinis, ne Clanis
alveo demotus in amnem Arnum transferretur, ne clamitatem ...
nicem adferret. ...

THE Spaniards were, upon their petit...
permitted to build a temple to AUGUSTUS,
the colony of Terragon; an example for all
provinces to follow. In answer to the Peop...
who prayed to be relieved from the *Centesim*...
a tax of one in the hundred, established at th...
end of the civil wars, upon all vendible com...
modities; TIBERIUS by an edict declared,
" that upon this tax depended the fund for
" maintaining the army: Nor even thus was...
" the Commonwealth equal to the expence,
" if the Veterans were dismissed before their
" twentieth year." So that the concessions
made them during the late sedition, to discharge
them finally at the end of sixteen years, as they
were made through necessity, were for the
future abolished.

IT was next proposed to the Senate, by AR-
RUNTIUS and ATEIUS, whether, in order to
restrain the overflowing of the Tiber, the
channels of the several rivers and lakes by which
it was swelled, must not be diverted? Upon
this question the deputies of several cities and
colonies were heard. The Florentines besought,
" that the bed of the Clanis might not be
" turned into their river Arnus; for that the
" same woul... ...utter ruin." The
...ramnates; " since
...would be
...the Nar,
...d them."
...against
...us into
...the

Lettres de Cicéron (lower book)

cum Antoniis et reliquis latronibus
jungeret. Cujus rei tanto in timore fui...
omnibus rebus relictis, cum paucior...
et minoribus navibus ad illas ire cona...
sim. Quæ res, si a Rhodiis non essem...
terpellatus, fortasse tota sublata ess...
men magna ex parte profligata est. Qu...
quidem classis dissipata est, adventu...
timore milites ducesque effugerunt: ...
rariæ omnes ad unam a nobis sunt exce...
Certe (quod maxime timui) videor ...
consecutus, ut non possit Dolabella i...
liam pervenire, nec sociis suis firmati...
rius vobis efficere negotium.

Rhodii nos et Rempublicam quam va...
desperaverint, ex Literis quas publice...
cognosces. Et quidem multo parcius n...
Mirari noli. Mira est eorum amentia: ...
meæ ullæ privatim injuriæ unquam: nec...
animus eorum in nostram salutem. Ma...
ditas partium aliarum, perseverantia ...
contentione optimi cujusque, ferenda ...
non fuit. Nec tamen omnes perditos ...
puto. Sed iidem illi, qui tum fugien...
patrem meum, qui L. Lentulum, qui P...

[margin note: moverunt]

dans la Syrie, et se joindre avec les Antoines
(45) et les autres brigands. Ce projet m'a
si vivement alarmé, que, perdant de vue tout le
reste, je n'ai pensé qu'à m'avancer vers lui avec
mes vaisseaux, quoique fort inférieurs aux siens
pour la grandeur et pour le nombre. Peut-être
l'aurois-je détruit sans ressource, si les Rhodiens
ne m'avoient interrompu : mais je l'ai du moins
beaucoup affoibli ; car sa flotte est dissipée. Chefs
et soldats, tous ont pris la fuite à mon approche ;
et les vaisseaux de transport sont tombés entre
mes mains, sans en excepter un. Je crois avoir
gagné, par cette expédition, de mettre Dolabella
dans l'impossibilité de passer en Italie, ce qui
faisoit ma principale crainte, et d'aller redoubler
vos embarras, en rendant la confiance à ses
Alliés.

Vous apprendrez, par ma lettre publique, à
quel danger les Rhodiens ont exposé la Répu-
blique et moi. J'en parle avec beaucoup de rete-
nue : mais vous n'en devez pas être surpris. Leur
ressentiment de mes
propres injures ne m'a jamais beaucoup tou-
ché : cependant, le fonds de malignité que ces
gens-là conservent contre moi, le penchant qu'ils
ont pour le parti opposé, leur mépris obstiné
pour tous les honnêtes gens, méritoient une cer-
taine rigueur. Ce n'est pas que je les croie tous
également coupables ; mais il se trouve, par une
sorte de fatalité, que ceux qui ont refusé de

Chapter 6

The Race of Life

FOR THE LAST TWO DECADES OF HIS LIFE Jefferson remained in Virginia, tending his plantations, corresponding broadly, entertaining countless visitors, encouraging scientific and philosophical studies, building his library, and creating his "academical village," the University of Virginia. One of the last survivors of the revolutionary era, he watched the great American experiment unfold in both favorable and dangerous directions.

In his retirement, his library became an even greater source of amusement and education for Jefferson, who once admitted to John Adams, "I cannot live without books." (TJ to Adams, June 10, 1815) Still, so distressed was Jefferson about the destruction of the original Library of Congress by the British in 1814, that he offered his own 6,500-volume collection as a replacement. He wrote to his friend Samuel H. Smith, former publisher of *The National Intelligencer* and now commissioner of revenue, "I learn from the Newspapers that the Vandalism of our enemy has triumphed at Washington over science as well as the Arts, by the destruction of the public library with the noble edifice in which it was deposited." (September 21, 1814) Jefferson's offer did not come without a price. Congress agreed to pay $23,950, a sum that surely eased Jefferson's impending insolvency as well as awarded the nation the "choicest collection of books in the U.S.," which Jefferson hoped would not be "without some general effect on the literature of our country." (TJ to Samuel H. Smith, May 8, 1815) This sale would become a lasting—and perhaps the most fitting—memorial to Thomas Jefferson. Former President Adams was well aware that his colleague had made another noble step to secure his place in history. He simply stated, "I envy you that immortal honour." (Adams to TJ, October 28, 1814)

(opposite) Books from the personal library of Thomas Jefferson. Photograph by Reid Baker, ca. 1980. Rare Book and Special Collections Division, Library of Congress.

When the original Library of Congress housed in the Capitol was burned by the British during the War of 1812, Jefferson offered to sell his own library to the nation. These volumes, from his original collection, reveal the breadth of Jefferson's learning. As seen here, some foreign-language translations were bound in on facing pages so that Jefferson could easily compare two versions of the same work. The library had taken Jefferson some fifty years to assemble. After the sale to Congress he set out to purchase new titles, which numbered about 1,000 at the time of his death.

Monticello, view of the West Front from the fish pond. Photograph by R. Lautman, 1992. Monticello/Thomas Jefferson Memorial Foundation, Inc.
Jefferson passed his final years at Monticello, from which he pondered the affairs of state at a comfortable distance from Washington and drew closer to the beauty of nature. In 1811, perhaps reflecting on his own life, he wrote one of his granddaughters, "The flowers come forth . . . have their short reign of beauty and splendor, and retire." (TJ to Anne Cary Bankhead, May 26, 1811)

Visitors were a constant source of entertainment, education, and aggravation for Jefferson. Every visiting dignitary as well as casual traveler made Monticello a "must stop" on his itinerary. Some people, such as the Portuguese scientist and refugee Abbé Correa da Serra and friend and neighbor James Madison, came so often that they laid claim to a bedroom, a fact which is related by today's docents at Monticello. Others, such as Margaret Bayard Smith, wife of Washington editor Samuel H. Smith, came intent on observing and recording Jefferson's lifestyle. Old friends, such as William Short, could not be prevailed upon to visit often enough. But of all the visits Jefferson enjoyed, that of the marquis de Lafayette during his triumphal tour of the United States in 1824 and 1825 must have been a highlight for both the sage of Monticello and his longtime revolutionary companion. They had not seen one another since 1789, after the fall of the Bastille.

There was now ample time for reflection and contemplation in Jefferson's life. He tried to avoid politics, but letters prove that he remained attentive to current events. Perhaps the greatest correspondence of his final years was with John Adams. Beneath the party politics that divided them was a firm foundation of affection that resurfaced as the two elder statesmen faced the inevitable end of their generation:

G. Thompson. *The Taking of the City of Washington in America.* Wood engraving. London, 1814. Prints and Photographs Division, Library of Congress.
On the evening of August 24, 1814, General Robert Ross led British troops into Washington and—encountering no resistance—burned some of the city's most notable public buildings, including the President's House, the U.S. Capitol, and the navy yard. This image, printed in London just weeks after the event, celebrated the British victory.

you & I have been wonderfully spared, and myself with remarkable health, & a considerable activity of body & mind. I am on horseback 3. or 4. hours of every day. visit 3. or 4. times a year a possession I have 90 miles distant, performing the winter journey on horseback. I walk little, however, a single mile being too much for me; and I live in the midst of my grandchildren, one of whom has lately promoted me to be a great grandfather. I have heard with pleasure that you also retain good health, and a greater power of exercise in walking than I do. but I would rather have heard this from yourself, & that, writing a letter, like mine, full of egotisms, & of details of your health, your habits, occupations & enjoiments, I should have the pleasure of knowing that in the race of life, you do not keep, in its physical decline, the same distance ahead of me which you have done in political honors & atchievements. no circumstances have lessened the interest I feel in these particulars respecting yourself; none have suspended for one moment my sincere esteem for you; and I now salute you with unchanged affections and respect. (TJ to Adams, January 21, 1812)

"I learn from the Newspapers that the Vandalism of our enemy has triumphed at Washington over science as well as the Arts, by the destruction of the public library with the noble edifice in which it was deposited."

TJ to Samuel H. Smith, September 21, 1814

The renewal of the Jefferson-Adams friendship was a source of pleasure and intellectual growth for both men and their correspondence remains a virtual gift to future generations.

Just before his seventy-fifth birthday, Jefferson tried to organize an account of the early history of the United States as he saw it. He wrote an informal explanation of three volumes of notes and papers he had assembled during his years as secretary of state. Jefferson's "Anas" remains one of the best sources of information on the founding of American political parties and the establishment of the national government. In another irony typical of Jefferson, his "Autobiography," on which he reluctantly embarked in 1821, only covers his life until 1790. For a man who penned thousands of letters and documents, this scant memoir serves only as a lean appetizer to his hearty accomplishments. He was more concerned that his role in founding the nation be remembered than his personal achievements.

There was time, too, for religion, always a sensitive matter for Jefferson; not the ritual of institutional church services but the examination and study of the Bible. By 1819 Jefferson had completed a long-term project to prove he was a real Christian. In his compilation "The Life and Morals of Jesus of Nazareth," Jefferson attempted to separate the true moral ethics of Jesus from the false writings of others.

Samuel F. B. Morse. *The Old House of Representatives.* **Oil on canvas. Washington, D.C., 1822. Corcoran Gallery of Art, Washington, D.C.**

While he was president, Jefferson often attended religious services in the Capitol: first in a hall in the North Wing and then, from 1807, in the chamber shown here, the former House of Representatives, now called Statuary Hall. Jefferson was not generally a churchgoer, but he did contribute to churches throughout his life. Services were held in the halls of Congress until after the Civil War.

(opposite) Thomas Sully. Thomas Jefferson. Oil on canvas, March 1821–1830. American Philosophical Society.

Sully's portrait of Jefferson, begun at Monticello in 1821, is considered a reliable record of Jefferson's looks and coloring in his old age. Jefferson sat for the artist during a twelve-day period, and this canvas was made in preparation for a full-length portrait commissioned by the U.S. Military Academy at West Point. This version from life was finally completed in 1830, by the commission of William Short, and presented to the American Philosophical Society, the institution over which Jefferson had long presided.

He wrote lengthy and frequent letters to intimates expounding his philosophy of religion and trying to explain his views of Jesus. As Jefferson communicated to William Short, he hoped to "justify the character of Jesus against the fictions of his pseudo-followers which have exposed him to the inference of being an impostor, for if we could believe that he really countenanced the follies, the falsehoods and the Charlatanisms which his biographers father on him, and admit the misconstructions, interpolations & theorisations of the fathers of the early, and fanatics of the latter ages, the conclusion would be irresistible by every sound mind, that he was an impostor." (TJ to Short, August 4, 1820)

Two years later, in a June 26, 1822, letter to Benjamin Waterhouse, he tried to summarize the doctrines of Jesus, which he said "are simple, and tend all to the happiness of man." After listing five basic beliefs, Jefferson queried the doctor: "Now which of these is the true and charitable Christian? he, who believes and acts on the simple doctrines of Jesus? or the impious dogmatists of Athanasius & Calvin?" Religious thought remains a complex part of the Jeffersonian mind.

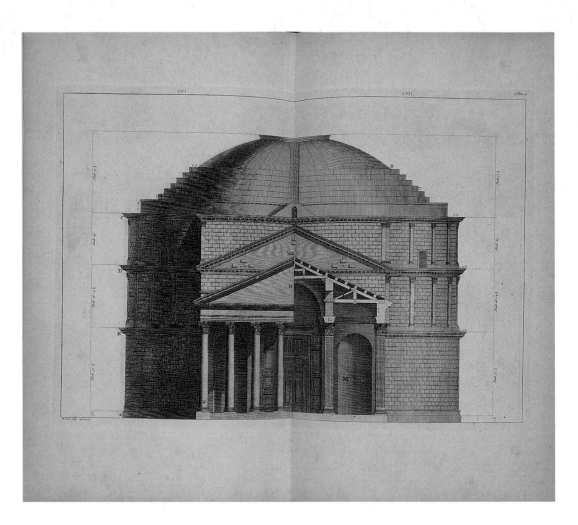

Andrea Palladio. "Half of the fore-front and Half of the front under the Portico of the Pantheon, now call'd the Rotunda." From Giacomo Leone, *Architecture of A. Palladio: In Four Books.* **Book IV (London, 1742). Rare Book and Special Collections Division, Library of Congress.**

Jefferson sold four editions of Palladio's works to Congress in 1815, and owned other editions as well. His knowledge of Palladio's work influenced the design of the U.S. Capitol, the Rotunda at the University of Virginia, and Monticello. Latrobe had suggested that a building at the head of the Lawn at the University of Virginia would give the "academical village" focus. It was Jefferson who determined that such a building be the finest example of spherical architecture and chose the Pantheon as the model.

From his early days in the Virginia legislature, Jefferson had been an ardent advocate of public education. His initial efforts to pass bills that would entitle all eligible males to university education had failed, primarily due to the expense involved. Of course, Jefferson's focus was on men. Women, such as his own daughters, should have "a solid education which might enable them, when become mothers, to educate their own daughters, and even to direct the course for sons, should their fathers be lost, or incapable, or inattentive." In his often-quoted letter to Nathaniel Burwell of March 14, 1818, Jefferson went on to list reading, French, music, drawing, and particularly household economy as skills and "inestimable treasures" for women.

By 1817, Jefferson was committed to creating a major public university near the village of Charlottesville. Known locally as "Mr. Jefferson's university," this institution's establishment allowed Jefferson a final opportunity to employ his ideas on the value of education to democracy. He saw to every detail, from lobbying the Virginia legislature for funds to employing a stonecutter from Italy to execute the architectural details. The building, grounds, curriculum, and faculty were all under his supervision. Although he believed that academic freedom would lead to the dis-

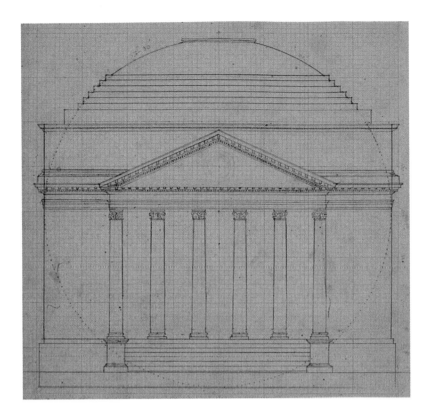

Thomas Jefferson. South Elevation of the Rotunda, begun 1818, completed March 29, 1819. Pricking, scoring, iron-gall ink, pencil on laid paper with coordinate lines, 1819. Thomas Jefferson Architectural Drawings, University Archives, Special Collections Department, University of Virginia Library.
The Rotunda at the University of Virginia was carefully planned by Jefferson to represent the authority of nature and the power of reason. To him, the classical architecture of Palladio best represented these ideals. It seems fitting that the Rotunda originally housed the University library, a source of enlightenment and wisdom.

semination of the principles of freedom he so cherished, he wanted to be sure that those principles would be republican in nature. To the end of his life he exerted characteristic and shameless control over academic matters, writing to Madison on February 17, 1826:

in the selection of our Law Professor we must be rigorously attentive to his Political principles. you will recollect that, before the revolution, Coke Littleton was the Universal elementary book of law-students, and a sounder Whig never wrote; nor of profounder learning in the orthodox doctrines of the British constitn, or in what were called English liberties. you remember also that our lawyers were then all Whigs. but when his black-letter text, and uncouth, but cunning learning got out of fashion, and the honied Mansfieldism of Blackstone became the Student's Horn-book, from that moment, that Profession (the Nursery of our Congress) began to slide into toryism, and nearly all the young brood of lawyers now are of that hue. they suppose themselves indeed to be whigs, because they no longer know what whiggism or republicanism means. it is in our Seminary that that Vestal flame is to be kept alive; it is thence it is to spread anew over our own state and the sister-states. if we are true and vigilant in our trust, within a dozen or 20. years a majority of our own legislature will be from our school, and many disciples will have carried it's doctrines home with them to their several states, and will have leavened thus the whole mass.

When the University of Virginia admitted its first class in 1825, Jefferson was eighty-two. He considered its founding a crowning achievement of his career, so much so that he included it in his epitaph.

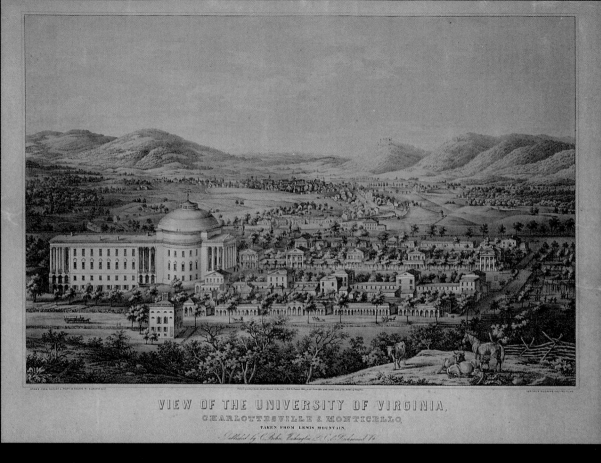

E. Sachse & Co. *View of the University of Virginia, Charlottesville & Monticello, Taken From Lewis Mountain.* **Panoramic map. Washington, D.C. and Richmond, Virginia, 1856. Geography and Map Division, Library of Congress.**

When the University of Virginia opened its doors to approximately thirty young men in March 1825, a visiting professor from Harvard proclaimed Jefferson's "academical village" "more beautiful than anything architectural in New England and more appropriate to an university than can be found, perhaps, in the world." This print shows the Rotunda and ten connected pavilions.

But for all that he and the nation had accomplished, Jefferson saw only a dark future ahead. The man who had entered political life with reluctance yet optimism knew that his ideals would gain only painful acceptance throughout the world. Sizing up the limited steps toward self-government that had been taken in Europe and South America, he correctly predicted to John Adams, "rivers of blood must yet flow & years of desolation pass over" before other nations would achieve "the blessings of liberty."

Thomas Jefferson to John Adams, Monticello, September 4, 1823. Manuscript Division, Library of Congress.

In this famous letter to John Adams, Jefferson predicts that only bloodshed would bring self-government to the nations of Europe and South America—a sacrifice he felt was necessary and justified.

the generation which commences a revolution rarely compleats it. habituated from their infancy to passive submission of body and mind to their kings and priests, they are not qualified, when called on, to think and provide for themselves and their inexperience, their ignorance and bigotry make them instruments often, in the hands of the Bonapartes and Iturbides to defeat their own rights and purposes. this is the present situation of Europe and Spanish America. but it is not desperate. the light which has been shed on mankind by the art of printing has eminently changed the condition of the world. as yet that light has dawned on the midling classes only of the men of Europe. the kings and the rabble of equal ignorance, have not yet recieved it's rays; but it continues to spread . . . to attain all this however rivers of blood must yet flow, & years of desolation pass over. yet the object is worth rivers of blood, and years of desolation. for what inheritance, so valuable, can man leave to his posterity?
(TJ to Adams, September 4, 1823)

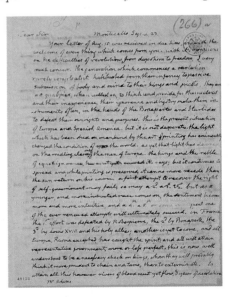

Similarly, when Jefferson looked ahead at the prospects of his country on the issues of slavery, states' rights, and western expansion, he saw only danger and self-destruction. The question of admitting Missouri into the Union as a slave state, raised in 1819, brought immediate concern:

. . . this momentous question, like a fire bell in the night, awakened and filled me with terror. I considered it at once as the knell of the Union. it is hushed indeed for the moment. but this is a reprieve only, not a final sentence. a geographical line, coinciding with a marked principle, moral and political, once concieved and held up to the angry passions of men, will never be obliterated; and every new irritation will mark it deeper and deeper . . . I regret that I am now to die in the belief that the useless sacrifice of themselves, by the generation of '76. to acquire self government and happi-

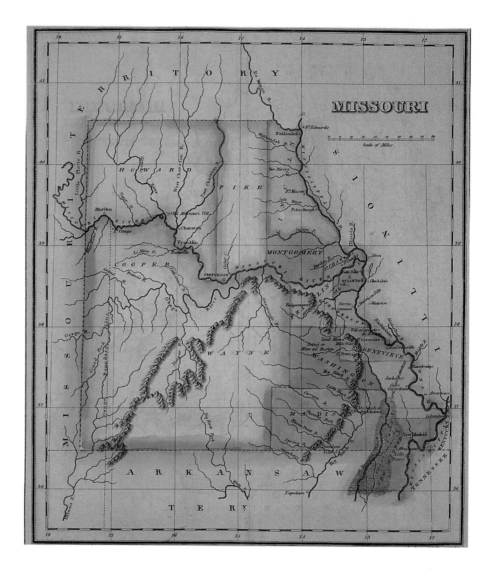

*ness to their country, is to be thrown away by the unwise and unworthy passions of their sons, and
that my only consolation is to be that I live not to weep over it. if they would but dispassionately
weigh the blessings they will throw away against an abstract principle more likely to be effected by
union than by scission, they would pause before they would perpetrate this act of suicide on themselves and of treason against the hopes of the world. (TJ to John Holmes, April 22, 1820)*

Another cause of continual despair to the master of Monticello was his personal debt. In what he knew of the future, he could only see burdensome and unre-
solved issues for both his nuclear family and his extended clan of workers and slaves.
Troubled finances would cost the members of his own family much of their inher-
itances and saddle them with lifelong struggles to repay the large debt owed by
Jefferson. And this dire situation cost his slaves their freedom, because he could not
afford to relinquish his only valuable asset nor could he afford the Virginia state
requirement to provide funds for the support of any slave he freed. Only a select
group of slaves was ever freed by Jefferson, or permitted to run away. Four of them
are thought by most people to have been the children of Jefferson and Sally
Hemings. The others were skilled artisans, also members of the Hemings family.
Sally Hemings was not among those freed by her owner.

Jefferson often claimed that slaves were not yet equipped by nature and experience to live in a free society. Ensnared by contradictions both societal and personal, he delegated the burden of resolving slavery to future generations:

I am sensible of the partialities with which you have looked towards me as the person who should undertake this salutary but arduous work. but this, my dear Sir, is like bidding old Priam to buckle the armour of Hector 'trementibus aevo humeris et inutile ferrumcingi.' no. I have overlived the generation with which mutual labors and perils begat mutual confidence and influence. this enterprise is for the young; for those who can follow it up, and bear it through to it's consummation. it shall have all my prayers, and these are the only weapons of an old man. but in the meantime are you right in abandoning this property, and your country with it? I think not. my opinion has ever been that, until more can be done for them, we should endeavor, with those whom fortune has thrown on our hands, to feed, & clothe them well, protect them from ill usage, require such reasonable labor only as is performed voluntarily by freemen, and be led by no repugnancies to abdicate them, and our duties to them. (TJ to Edward Coles, August 25, 1814)

Anne Cary Bankhead. Household accounts for Monticello, Sunday, August 9, 1807. Manuscript Division, Library of Congress.

Household accounts kept by Jefferson's granddaughter show purchases made from slaves at Monticello, including eleven eggs from John Hemings, Sally Hemings's half-brother. Slaves were allowed to supplement their diets and their income by growing vegetables and raising chickens on their own time, usually in the evening. John, who was master carpenter at Monticello, was one of only five slaves freed in Jefferson's will because of his loyal service and great skill as a builder.

157 THE RACE OF LIFE

The American Colonization Society was one of many groups seeking to find a solution to the conundrum of slavery in the early nineteenth century. Jefferson did not join or formally endorse the American Colonization Society after it was established in December 1816, but he did favor the idea of foreign colonization by free African Americans. In an 1811 letter to John Lynch, he expressed his support of the establishment of such a colony in Africa:

You have asked my opinion on the proposition of Mrs. Mifflin to take measures for procuring on the coast of Africa an establishment to which the people of color of these states might from time to time be colonised under the auspices of different governments. having long ago made up my mind on this subject, I have no hesitation in saying that I have ever thought it the most desirable measure which could be adopted for gradually drawing off this part of our population most advantageously for themselves as well as for us. going from a country possessing all the useful arts, they might be the means of transplanting them among the inhabitants of Africa, and would thus carry back to the country of their origin the seeds of civilisation, which might render their sojournment and sufferings here a blessing in the end to that country.

I recieved in the 1st. year of my coming into the administration of the general government, a letter from the governor of Virginia (Colo. Monroe) consulting me, at the request of the legislature of the state, on the means of procuring some such asylum, to which these people might be occasionally sent. I proposed to him the establishment of Sierra Leone, to which a private company in England had already colonised a number of negroes, & particularly the fugitives from these states during the revolutionary war; and at the same time suggested, if this could not be obtained, some of the Portuguese possessions in South America, as next most desirable. (TJ to John Lynch, January 21, 1811)

> **"the revolution in public opinion which this cause requires, is not to be expected in a day, or perhaps in an age. but time, which outlives all things, will outlive this evil also."**
>
> *TJ to James Heaton, May 20, 1826*

Plagued forever by his inability to resolve the slavery question, he could only lament at the end of his life:

a good cause is often injured more by ill timed efforts of it's friends than by the arguments of it's enemies. persuasion, perseverance, and patience are the best advocates on questions depending on the will of others. the revolution in public opinion which this cause requires, is not to be expected in a day, or perhaps in an age. but time, which outlives all things, will outlive this evil also. my sentiments have been 40. years before the public. had I repeated them 40. times, they would only have become the more stale and thread-bare. altho I shall not live to see their consummation, they will not die with me. but living or dying they will ever be in my most fervent prayers. (TJ to James Heaton, May 20, 1826)

(opposite) "Executor's Sale." From the *Charlottesville Central Gazette*. January 13, 1827. Courtesy, American Antiquarian Society.
At the time of his death Jefferson owed over $107,000 to creditors. Jefferson's surviving daughter, heir to Monticello, was forced to auction the contents of the entire house, including Jefferson's personal belongings. The sale, as noted in this advertisement, took place on January 15, 1827, and even the family members were required to bid for most of the items they wanted because the financial need was so great. Sadly, the earnings were not sufficient to pay off the debt, and the family was pressed to sell Monticello itself, for which they received a mere $4,500.

EXECUTOR'S SALE.

Will be sold, on the fifteenth of January, at Monticello, in the county of Albemarle, the whole of the residue of the personal estate of Thomas Jefferson, dec., consisting of

130 VALUABLE NEGROES,

Stock, Crop, &c. Household and Kitchen Furniture. The attention of the public is earnestly invited to this property. The negroes are believed to be the most valuable for their number ever offered at one time in the State of Virginia. The household furniture, many valuable historical and portrait paintings, busts of marble and plaister of distinguished individuals; one of marble of Thomas Jefferson, by Caracci, with the pedestal and truncated column on which it stands; a polygraph or copying instrument used by Thomas Jefferson, for the last twenty-five years; with various other articles curious and useful to men of business and private families. The terms of sale will be accommodating and made known previous to the day. The sale will be continued from day to day until completed. This sale being unavoidable, it is a sufficient guarantee to the public, that it will take place at the time and place appointed.

THOMAS J. RANDOLPH,
Executor of Th: Jefferson, dec.
January 6, 1827—2t

The paintings and busts of Thos. Jefferson, dec. will not be offered for sale on the 15th of January next; but will be sent to some one of the large cities and then sold, after due notice.

Metropolitan—EXTRA.

METROPOLITAN OFFICE,
July 12th, 1826.

Scarcely had the mournful intelligence reached us of the death of the sage and venerable father of our Independence, ere a fresh draught is drawn upon our sympathies, for his like venerable compeer JOHN ADAMS. *Jefferson* and *Adams* were twin stars that shone with resplendent glory, during the whole eventful struggle of the revolution. They have descended together to the tomb, and the prayers and blessings of their countrymen follow them. Their services, in conjunction with the happy coincidence of their deaths, have secured them an imperishable niche in the temple of fame. The late anniversary will be hailed as a glorious era in the annals of liberty, and we most sincerely trust will be 'solemnized with pomps, shows, games, 'sports, guns, bells, bon-fires and illuminations,' until the end of time.

It is our greatest gratification to record, that from the moment the melancholy tidings were received, every political feeling was banished; our citizens only remembered that these illustrious men were the promoters of their country's independence, and had hallowed it by their death. Indeed, if the world had asked a sign to prove the *divina origine* of our compact, it would have it in the *miracle* of their simultaneous demise, on the Jubilee of American Freedom.

The very day after our worthy Mayor had called the attention of the Town Councils in his truly feeling and eloquent address upon the death of Jefferson, he had to exercise his solicitude anew upon a like mournful occasion, which he did on Monday last, in the following words.

Mayors Office Georgetown,
10th July 1826.

To the Honorable, the Board of Aldermen and Board of Common Council.

Gentlemen: The Committee appointed by your honorable body, to adopt measures in relation to the death of the venerable *Thomas Jefferson*, met, and were proceeding with the arrangements to comply with your wish, when, this morning, it was announced that his compatriot, the venerable JOHN ADAMS, had also died on the same day. They deemed it respectful and decorous to suspend their proceedings until the Corporation should have an opportunity to express their sentiments in relation to this additional event, so well calculated to excite our feelings.

The character of the illustrious deceased is too well known to you, Gentlemen, and to his country, to render necessary any remarks from me; suffice it, that he was the efficient, energetic, and eloquent compeer of the illustrious *Jefferson*, and, in all that related to invaluable services to our country, his firm and faithful ally.

Very respectfully,
I am, Gentlemen,
Your obt. servt.
JOHN COX, Mayor.

Mr. Addison then introduced a resolution expressive of the high sense which was entertained by the Board of Common Council, and by every American, for the services of these compeers in glory, and a wish, that as in their lives they had been united in the great cause of liberty, so in their deaths the honors due their memory should not be divided. It is needless to add, that it was passed without one dissenting voice.

The Committee to whom was referred the necessary ceremonials, passed the following resolution:

At a meeting of the Committee of Citizens, appointed by the Corporation of Georgetown, for the purpose of adopting measures and making arrangements for paying all suitable respect to the memory of *Thomas Jefferson* and of *John Adams*,

PRESENT

John Cox, Mayor---John Mason---Walter Smith---John Threlkeid---Thomas Corcoran, Sen.---John Laird---William Marbury---Leonard Mackall---Clement Smith---Charles King---James S. Morsell---Charles Worthington and Charles A. Beatty.

Resolved, That a day be set apart (of which due notice will be given) for the observance of such solemn ceremonies, as may evince the deep regret felt for the death, and the high sense entertained of the virtues, the patriotism, and the extraordinary usefulness during the long lives of these highly distinguished men—in which the citizens of the town and of the adjacent country of the district, and the strangers residing in the town and vicinity shall be invited.

That Francis S. Key be requested to deliver an oration on the occasion, at such time and place as shall hereafter be determined on.

That the members of this committee will wear crape on the left arm for thirty days, and that our fellow citizens be, and they are hereby respectfully invited to do the same.

JOHN COX, Mayor,
Chairman.

WALTER SMITH,
Secretary.

View of the obelisk,
Thomas Jefferson's burial place at
Monticello. Photograph by James
T. Tkatch. Monticello/Thomas
Jefferson Memorial Foundation, Inc.

Although Jefferson ordered that his tombstone
be made of "coarse stone" so that no one would
be "tempted hereafter to destroy it for the value
of the materials," visitors to Monticello after his
death hacked chips off the monument to keep as
souvenirs. Eventually, the original marker was
replaced by the granite obelisk shown at right.

(opposite) *Metropolitan-Extra.*
Broadside. Washington, D.C.,
July 12, 1826. Rare Book and
Special Collections Division,
Library of Congress.

The amazing coincidence of the deaths of
Thomas Jefferson and John Adams on the
same day is noted in almost religious tones in
this announcement, which calls the two
fathers of independence "twin stars that
shone with resplendent glory."

> **"to my self you have been a pillar of support**
> **thro' life. take care of me when dead, and**
> **be assured that I will leave with you my last**
> **affections."**
>
> *TJ to James Madison, February 17, 1826*

Sadly, Jefferson was a personal captive to the slavery issue. His troubled finances caused him to sell slaves throughout his life, and it was money that prevented him from following the example of other notable Virginians, such as George Washington, who freed his slaves at his Mount Vernon estate in his will. And after his death it was debt again that led to the sale of all but five slaves (those of the Hemings clan freed in his will) at a five-day auction in early 1827.

Jefferson died at age eighty-three. Though ailing for weeks, he somehow managed to hold on to life until July 4, 1826, the fiftieth anniversary of American independence from British rule. In one of history's great coincidences, John Adams died later that same day. With those two deaths, the revolutionary generation virtually disappeared, but it left a sure legacy that seems to grow and renew itself with each generation of Americans. Adams's last words, "Thomas Jefferson survives," are doubly ironic and meaningful now because his junior colleague from Virginia seems to have stolen the spotlight from others of the revolutionary era. Two centuries later, it is Jefferson's words—and words that might not even have been entirely his—that are remembered.

On his deathbed, with his estate in jeopardy and his heirs' futures in the balance, Jefferson had managed to conjure the inspirational prose for which he is still loved. He knew he would be too ill to attend the fiftieth anniversary of American independence in Washington so he sent what would be his last public statement:

> "the general spread of the light of science has already laid open to every view the palpable truth that the mass of mankind has not been born, with saddles on their backs, nor a favored few booted and spurred, ready to ride them legitimately, by the grace of god."
>
> *TJ to Roger Weightman, June 24, 1826*

may it be to the world what I believe it will be, (to some parts sooner, to others later, but finally to all.) the Signal of arousing men to burst the chains, under which Monkish ignorance and superstition had persuaded them to bind themselves, and to assume the blessings & security of self government. that form which we have substituted restores the free right to the unbounded exercise of reason and freedom of opinion. all eyes are opened, or opening to the rights of man. the general spread of the light of science has already laid open to every view the palpable truth that the mass of mankind has not been born, with saddles on their backs, nor a favored few booted and spurred, ready to ride them legitimately, by the grace of god. these are grounds of hope for others. for ourselves let the annual return of this day, for ever refresh our recollections of these rights, and an undiminished devotion to them. (TJ to Roger Weightman, June 24, 1826)

It is another wonderfully Jeffersonian quirk that his last known words on liberty are in principle and spirit so much like his first.

(opposite) Thomas Jefferson to Roger Weightman, Monticello, June 24, 1826. Manuscript Division, Library of Congress.

Jefferson carefully crafted the language of this letter to Washington mayor Roger Weightman in the last official communication before his death. Although Jefferson knew he would not be present at the fiftieth anniversary of independence, to which Weightman had invited him, he was aware that his words would mark the occasion and elegantly conveyed his firm faith in the principles of the Declaration of Independence.

Respected Sir   Monticello June 24. 26   (3

The kind invitation I recieve from you on the part of
the citizens of the city of Washington, to be present with them at
their celebration of the 50th anniversary of American independance;
as one of the surviving signers of an instrument, pregnant with our own,
and the fate of the world, is most flattering to myself, and heightened
by the honorable accompaniment proposed for the comfort of such a
journey. it adds sensibly to the sufferings of sickness, to be deprived by it
of a personal participation in the rejoicings of that day. but acquiescence
is a duty, under circumstances not placed among those we are permitted
to controul. I should indeed, with peculiar delight, have met and
exchanged there, congratulations personally, with the small band,
the remnant of that host of worthies, who joined with us, on that
day, in the bold and doubtful election we were to make, for our country,
between submission, or the sword; and to have enjoyed with them the
consolatory fact that our fellow citizens, after half a century of experience
and prosperity, continue to approve the choice we made. may it be to
the world what I believe it will be, (to some parts sooner, to others later,
but finally to all) the Signal of arrousing men to burst the chains, under
which monkish ignorance and superstition had persuaded them to bind
themselves, and to assume the blessings & security of self government. the
form which we have substituted restores the free right to the unbounded exercise
of reason and freedom of opinion. all eyes are opened, or opening to the
rights of man. the general spread of the light of science has already
laid open to every view the palpable truth that the mass of mankind has not been
born, with saddles on their backs, nor a favored few booted and spurred, ready to
ride them legitimately, by the grace of god. these are grounds of hope for others. for
selves let the annual return of this day, for ever refresh our recollections of these ri
and an undiminished devotion to them.

Why Jefferson Lives:
A Meditation on the Man
and the Myth

by Joseph J. Ellis

HE SPEAKS TO US ACROSS THE AGES, in part because he knew we would be listening. Like all the other vanguard members of the revolutionary generation, Thomas Jefferson had a keen interest in what he called "posterity's judgment," meaning his place in the history books. Like most of his prominent peers, he started keeping copies of all his letters early on, and towards the end of his long career, most memorably in his correspondence with John Adams in their twilight years, each letter became a self-conscious performance. He was, in short, sending his letters to us as much as to his irascible colleague in Quincy, Massachusetts.

Jefferson was an agnostic about everlasting life with God in heaven, but a devout believer in his persistence within the collective memory of posterity. One of the reasons why the words etched on the tablets inside the Jefferson Memorial strike us as eloquent and inspirational is that many of them were crafted for precisely that purpose. To be sure, he had no way of knowing the specific manifestations of his immortality, no way of foreseeing his memorial on the Tidal Basin, his head on Mount Rushmore, his face on the nickel—it displaced his beloved buffalo—or his name given to the main building of the Library of Congress. But he did know that the founders of nations tended to become heroic figures of mythological proportions, for the same reasons that the earliest Christians were usually canonized as saints. Jefferson never said, as Abraham Lincoln said at Gettysburg, that "the world will little note nor long remember what we say here." If there was a Mount Olympus in the American future, he expected to occupy a spot near the summit.

As mentioned earlier, Jefferson was not distinctive in this regard. One of the reasons that the several modern editions of the papers of Jefferson, Adams, George Washington, Benjamin Franklin, and James Madison seem destined to stretch out to the crack of doom is that they all felt the same intimations of immortality and preserved every scratch of their respective pens, or quills, accordingly. Recently, as we all prepare to cross over to the other side of the millennium, there has been a spate of books looking back at the twentieth century, and one best-seller arguing that the generation that came of age in World War II was "the greatest generation." One can make spirited and plausible claims of greatness about several age cohorts in American history, but let me assure you that all will eventually lose out to Jefferson's generation. As Ralph Waldo Emerson once put it, they were the patriarchs who "beheld God and nature face to face."

Even within the revolutionary generation, however, Jefferson casts a special spell. The rest of them are "back there," safely interred in the ground and in our memories as venerable relics or statues, their wise words like distant echoes of a bygone era, ancestral voices, their clothing, hairstyles, and language reminiscent of a costume ball in a lushly staged Merchant and Ivory film. Jefferson, on the other hand, is "up here" with us, a regular participant in our ongoing conversations about race, gun control, impeachment, religious freedom, social security, the deficit. He is politically ubiquitous and ideologically promiscuous, claimed by the right wing of the Republican party as the chief spokesman for limited government and the everlasting enemy of higher taxes, recognized by Democrats as the founding father of their party and the chief inspiration for the egalitarian goals of their liberal agenda. Ronald Reagan said that we should "pluck a flower from Jefferson's garden and wear it in our lapels forever." William Jefferson Clinton visited Monticello for inspiration before his first inaugural and described the tingling sensation

Charles Balthazar Julien Fevret de Saint-Mémin. Thomas Jefferson. Medallion engraving after life portrait, ca. 1804. Prints and Photographs Division, Library of Congress.

Saint-Mémin made the graceful crayon portrait on which his engravings were based from life with the help of a physiognotrace. The sitting took place on November 27, 1804, probably at the artist's rooms on F Street in Washington, since the tracing device was cumbersome. Jefferson was sixty-one years old and approaching the end of his first term. The widely distributed image contributed significantly to Jefferson's iconic status.

he felt whenever he gazed out from the Oval Office across the Tidal Basin and glimpsed Jefferson's profile. When a DNA study confirmed that Jefferson most probably fathered a child by Sally Hemings, it was front-page news and the main subject of prime time talk-shows. Op-ed writers in the *New York Times* and the *Wall Street Journal* smelled a left-wing conspiracy designed to rescue President Clinton from his Monica Lewinsky woes by suggesting that such sexual indiscretions had a distinguished presidential pedigree.

Jefferson also seems to possess the unique capacity to live on with disarming potency in the hearts and minds of ordinary Americans. My furnace broke down while I was working on the book that became *American Sphinx*. The repairman arrived and, seeing the books on Jefferson littered across my desk, asked me to follow him down to the basement so he could fully apprise me of Jefferson's abiding convictions as a devout Christian, an important truth that other biographers had gotten wrong and that he wanted to be sure I got right. Or there was an evening in Richmond when a well-spoken, elderly woman in the audience arose to protest my claim that Jefferson was capable of deep duplicity on occasion. No, she insisted, that was simply not true. Jefferson visited her every night in her dreams and always behaved honorably. She concluded with a wonderful flourish, noting with disdain that I was "a mere pigeon on the great statue of Thomas Jefferson."

John Adams may have been literally incorrect when he uttered his last words on that providential day of July 4, 1826, "Thomas Jefferson survives." In fact, Jefferson had died about four hours earlier on that very day. But Adams was right for the ages. We never ask, "What is still living in the political philosophy of George Washington?" We never wonder what Benjamin Franklin would say about health care, abortion, or campaign finance reform. Only Jefferson among all the founders is so routinely resurrected, his spirit and avowed legacy alive and well and dwelling amongst us. Why is that so? How does he levitate so easily from his time to ours?

In order to appreciate the Jeffersonian levitations for the magical feats they truly are, we need to recognize how far his legacy has to travel before it can land up here in the present. For we live in a post-Jeffersonian world. The demographic and economic changes that swept through the United States between 1890 and 1920 transformed the material and mental landscape that Jefferson recognized as familiar terrain. Once we became an urban, industrial, modern society without an expanding frontier and with what we might call a self-evident need for federal regulation of our economy and environment, Jefferson's agrarian vision became anachronistic, his world truly "lost." Jefferson was resolutely premodern. That means he was pre-Darwin, pre-Marx, pre-Freud, pre-Einstein, pre-Stravinsky, pre-Picasso, pre-Keynes, pre-*Brown v Board of Education*. His version of liberalism presumed a minimalist state and white Anglo-Saxon male superiority. Our version of liberalism presumes a post-New Deal federal government and a multiracial, gender-blind ideal. All conjurings of Jefferson in the present that ignore the chasm between his world and ours, or that simply finesse the translation by presuming that his words have eternal meaning, are fatally flawed from the start, like trying to plant cut flowers.

Let me offer the three most salient examples of the translation problem which, taken together, make the routinized resurrections of Jefferson even more stunning, indeed almost miraculous. First, in several of Jefferson's most famous statements, for instance the natural rights section of the Declaration of Independence and his First Inaugural Address, he asserts his belief in the capacity of individual citizens to govern themselves and their right to pursue happiness unfettered by institutions of any kind. But as Edmund Morgan pointed out most trenchantly in *American Slavery, American Freedom*, both of Jefferson's convictions about personal freedom depended on the unspoken presumptions that slave labor would produce the requisite abundance, class conflict would therefore be avoided within the white population, and blacks would forever be excluded from the citizenry. The intensity of his political radicalism, in short, was inextricably tied to the intensity of his white racism. You cannot get the former without the latter unless you distort the historical Jefferson. And this holds true for Jefferson's personal life, which was so dependent for its own pursuits of happiness on slave labor, as well as for his larger vision for American society as a whole.

Second, Jefferson is commonly described as "the apostle of democracy," a phrase meant to convey his faith in majority rule and in the capacity of ordinary Americans to make sensible judgments about national policy. Now, there is clearly something to this designation, since Jefferson really did regard the House of Representatives as the sovereign branch of the government and mistrusted the executive and judicial branches because they were further removed from popular opinion. But Jefferson himself seldom used the word "democratic" until the very end of his life, and for good reason. In the late eighteenth century the term was used as an epithet, to mean the surrender of what was in the public interest to popular opinion. Jefferson's enemies within the Federalist camp often accused him of being a democrat, meaning a political leader who pandered to shallow and short-term popular movements. He, of course, rejected the charge and the term. Moreover, Jefferson did not favor extending the vote to white males without property, until he retired from public office himself. Women and blacks, of course, remained forever beyond the pale. Nor did he ever think that ordinary American citizens should hold office at the national level. He went to his death regarding Andrew Jackson and his followers as a motley band of barbarians who contaminated the original intentions of the Revolution. The word "democracy" accumulated a multiple set of semi-sacred meanings in the course of the nineteenth century. Jefferson would have rejected most of them. The world that Alexis de Tocqueville described and Andrew Jackson symbolized was much too hurly-burly and crudely materialistic a place to fit his prescription for America.

Third, and finally, there is the important principle of religious freedom, which he and Madison established in Virginia and which Jefferson made memorable with the phrase "wall of separation" between church and state. This is one Jeffersonian idea that translates pretty well into the present, since he truly meant a total separation and non-negotiable freedom to worship whatever god one wished. Within the revolutionary generation Jefferson was truly distinctive on this score. Virtually every other statesman, save perhaps Franklin, presumed that the United States would and should remain a Christian, indeed a Protestant country, and that toleration ought not extend to Catholics and Jews, much less to deists or atheists. They believed that shared religious convictions were the essential glue to bind the citizenry together. Jefferson did not believe that such ideological or theological cement was necessary. Like Voltaire, he wished to see the last king strangled with the entrails of the last priest.

That said, very little in our contemporary religious landscape would be familiar to Jefferson, who presumed that within fifty years of his death virtually everyone in America would be a practicing Unitarian (if that is not a contradiction in terms). He did not foresee the potency of the evangelical movement, which in fact was building strength even as he lived. Evangelical Christians who claim him as a spokesman, like my furnace repairman, have the wrong man. Jefferson thought that Jesus was an admirable role model, but not the Son of God. Moreover, Jefferson would find it extremely awkward to concede that the chief defender of his cherished "wall of separation" was the Supreme Court, which he described as a gang of "sappers and miners" dedicated to blowing up the foundations of the American republic. Jefferson believed that his principle of unrestricted religious freedom should be put to a popular vote. He did not regard the judiciary as the ultimate interpreter of the Constitution. And, based on all polls of contemporary popular opinion, his Jeffersonian religious ideal would be defeated by his Jeffersonian political faith in the people.

Where does that leave us? Well, it should heighten our sense of the daunting task facing anyone wishing to appropriate Jefferson for modern political purposes while also remaining faithful to the eighteenth-century context. Unless you believe that ideas are like migratory birds that can take off in one century and land intact and unchanged in another, claiming the Jeffersonian legacy is a highly problematic enterprise. Any literal translation of Jefferson from then to now is, in fact, impossible. Indeed, Jefferson himself would have been the first to warn us away from the effort, believing as he did that each generation is sovereign, needs to free itself

JOSEPH J. ELLIS

**Washing down the
Thomas Jefferson Memorial,
Washington, D.C. Photograph by
William K. Geiger, April 1985.**
*As a new generation of scholars reexamines
apparent disparities between Jefferson's avowed
principles and apparent contradictions in his
policies and lifestyle, his reputation as a genius
of liberty endures in the popular imagination.*

from what he called "the dead hand of the past" and strike out, unencumbered and open-minded, in its own direction. In that sense, the core Jeffersonian legacy is to repudiate all legacies. If, somehow, he were miraculously resurrected in the well of the Senate and asked to dispense his wisdom on Social Security, Kosovo, or welfare legislation, he would decline, arguing that this is not his time, but ours; we are on our own.

Before we permit him to recede into the misty past, or perhaps into those fogbanks that envelop Monticello in the morning and that the Ken Burns documentary for PBS captured so lovingly on film, the evidence presented thus far allows us to note for the record the deeper sources of his inherent elusiveness, the elemental reasons why his legacy floats, like the fog, so easily among different ideological camps.

The most obvious explanation is that he is famous for his eloquent rendering of timeless truths about freedom and equality, but he was not a political philosopher so much as an active political practitioner. Over a career that lasted for almost fifty years as a diplomat, statesman, and party leader, Jefferson was consistently forced by the imperatives imposed on a wielder of power to make real-life choices that compromised his cherished ideals. Despite his lyrical denunciations of slavery, he found himself trapped in a Virginian society where it was deeply rooted. Despite his strong expressions of hostility to the monarchical character of the American presidency throughout the 1790s, he made the most significant executive decision in American history, the Louisiana Purchase, in 1803. Despite his celebration of a free press, he unleashed his state attorney-generals against Federalist editors in 1804. The list could go on to include his support for the Embargo Act of 1807, which violated all his exaltations of a free market unfettered by government regulation. Unlike Voltaire or Rousseau, Jefferson was not a closeted intellectual. The purity of his principles was regularly forced to engage the messy reality of political power in the world. Think of an eloquent academic dissenter, protesting all the oppressions and degradations of the university administration, then suddenly promoted to provost.

A second and less obvious reason for his disarming capacity to show up on all sides of a political debate comes into focus if we listen attentively to the message projected by the most famous words he ever wrote. This, of course, is the natural rights section of the Declaration of Independence, the magic words of American history and the motherlode of Jeffersonian wisdom that all claimants of the legacy acknowledge as the primal source. It is, in fact, not easy to listen to these words dispassionately. They are the rhapsodic refrain of the American Song that, like a catechism recited over and over or a golden oldie listened to countless times, resists careful scrutiny. So muster your maximum measure of detachment as these ringing words roll past:

We hold these truths to be self-evident, that all men are created equal, that they are endowed by their Creator with certain unalienable Rights, that among these are Life, Liberty and the pursuit of Happiness. That to secure these rights, Governments are instituted among Men, deriving their just powers from the consent of the governed, ...

These are the core tenets of America's original promise to itself and to the world. These words provided the inspiration for Lincoln at Gettysburg in 1863 and Martin Luther King, Jr. a hundred years later when he referred to "the promissory note" issued to all Americans. It therefore seems almost sacrilegious to observe that the promise is inherently utopian and incapable of being realized on this earth because it is based on a fundamental contradiction. Jefferson could not see the contradiction because, coming at the start of modernity's war against entrenched privilege and power, he presumed that the destruction of those vestiges of medieval tyranny would lead naturally and inevitably to both liberty and equality. And there is the core contradiction, which, thanks to Jefferson's lyrical formulation, became the central contradiction of American political thought. Our twin ideals are freedom and equality. They are in fact logically and historically incompatible. Freedom leads to social and economic inequality. And restoring a measure of equality means limiting freedom. Jefferson's magic words really do work magic, for they articulate irreconcilable human urges at a sufficiently abstract level to mask their mutual exclusiveness. Modern-day conservatives and libertarians can embrace the freedom side of the Jeffersonian formulation. Modern-day liberals can embrace the equality side. To paraphrase Jefferson's famous line in his First Inaugural: we are all conservatives, we are all liberals, because we are all Jeffersonians.

As this analysis suggests, the source of Jefferson's abiding relevance and persistent leverage on our political debates is his genius with language. There is a sense in which Jefferson did not think in terms of ideas, but in terms of words. Although he should not properly be regarded as the father of American democracy, he should be credited with inventing the rhetoric which allows democracy to work. Here an appreciation of the historical context makes his achievement even more stunning. For Jefferson recognized earlier than almost anyone else—Tom Paine might be accorded primacy—that a society in which political sovereignty rested with the people-at-large would require a new vocabulary that was simultaneously more accessible and more elusive. In all previous political cultures, the elite leaders only needed to persuade one another. In the American republic, a mass electorate needed to be mobilized. Jefferson constructed a kind of verbal canopy under which different constituencies could gather, speaking the same words while meaning quite different things by them. He invented the consensual vocabulary of mainstream American politics.

If he is more a rhetorician than a philosopher, he is also more a visionary than a thinker. Specific applications of his ideas to our contemporary political problems will almost always be historically (if not politically) incorrect. But the larger vision appeals to a timeless and universal struggle that each era must rediscover and confront on its own terms; it projects a distinctively Jeffersonian way of thinking about that structure that remains relevant both within the United States and in the larger world. The Jeffersonian vision frames political choices in a dramatic format that stigmatizes concentrated political power, what he called "consolidation." It celebrates decentralized and wholly voluntary networks of governance, what he called "diffusion."

At the domestic level, it places the power of the federal government on the permanent defensive and makes our evolution toward a more proto-socialistic society along European lines exceedingly more difficult and complicated. In the absence of any great crisis, like the Great Depression, World War II, or the Cold War, it casts a shadow of suspicion over all requests for allegiance and support coming from Washington, which becomes the Evil Empire where courtiers and lobbyists plot their inside-the-beltway schemes. Beyond the purely elective arena, one can see the Jeffersonian impulse operating nicely in American higher education, which is wholly unregulated, decentralized, protean, and the envy of the world. Or think of Jefferson smiling at the technological and economic revolution wrought by the personal computer. The mainframe, he could have told the corporate leadership at IBM, was the wrong way to go. The lap top is the ideal Jeffersonian instrument, and cyberspace, with its free-floating access to multiple websites and internet cruising, is the perfect Jeffersonian atmosphere.

At the global level, Jefferson's vision levitates above the tangled particularities of regional or national conflicts to provide a confident if almost cosmic sense of where history is headed. In the last letter he wrote, the vision came through loud and clear: "in short, the flames kindled on the 4th of July 1776 have spread over too much of the globe to be extinguished by the feeble engines of despotism. on the contrary, they will consume those engines, and all who work for them." (TJ to Roger Weightman, June 24, 1826) This places Jefferson squarely on the side of the dissident Polish workers in the Gdañsk shipyard, on the Berlin Wall with the East and West Germans who were tearing it down, with the youthful Chinese protesters in Tianenmen Square, with the Tibetan monks resisting Chinese domination, with the black majority in South Africa opposing apartheid, though this latter venue is loaded with ironies. These are the kinds of giant struggles between the Forces of Light and the Forces of Darkness that Jefferson would understand best because they recapitulate the dramatic conditions he experienced while living through the American and French Revolutions. Though he proved a poor predictor of the specific course taken by the French revolution, his prophecy for the long-term global triumph of liberal values has proven correct in the twentieth century, from the defeat of totalitarianism in the 1940s to the collapse of Soviet-styled communism in the 1980s. Francis Fukuyama's book, somewhat unfortunately entitled *The End of History and the Last Man* (1992), might more accurately have been called "Jefferson Was Right." In a very real sense, then, his legacy is most at home abroad.

In the end, to echo his own cadences, prudence dictates, and a decent respect for the opinions of mankind requires, that we celebrate his astonishing immortality. The ultimate Jeffersonian legacy is the perpetual and unbridgeable gap between our ideals or dreams and the more fallible and sometimes sordid lives we live. Jefferson always speaks to us across the gap from the idealistic side, beckoning us, like the great green light in *The Great Gatsby*, toward our different dominions in the Promised Land. Always receding just beyond our grasp into the middle distance of a better future, Jefferson remains relevant and resonant for the same reason that eternal and everlasting life remains a human hope. The man who walked the earth from 1743 to 1826, if you come to know him well, will always disappoint. The myth he has become, on the other hand, for all its contradictions and elusive abstractions, has occupied the high ground in all our national and international battlegrounds and still remains the seminal source of our will to believe.

Select Bibliography

Primary Sources

Betts, Edwin M., ed., *Thomas Jefferson's Farm Book* (Princeton: Princeton University Press, 1953).

Boyd, Julian P., *The Declaration of Independence: The Evolution of the Text*. Gerard W. Gawalt, ed. (Washington, D.C., and Charlottesville, Virginia: Library of Congress and Thomas Jefferson Memorial Foundation, Inc., 1999).

Boyd, Julian et al, eds., *The Papers of Thomas Jefferson*, 27 vols. to date (Princeton: Princeton University Press, 1950-).

Jefferson, Thomas, *Notes on the State of Virginia* (Philadelphia: Prichard and Hall, 1788), and William Peden, ed. (Chapel Hill: University of North Carolina Press, 1954).

Lipscomb, Andrew A. and Albert Ellery Bergh, eds., *The Writings of Thomas Jefferson*, 20 vols. (Washington, D.C.: Thomas Jefferson Memorial Association, 1903-4).

Padover, Saul K., *The Complete Jefferson* (Freeport, New York: Books for Libraries Press, 1943).

Peterson, Merrill D., ed. [Jefferson, Thomas], *Writings* (New York: Library of America, 1984).

Wilson, Douglas, ed., *Jefferson's Literary Commonplace Book* (Princeton: Princeton University Press, 1989).

Manuscripts

Thomas Jefferson Papers at the Library of Congress, Missouri Historical Society, Massachusetts Historical Society, University of Virginia, and the Huntington Library.

Note: Spelling, punctuation, and orthography follow the original manuscripts and have not been modernized.

Secondary Sources

Adams, Henry, *History of the United States of America during the Administrations of Thomas Jefferson* (New York: Literary Classics of the United States/Viking, 1986).

Adams, William Howard, ed., *The Eye of Thomas Jefferson* (Washington, D.C.: National Gallery of Art, 1976).

Ambrose, Stephen E., *Undaunted Courage* (New York: Simon & Schuster, 1996).

Brodie, Fawn M., *Thomas Jefferson: An Intimate History* (New York: W. W. Norton, 1974).

Brown, David S., *Thomas Jefferson: A Biographical Companion* (Santa Barbara, California: ABC-CLIO, 1998).

Buckley, Thomas E., S.J., *Church and State in Revolutionary Virginia, 1776-1787* (Charlottesville: University Press of Virginia, 1977).

Burstein, Andrew, *The Inner Jefferson: Portrait of a Grieving Optimist* (Charlottesville: University Press of Virginia, 1995).

Bush, Alfred L., *The Life Portraits of Thomas Jefferson* (Charlottesville, Virginia: Thomas Jefferson Memorial Foundation, 1962).

Cremin, Lawrence A., *American Education: The National Experience, 1783-1876* (New York: Harper and Row, 1980).

Cresswell, Donald H., *The American Revolution in Drawings and Prints* (Washington, D.C.: Library of Congress, 1975).

Cunningham, Noble E., Jr., *The Image of Thomas Jefferson in the Public Eye: Portraits for the People, 1800-1809* (Charlottesville: University Press of Virginia, 1981).

Cunningham, Noble E., Jr., *In Pursuit of Reason: The Life of Thomas Jefferson* (Baton Rouge: Louisiana State University Press, 1987).

Ellis, Joseph J., *American Sphinx: The Character of Thomas Jefferson* (New York: Alfred A. Knopf, 1997).

Gordon-Reed, Annette, *Thomas Jefferson and Sally Hemings: An American Controversy* (Charlottesville: University Press of Virginia, 1997).

Hellenbrand, Harold, *The Unfinished Revolution: Education and Politics in the Thought of Thomas Jefferson* (Newark: University of Delaware Press, 1990).

Hutson, James H., *Religion and the Founding of the American Republic* (Washington, D.C.: Library of Congress, 1998).

Jackson, Donald, *Thomas Jefferson and the Stony Mountains: Exploring the West from Monticello* (Urbana: University of Illinois Press, 1981).

Kaestle, Carl F., *Pillars of the Republic: Common Schools and American Society, 1780-1860* (New York: Hill and Wang, 1983).

Lewis, Jan, *The Pursuit of Happiness: Family and Values in Jefferson's Virginia* (New York: Cambridge University Press, 1983).

Maier, Pauline, *American Scripture: Making the Declaration of Independence* (New York: Alfred A. Knopf, 1997).

Malone, Dumas, *Jefferson and His Time*, 6 vols. (Boston: Little, Brown, 1948-81).

Mayer, David, *The Constitutional Thought of Thomas Jefferson* (Charlottesville: University of Virginia Press, 1994).

McLaughlin, Jack, *Jefferson and Monticello: The Biography of a Builder* (New York: Henry Holt, 1988).

Miller, Charles A., *Jefferson and Nature: An Interpretation* (Baltimore: The Johns Hopkins University Press, 1988).

O'Brien, Conor Cruise, *The Long Affair: Thomas Jefferson and the French Revolution, 1785- 1800* (University of Chicago Press, 1996).

Onuf, Peter S., ed., *Jeffersonian Legacies* (Charlottesville: University Press of Virginia, 1993).

Pangle, Lorraine Smith and Thomas L. Pangle, *The Learning of Liberty: The Educational Ideas of the American Founders* (Lawrence: University Press of Kansas, 1993).

Peterson, Merrill D., *The Jefferson Image in the American Mind* (New York: Oxford University Press, 1960).

Peterson, Merrill D., *Thomas Jefferson and the New Nation: A Biography* (New York: Oxford University Press, 1970).

Peterson, Merrill D., ed., *Thomas Jefferson: A Reference Biography* (New York: Charles A. Scribner's Sons, 1986).

Randolph, Sarah N., *The Domestic Life of Thomas Jefferson* (Charlottesville: University of Virginia Press, 1978).

Risjord, Norman K., *Jefferson's America* (Madison, Wisconsin: Madison House, 1991).

Risjord, Norman K., *Thomas Jefferson* (Madison, Wisconsin: Madison House, 1994).

Sanford, Charles B., *Thomas Jefferson and His Library: A Study of his Literary Interests and of the Religious Attitudes Revealed by Relevant Titles in his Library* (Hamden, Connecticut: Archon Books, 1977).

Sloan, Herbert E., *Principle and Interest: Thomas Jefferson and the Problem of Debt* (New York: Oxford University Press, 1995).

Smith, James Morton, *The Republic of Letters: The Correspondence between Thomas Jefferson and James Madison, 1776-1826* (New York: W. W. Norton, 1995).

Sowerby, E. Millicent, *Catalogue of the Library of Thomas Jefferson*, 5 vols. (Washington: Library of Congress, 1952-59).

Stanton, Lucia, *Slavery at Monticello* (Charlottesville, Virginia: Thomas Jefferson Memorial Foundation, Inc., 1996).

Stein, Susan R., *The Worlds of Thomas Jefferson at Monticello* (New York: Harry N. Abrams, Inc., 1993).

Tyler, Ron, *Prints of the West* (Golden, Colorado: Fulcrum Publishing, 1994).

Virga, Vincent, and the curators of the Library of Congress, *Eyes of the Nation: A Visual History of the United States* (New York: Alfred A. Knopf, 1997).

Wallace, Anthony J. C., *Jefferson and the Indians: The Tragic Fate of the First Americans* (Cambridge, Massachusetts: Harvard University Press, 1999).

Wills, Garry, *Inventing America: Jefferson's Declaration of Independence* (New York: Doubleday, 1978).

Wolf, Edwin 2nd., *Philadelphia: Portrait of a City* (Philadelphia: Camino Books, 1990).

Wood, Gordon S., *The Radicalism of the American Revolution* (New York: Vintage Books, 1992).

Index

Page references in boldface type are to illustrations.
The abbreviation TJ has been used for Thomas Jefferson.

white supremacy, xix, 83, 166

Wilkinson, Gen. James, 108, 128

will, TJ's. *See* codicil to

Willard, Joseph, letter from TJ, 106

Williamsburg (Virginia), Bodleian plate
  views of, **7**

Wills, Garry, introduction by, xiii-xxii

Wise, John, letter from TJ, 77

Wistar, Caspar, letter from TJ, 61

women
  education of, views on, 152
  inheritance law reform and, 29
  voting rights denied to, 167

Wood, Gordon, on TJ, 83

writings, TJ's. *See*
  "Anas,"
  Annual Address to Congress,
  "Autobiography,"
  Bill for establishing Religious Freedom,
  "Bill for the More General Diffusion of
    Knowledge,"

"bill for new-modelling the form of
  Government . . . . ,"
Continental Congress, instructions to
  Virginia delegates,
Declaration of Independence,
"Declaration . . . Setting forth the
  Causes and Necessity of their taking
  up Arms,"
inaugural addresses, first and second,
Kentucky resolution, draft of,
letters (TJ), under correspondents' names
"Life and Morals of Jesus of Nazareth,"
*Manual of Parliamentary Practice For the Use
  of the Senate of the United States,*
Message from the President of the United States,
Notes on the State of Virginia,
"Plan for Establishing Uniformity in the
  Coinage, Weights, and Measures of the
  United States,"
*Summary View of the Rights of British
  America,*

Virginia, constitution, drafting, and
  legal code revisions
Wythe, George
  attendance at Virginia convention, 27
  manual of parliamentary practice, 75
  portrait by John Trumbull, **6**
  revision of legal code, 35
  TJ's mentor and tutor, 6, 9, 12, 86

X

XYZ affair, 77

Y

Yorktown, battle of, **38**, 39
Young, James H., 157

Object list and reproduction numbers

The following list provides the reproduction numbers for Library of Congress items in this publication where such numbers are available. Color transparencies are indicated by the prefix LC-USZC4, while the prefixes LC-USZ62 and G&M Neg. indicate a black and white negative. Color copy transparencies or black and white prints may be ordered directly from the Library's Photoduplication Service, Washington, D.C., 20540-5230 (telephone 202-707-5640). If a Library of Congress item does not have a reproduction number listed below, contact the custodial division listed in the object's caption for further instructions on how to obtain a copy. The Library's general telephone number is 202-707-5000. Its Internet address is http://www.loc.gov.

xxiv: LC-USZC4-1476

7: LC-USZ62-2104

11: LC-USZC4-5326

16 (bottom): LC-USZC4-3146

34 (bottom): LC-USZ62-60690

35 (left): LC-USZ62-10474

35 (right): LC-USZ62-31864

37: LC-USZC4-5310

41 (top): LC-USZC4-5277

48: LC-USZ62-59512

51 (top): LC-USZ62-92869

62: LC-USZC4-4547

64: LC-USZC4-530

66 (left): LC-USZC4-4602

67 (top): LC-USZ62-4823

69 (top): G&M Neg. #2440

76: LC-USZC4-550

93 (top): LC-USZC4-280

93 (bottom): LC-USZC4-1495

94: LC-USZC4-247

95 (top): LC-USZC4-1098

95 (bottom): LC-USZC4-1090

96: LC-USZC4-2705

107: LC-USZ62-52550

114: LC-USZC4-683

116: LC-USZC4-4804

129 (top): LC-USZ62-45726

130: LC-USZC4-4544

133 (left): LC-USZ62-19231

133 (right): LC-USZ62-17372

148 (bottom): LC-USZC4-4555

160: LC-USZ62-60776

165: LC-USZC4-5179

3|01

GAYLORD S